Blacks and Jews in Literary Conversation

In an attempt to lend a more nuanced ear to the ongoing dialogue between African and Jewish Americans, Emily Budick examines the works of a range of writers, critics, and academics from the 1950s through the 1980s. *Blacks and Jews in Literary Conversation* records conversations both explicit, such as essays and letters, and indirect, such as the fiction of Bernard Malamud, Philip Roth, Alice Walker, Cynthia Ozick, Toni Morrison, and Saul Bellow. The purpose is to understand how this dialogue has engendered misconceptions and misunderstandings, and how blacks and Jews in America have both sought and resisted assimilation and ethnic autonomy.

In analyzing the history of this discourse, Budick explores the ways in which ethnic fiction works in multicultural America, the effects of identity politics on cultural pluralism, and the tensions and bonds created as African and Jewish Americans continue to construct their ethnic and religious identities in the United States.

Emily Miller Budick is a professor of American Literature at the Hebrew University of Jerusalem, Israel. Her previous books include *Emily Dickinson and the Life of Language, Nineteenth-Century American Romance, Fiction and Historical Consciousness,* and *Engendering Romance.*

Blacks and Jews in Literary Conversation

Emily Miller Budick

CAMBRIDGE
UNIVERSITY PRESS

PUBLISHED BY THE PRESS SYNDICATE OF THE UNIVERSITY OF CAMBRIDGE
The Pitt Building, Trumpington Street, Cambridge CB2 1RP, United Kingdom

CAMBRIDGE UNIVERSITY PRESS
The Edinburgh Building, Cambridge CB2 2RU, UK   http: //www.cup.cam.ac.uk
40 West 20th Street, New York, NY 10011-4211, USA   http: //www.cup.org
10 Stamford Road, Oakleigh, Melbourne 3166, Australia

First published 1998

Printed in the United States of America

Typeset in Baskerville 10.5/12.5 pt, in Penta [RF]

A catalog record for this book is available from the British Library

Library of Congress Cataloging-in-Publication Data
Budick, E. Miller.
Blacks and Jews in literary conversation / Emily Miller Budick.
p.   cm. – (Cambridge studies in American literature and
culture)
Includes index.
ISBN 0-521-63194-7 (hardcover). – ISBN 0-521-63575-6 (pb.)
1. American fiction – Afro-American authors – History and criticism.
2. American fiction – Jewish authors – History and criticism.   3. Afro-
American authors – Political and social views.   4. Jewish authors –
Political and social views.   5. Afro-Americans – Relations with
Jews.   6. Afro-Americans in literature.   7. Race relations in
literature.   8. United States – Race relations.   9. Jews in
literature.   I. Title.   II. Series.
PS153.N5B83   1998
813'.54098924–dc21   98-3676
                                                                     CIP

ISBN 0-521-63194-7 hardback
ISBN 0-521-63575-6 paperback

For Rachel, Ayelet, Shaul, and, last but not least, Hananel

Contents

Acknowledgments

There is for every true statement the formulation that best realizes its truth. Literary criticism, as I understand it, is, like dialogue, the attempt to enter into other people's discourse in order, through a process of mutual construction, to facilitate the realization of other people's truths as well as one's own. Whether I have succeeded in my own intervention into the literary conversations of African and Jewish Americans to clarify intentions and desires is for others to determine. But those who have read, commented on, and discussed this work with me up until now have certainly helped me find those formulations that most nearly express my particular truths. I thank my colleagues and friends: Sharon Baris, Lawrence Besserman, Judith Besserman, Marcus Klein, Michael Kramer, Jeffrey Rubin-Dorsky, Shaindy Rudoff, William Howarth, Janine Woolfson (research assistant par excellence – and here let me thank the Israel Academy of Arts and Sciences, who funded this assistance, and more), Chava Burshtein-Rothenberg (a superb proofreader), the still anonymous Cambridge Press reader, my copy editor, Nancy Landau, Anne Sanow of the Press, and Eric Sundquist, who set the entire publication process in motion. I thank them, my many other friends, and my family – Rachel Elmakeyes and Shaul Elmakeyes, Ayelet Budick, and (especially) my husband, Sanford Budick – who not only consented to endless dialogue but also sustained me in the belief that I might, after all, have something to say. Hananel Haim Elmakeyes arrived before this book went to press: he is reason enough to keep faith that conversation never ceases.

Portions of the readings of Morrison, Ozick, and Paley have appeared in: "On the Mutual Displacements, Appropriations, and Accommodations of Culture: Toni Morrison, Grace Paley, and Cynthia Ozick," *Prospects: An Annual of American Culture Studies,* ed. Jack Saltzman (New York: Cambridge University Press, 1995), pp. 387–404.

Introduction: *"Because you were strangers in the land"*

Even though both blacks and Jews have been strangers of sorts in the land of America and have cast themselves and each other as such in their writings, for the most part their histories have had very little in common. Such interaction as did exist occurred only among slender elements of both populations, and, even then, only at very specific moments and under highly particular circumstances. Notable among these is 1930s and 1940s activism in the Communist Party or labor unions and in the Civil Rights movement of the 1950s and early 1960s. Still, black and Jewish writers, intellectuals, and academics have tended to keep each other in mind, as if, indeed, there were a revelation for each of them in the existence of the other. For a significant number of African and Jewish American writers, the other group becomes a vehicle by which to think through their own ethnic identities. What is not obvious is how blacks and Jews function in each other's thinking and writing. More importantly, perhaps, it is not clear what this relationship means for interethnic dialogue and for the construction of American culture.

This study attempts to record several conversations among prominent African and Jewish Americans. Sometimes the dialogue is explicit, proceeding through essays, letters, and symposia. Sometimes, especially as manifested in fictional writings, it is more indirect. I am not concerned with all black and Jewish writers, or even with all those writers who engage the other ethnic community. Rather, I am primarily interested in writers who evidence concern with their own ethnic identity *and*, at the same time, engage the ethnic identity of the other group. My focus, in other words, is on how writers construct their separate, ethnic identities, textually, *in relation to each*

1

other, in a series of such constructions, which produce greater and greater entanglements of the two ethnicities.

Hence my idea of *mutuality,* to which I will be recurring throughout this book. The influence of blacks on Jews and Jews on blacks is never unidirectional or unidimensional, even within single pairs of writers or texts. Everywhere present are other black- and Jewish-authored texts. These texts are themselves already in the condition of some degree of black–Jewish intertextuality. For this reason, black–Jewish relations can be taken as a figure for American ethnic relations generally, though I would prefer to keep my claims specific to the texts and individuals I will be discussing. At the same time, since Jews and blacks differ in regard not only to race but to religion as well (a factor often overlooked in studies of black–Jewish dialogue), African–Jewish American relations can also be understood within the larger, extra-territorial, contexts of Jewish–Christian tensions. In terms of both race and religion, we discover on the parts of the black and Jewish participants to dialogue who interest me neither racism nor anti-Semitism. Rather we find the embeddedness of language and culture within histories no one can forget or disavow. As Jews and blacks attempt to manage the subjects of racial and religious antagonism, they find themselves inevitably drawn into other, older disputes. These cannot but affect their own constructions of self and other.

At some moments in the following pages, my tracing of the mutual textual constructions of black and Jewish identities will mean nothing more than recording and listening to dialogues between particular blacks and Jews. To some extent, my purpose is to put aside some popular assumptions concerning black–Jewish relations and simply to attend once again to what individuals have said to each other. Even here, however, my motivation is somewhat deeper. Dialogue already involves mutual construction. It means granting and accommodating another individual's perceptions of you as much as of the issues the two of you debate. This is one of the dangers of conversation, which sometimes produces the avoidance of dialogue. It is also one of its great gifts. I take as a starting assumption about all of the statements and conversations I am going to discuss that they are sincerely intended. I also assume, however, that much is left unsaid. Often, in fact, these silences or omissions provoke the angriest responses and counterresponses in their wounded interlocutors. In all of these texts, especially those that go beyond mere conversation or dialogue, such as the fictions discussed in Chapters Three, Four, and Five, the larger contexts of racial and religious sensibility function to produce meanings that the individual participants to the dialogue may not wholly intend. My major subject is the body of writings (fictional and nonfictional) produced by blacks and Jews that evidence ethnic identity as a larger American cultural construction, in which individuals proceed through one another on the way to declaring a self.

In order to bring out these processes and consequences of mutual construction, my readings, for the most part, will proceed as conversations, some of them real, some of them staged by my placing in juxtaposition affiliated statements by black and Jewish writers. I make no claims for the representativeness of these conversations. I do, however, believe in the importance of these moments of mutual ethnic construction. They crystallize processes occurring elsewhere and in differing forms in the society at large. Reciprocally, they are themselves forces within the ethnic constructions of America.

Let me put forward a few underlying assumptions. I take for granted that there is no such thing as pure ethnic identity, black or Jewish, even in hyphenated form: Jewish-American, African-American. Rather, all ethnic identities, in the United States at least, are mutually constructed. Nonetheless, I accept that ethnic difference does exist, that it is significant to many Americans, and that it functions for many individuals as the base and structure of their intellectual, moral, and spiritual lives. For many African Americans the term "African" or "black" represents, as does the term "Jew" for many Jewish Americans, a discrete and identifiable set of characteristics which are *not* American and are *not* those of any other ethnic group within the United States. Hyphenated identity (even with the hyphen omitted, as is today's fashion) constitutes for them a real identity – Jewish American, African American, Native American, and so on. This identity matters, and it is differentiable from other such identities. It brings with it certain ethical and historical responsibilities. It also makes inevitable conflict and competition for cultural materials and power – and it this aspect of ethnic expression that I want to highlight.

Both Werner Sollors and Sacvan Bercovitch have provided models of American multiculturalism and pluralism in which expressions of individual positions, whether ethnically or individualistically conceived, are not so much radical or revolutionary challenges to or deviations from the dominant status quo as they are affirmations of what, in the final analysis, emerge as recognizable forms of American cultural expression.[1] In Sollors's taxonomy of ethnicities, African American and Jewish American and Italian American groups will have more in common with each other as Americans than with the ethnically other group (African, Jewish, or Italian) from which they take their specific, hyphenated, identities. Similarly, for Bercovitch, individualism and marginality function within American literature, not to subvert the idea of America but, in some significant way, to constitute it, producing consensus out of the enactment of dissensual possibilities.

While preserving Sollors's and Bercovitch's cultural models, I want to suggest that mutualities of ethnic construction may evidence genuine conflict for cultural domination, as writers respond to, appropriate, and often displace each other's cultural materials. It is possible that this conflict may produce an interactive relationship between the two sides to the conflict, which effectively prevents the consolidation of cultural authority. For this reason, I use some of these ideas of conflict, in particular within literary texts, to counter aspects of Walter Benn Michaels's assertions concerning what he calls the "race" and "culture" dynamic of American nativism. Michaels's idea is that, in complicated and not necessarily intentional ways, culture, in the United States, is "put forward as a way of preserving the primacy of identity while avoiding the embarrassments of blood."[2] Ethnic writing, I will insist, at least in the later texts that concern me, keeps in view the elements of cultural construction that culture, viewed from positions of dominance or presumed dominance, can obscure. Since Michaels deals specifically with blacks and Jews both in his book and in several later essays, I return to his arguments later in my analysis.

Nonetheless, for the major part of my study I want to insist that such cultural conflict as may eventually do the valuable work of preventing the sedimentation of culture into a hegemonic totality may also reflect and even unleash genuine hostilities. Specifically, it may produce the repetition within each individual ethnic construction of those elements of the other's ethnic position (and of American culture generally) that each group, in insisting on its ethnic position, would most like to disown or displace. In this way, the dynamics of ethnicity confirm, albeit ironically and inadvertently, Sollors's and Bercovitch's theses concerning American consensus. American writers may seem never so American as when they are resisting that designation. And they may never so fully embody what they least respect in American culture as when they are protesting it.

A similar insistence on the tensions or dissensions that threaten more damage than benefit also controls my relationship to the ideas of Paul Gilroy.[3] In *The Black Atlantic: Modernity and Double Conscious-*

ness Gilroy powerfully describes the biracial construction of modernity. He argues against both Eurocentricism *and* Afrocentricism (especially in its exceptionalist African American variety). Gilroy produces this argument by exploring the ways in which Western thought already incorporates a thinking about race. This already racialized thinking produces in the Western descendants of Africa modes of thought and discourse already constituted by, and contributory toward, the larger philosophical and political debates of Western civilization. Since Gilroy specifically discusses this phenomenon of Black Atlantic cultural construction in relation to Jews and Jewish history, his ideas appear at various moments in my own investigation of African and Jewish American dialogue. For the moment I want simply to invoke the rich context of his thought and also to stress my relation to it. My own focus is not the seams of black–white mutualities. Instead, I want to bring pressure to bear on the active ruptures by which two segments of the world's population, blacks and Jews, strain apart.

In short, my purpose in looking at mutual textual constructions of African and Jewish American writers is to see how individual authors manufacture their hyphenated identities, as they both insist on the legitimacy of the ethnic component of that identity and yet apply in their constructions to the very specific, ethnically different, materials of another ethnic group, which is itself engaged in its own parallel processes of ethnic construction. The production of friction, fracture, and antagonism within these processes of mutual ethnic, cultural, construction may, in the end, yield some very positive results. I will try to locate these at the end of the book. Nonetheless, for these constructions to be constructive, it may be necessary to isolate and even highlight them, if only to disabuse ourselves of a certain innocence or disingenuousness. Such innocence, rather than encouraging multiethnic aspiration and idealism, may simply stand in the way of their fulfillment.

Let me immediately add, therefore, that I do not imagine my own 1990s intervention into these earlier cultural conversations as being without ideological motivation. Nor do I mean to "catch" anyone in his or her intellectual inattentiveness. In the first place, all of the texts I discuss are, in my opinion, extraordinarily insightful and well-meaning. Each is informed by what I would call *textual intelligence,* by which I mean that knowledge exceeding authorial intention that pieces of writing can achieve through the sheer intensity of their involvement in the issues that inspire them. Second, we all write out of our cultural moment. My own take on these Jewish- and black-authored texts is informed by the literary critical strategies and cultural assumptions of the contemporary American academy. In particular, this means that my thinking is informed by the attitudes of multiculturalism, which were largely put into place in the United States by black studies programs and the black power movement. In the 1990s we grant in ways that we did not concede earlier the importance of ethnic expression. We may not all agree on the legitimate contours of identity politics, but most of us acknowledge that ethnic expression is a legitimate, even valuable, aspect of our Americanism.

This last point is especially important in relation to what emerges as my major criticism of Jewish American intellectuals in the 1960s and 1970s. Blacks, I suggest, were during these decades maintaining a careful course of cultural preservation and separateness, which succeeded in transforming our idea of America. Jews, during the same period, were committed to assimilation for themselves and integration for blacks, although whether assimilation and integration are, in the Jewish imagination, identical phenomena remains to be seen. Nonetheless, the consequence of these divergent trajectories is that it is by no means clear whether Jews, when they address national issues such as racism, do so as Jews or as Americans.

For a 1990s Jewish-American-Israeli the willingness of Jewish Americans to forfeit the specificity of their Jewish identity or to submerge it within a larger national identity might well seem problematic. Therefore, in my analysis of black and Jewish mutualities and divergences, I do not occupy a neutral or unimplicated position. As a Jew, I already stand on one side of an interactive relationship. At the same time, as a religiously observant Jew now residing in Israel, I also separate out from the Jewish American community. Just as blacks and Jews see each other through the lenses of their differing ethnic agendas, so I see both groups, but especially Jewish Americans, through my own ideologically informed critical distance. And if Jews and blacks in the United States construct themselves through their constructions of each other, I no less discover my own identity through my incorporation of and opposition to theirs.

In many ways, my own position represents, like some of the earlier Jewish positions I record, a response to the urgencies of black needs and demands in an America that is still not free of racism. But whereas an earlier generation of Jews committed itself to the dissolution of both black and Jewish identity into what was imagined as "American" identity (as if this identity could be isolated from its black and Jewish components), I, influenced by both the black culture movement and the post-1967 Zionism of American Judaism, imagine the maintenance of ethnic specificity as a major goal of American, indeed of world, culture (post-1967 Judaism was itself, in some ways, galvanized by the black movement, which rejected white American, Jewish and non-Jewish, participation). At the same time, since my ethnic commitment takes me out of the United States into a different Jewish community, my agenda conflicts with not only that of other Jewish Americans but specifically that of American blacks. Black goals, or at least some of the forms of their expression, sometimes seem to me to stand in diametrical opposition to my own. This is the case both in terms of domestic American politics and also in relation to international issues, such as the Palestinian–Israeli conflict.

I argue that many Jewish Americans, like many other Americans, did not hear what blacks were saying in the 1950s and early 1960s concerning black culture. In the 1990s I find myself, with other Americans, finally being able to hear and respond to the claim that American culture is and always has been biracial. What was necessary in the United States from the nineteenth century on was, from the black perspective, not integration but the recognition, on the cultural level, that this integration had already occurred, even though it remained, to use Ellison's word, "invisible," at least to whites. But hearing this message, I respond as well to aspects of black identity politics that seem to endanger both my own identity and that of my group. These politics have to do with the ways in which black strategies, aimed primarily at challenging the supremacy of white Christian culture in the United States, participated in earlier moves within the history of Christian thought, which had as their basis a supersessionist claim against Judaism. Sometimes the Jew in the black text is not a contemporary Jewish American or Israeli but an Israelite.

In Chapter Five of this study I deal directly with the implications of bringing to bear upon the already mutually constructed discourse of African and Jewish Americans the third position of the expatriate Israeli American Jew, whose position is also mutually constructed and constructing. Here, as throughout this book, I maintain that whatever the understandings or misunderstandings between the participants to dialogue (black–Jewish and Jewish–Jewish), the conversation transforms all of its members. My main objective is to bring into view these processes of mutual construction, and their consequences, those deep internal transformations that occur in one's self-consciousness (including my own) when, expressing one's own point of view, one also sees the world through someone else's per-

spective. Although such process often marks the beginnings of productive communal sharing, it can also signal missteps and trespasses,
as, losing the distinctions between self and other, one constructs the
other as oneself and causes the other similarly to misconstrue and
misconstruct oneself.

1

Mutual Textual Constructions of Black–Jewish Identity

If we blow into the narrow end of the *shofar,* we will be heard far. But if we choose to be Mankind rather than Jewish and blow into the wider part, we will not be heard at all; for us, America will have been in vain.

> Cynthia Ozick, "Toward a New Yiddish"

The story of the Negro in America is the story of America . . . Our dehumanization of the Negro . . . is indivisible from our dehumanization of ourselves: the loss of our own identity is the price we pay for our annulment of his.

> James Baldwin, "Many Thousands Gone"[1]

According to an extraordinarily lengthy series of books, collections, articles, and symposia published in the late 1960s and early 1970s, the 1960s witnessed a baffling and painful demise of what many intellectuals of the period referred to as the "Negro–Jewish alliance."[2] This lament for the end of the black–Jewish alliance is odd, for at least two reasons. First of all, by most responsible accounts, the alliance hardly existed before the Civil Rights activism of the 1950s.[3] This is not in any way to deny the significant intervention of certain prominent Jews in the NAACP and other black organizations. Nor is it to erase black–Jewish involvement in the Communist Party or the labor unions. It is, however, to suggest that the term "alliance" misstates or overstates the nature of the exchange. Second, *before* the latter 1960s, when this presumed alliance seems finally and irrecoverably to have fallen apart (although, to read some

9

recent commentaries, one would think this only happened in the 1990s), there is nothing even approximating the 1960s proliferation of written concern for the relationship between blacks and Jews. Whatever the black–Jewish alliance was, and whenever it occurred, Jewish–black *dialogue* as such does not commence in earnest until the 1960s. Unless we imagine alliance as somehow preceding or transcending dialogue, we may properly feel that the conversation between blacks and Jews is a more recent and more enduring phenomenon. We may feel, further, that it has exactly not yet come to an end.

I suggest that the important relationship between African and Jewish Americans does not end in the 1960s but, rather, begins there. I want to assert further that such conversation as persists into the present time builds on those earlier 1960s exchanges. Why so many Americans, both black and Jewish, should have mourned the beginning of this dialogue as the end of a special relationship is a question I will be trying to answer throughout this study. As Kenneth Clark pointed out as early as 1946, well in advance of the fabled decline in the black–Jewish alliance, "in practically every area of contact between the Negro and Jewish peoples some real or imagined grounds for mutual antagonism exist." Yet, he continued, there is "a general reluctance to deal with those aspects of Negro life in America that directly and concretely involved Negro-Jewish relations."[4] This reluctance may indicate nothing more than a natural desire on the parts of the two minorities to avoid conflict. But it may also reveal a tendency to prefer fantasy to fact and to discover, under the cover of fraternal feeling, even more powerful bases for disagreement and dissension.

Whatever the reasons, the *decline* of the fabled alliance between blacks and Jews came to structure much of the angry thinking of the 1960s concerning African and Jewish American relations. It figures prominently in an important essay by Cynthia Ozick, written in 1972 and concerning a 1971 novel on blacks and Jews by Bernard Malamud, which returns us (as Ozick notes) to a 1963–64 conversation between Ralph Ellison and Irving Howe and to a somewhat earlier exchange (which Ozick does not take up) between Ellison and another Jewish critic, Stanley Edgar Hyman. These dialogues dip in and out of a set of other statements and conversations, involving Hannah Arendt, Norman Podhoretz, and, most importantly, James Baldwin.[5] What the issues are in these moments of African and Jewish American confrontation – and what is at stake for blacks and Jews and American culture in this dialogue and in the mutual ethnic constructions that it produces and denies – are my concerns in the following discussion. They have to do with a competition between blacks and Jews for authority in American culture. This competition powerfully resonates with earlier conflicts concerning Jews in Western culture, in particular the tensions, anxieties, and assumptions of chosenness and supersessionism that divide Judaism and Christianity. At the same time, it reflects black–white relations in America generally, making the black–Jewish dialogue something of a model both for a more general debate between Christians and Jews and a more local, American, conversation between blacks and whites.

Let me proceed from later to earlier texts.

"I got to find the [promised] end": The Problem of Jewish American Identity in Bernard Malamud's Tenants[6]

In 1971 Bernard Malamud published a book about two writers, one black, the other Jewish, both of them tenants of a condemned New York City apartment building, both struggling unsuccessfully to complete their novels, and both, after a brief collegial relationship, dedicated to the destruction of each other and of the other's art. This is the brutal, violent, *penultimate,* conclusion of *The Tenants,* for which, I think, the book is largely remembered:

> "Bloodsuckin Jew Niggerhater."
> "Anti-Semitic Ape."
> Their metal glinted in hidden light, perhaps starlight filtering greenly through dense trees. Willie's eyeglass frames momentarily gleamed. They aimed at each other accurate blows. Lesser felt his jagged ax sink through bone and brain as the groaning black's razor-sharp saber, in a single boiling stabbing slash, cut the white's balls from the rest of him.
> Each, thought the writer, feels the anguish of the other.
> THE END

Although for Cynthia Ozick this ending is the point and purpose of the book, I call it the *penultimate* ending for two reasons. First of all, as the passage makes very clear, this may not be the ending at all of Harry Lesser's and Willie Spearmint's actual relationship in the world within the text. Rather, it may be a fantasy ending, one among several other such endings, including two African and Jewish American marriages. And the ending may be imagined as having been written either by Harry or by Willie or, of course, by Malamud himself (the identity of the "writer" remains deliberately unspecified in the text's final paragraphs).

Second, the words THE END have already appeared several times in the novel, and they are not now the end of the book. Immediately following the mutually destructive encounter between Harry and Willie comes the following, spoken by the Jewish landlord of the building in which the two are tenants: "Mercy, the both of you, for Christ's sake, Levenspiel cries. Hab rachmones, I beg you. Mercy on me." And then the word *mercy* is repeated 113 times, no period at the end of this run-on sentence/paragraph.

There is certainly much evidence in Malamud's novel to support reading it as being primarily about deteriorating African–Jewish American relations after the 1960s black power movement, with its explicit injunction to white intellectuals to stay out of black politics, literature, and culture.[7] Nonetheless, in order to get at the novel's truly high stakes, both for blacks and, perhaps (since this is a Jewish-authored novel about a Jewish protagonist), even more critically for Jews, I want to leave for a moment the primary story this novel seems to tell and propose an alternate, related, reading. This reading hinges on the second important relationship in the novel, which is thrown into prominence by its concluding words, the relationship between the two Jews, Levenspiel and Lesser. This Jewish–Jewish relationship (which is to some degree duplicated in the relationship between Lesser and Willie's Jewish girlfriend, Irene Bell) precedes the Lesser–Spearmint one. It also frames it, Levenspiel's appeal to mercy at the end already having made its appearance only several pages into the text: "Have a little mercy, Lesser, move out so I can break up this rotten house that weighs like a hunch on my back. . . . Hab rachmones, Lesser" (pp. 17–18).

Malamud's novel, I suggest, is no less about this Jewish–Jewish relationship than it is about race relations. Indeed, its interest in race may well be a cover (perhaps more unintentional than willed) for its more fraught intra-Jewish message. From this point of view, African–Jewish American relations may have less to do with external, objective socioeconomic, political, or even cultural realities than they do with Jewish self-conceptions and with the place of the African American in these self-conceptions. On the *Jewish* side of things, what precedes and produces the black–Jewish crisis may be a prior failure to consolidate ethnic identity within the Jewish community itself. I should say now that although this is not the whole meaning of this text, it is an important aspect of it, without which *The Tenants'* startling interpretation of contemporary race relations cannot be broached.

In Chapters Three, Four, and Five of this book, I discuss a set of fictions by blacks and Jews that both describe the mutual construction of African and Jewish American identity and are themselves constituted by such acts of mutual construction. At the risk of anticipating my subject there, I want to read Malamud's novel as a work of American Jewish fiction that produces its portrait of American Jewish identity – or, rather, the *failure* of American Jews to consolidate an American identity that preserves Jewish content – through its application to African American cultural materials. Malamud's book has a charge to make against Jews, and it is as much against Malamud himself as against other Jewish intellectuals.

That *The Tenants* should end with the word "mercy" strung out across and down the page is not surprising. From the beginning of his career, Malamud wrote about American Jews less from within Jewish history or with an intention of clarifying something about Jewish or Jewish American life than by reference to Christian culture. He wished to establish the Jew as a metaphor of spirituality and suffering, of grace achieved and denied. Malamud always resisted being labeled an American Jewish writer.[8] His fiction is less concerned to define and preserve something called Jewish identity than to allegorize and universalize it. And this makes Malamud, for all of his closeness to Jewish sources, the most Christian of the major Jewish American authors (Saul Bellow, Philip Roth, and Cynthia Ozick are the other three).

Indeed, the major difference, perhaps, between Roth and Malamud is that while Malamud writes an intrinsically Jewish prose, replete with Yiddishisms and resonant of Jewish lore and legend (something like Ozick's prose style), he is essentially unconcerned with the American Jewish community. On the other hand, Roth, whose writings exhibit far less Jewish texture, is intent on portraying American Jewish life, and thereby analyzing and constructing American Jewish identity.[9] As Roth himself observes about Malamud:

> The Jews of *The Magic Barrel* and the Jews of *The Assistant* are not the Jews of New York or Chicago. They are Malamud's invention, a metaphor of sorts to stand for certain possibilities and promises, and I am further inclined to believe this when I read the statement attributed to Malamud which goes, "All men are Jews." In fact, we know this is not so; even the men who are Jews aren't sure they're Jews. But Malamud as a writer

of fiction has not shown specific interest in the anxieties and dilemmas and corruptions of the contemporary American Jew, the Jew we think of as characteristic of our times.[10]

In its insistence that moral relatedness has solely to do with the ethical exchanges of individuals, and in its universalization of the Jew as Christ-sufferer, *The Tenants* is no different from many other Malamud fictions. Nor is *The Tenants* unique in the Malamud canon in formulating this thesis in relation to blacks and Jews as opposed to Jews and Christians. Malamud wrote three earlier fictions that utilize black and Jewish characters (in one case, a bird who is both black and Jewish). These texts are: "Black Is My Favorite Color," which specifically deals with American race relations, and the two stories that seem to me to provide the philosophical background for *The Tenants:* "The Jewbird" and "Angel Levine." Although most critics do not include "The Jewbird" among Malamud's contemplations of black Americans, the fact that the Jewbird is a blackbird, named Schwartz, seems to me to make this link inevitable (*schwartzer* is the Yiddish word Jewish Americans use to refer, usually condescendingly, to blacks). The story's deathly conclusion eerily anticipates the penultimate scene of *The Tenants.*[11]

Both "The Jewbird" and "Angel Levine" metaphorize blacks as Jews, and therefore, insofar as they are Jews, their stories (in a process similar to the conversion, in *The Assistant,* of the Christian Frank Alpine) represent blacks as the Christs of our contemporary moment. "A wonderful thing, Fanny," says the Jewish sufferer in "Angel Levine" about the black Jewish angel of that story, "Believe me, there are Jews everywhere" (p. 289). By this the story means as well what Malamud says elsewhere, that "every man is a Jew" and every Jew is a Christ: "I try to see the Jew as a symbol of the tragic experience of man existentially," explained Malamud. "I try to see the Jew as universal man. Every man is a Jew though he may not know it."[12]

How African Americans may feel about the Jewish writer's metaphorical rendering of them, their incorporation within the economy of Jewish thinking about Judaism and its relation to Christianity, I try to assess later in the book. What concerns me for the moment is the implication for Jews of Malamud's strategy. By claiming that all men are Jews, Malamud certainly intends a response to the dominant pattern of Christianity's treatment of the Jews, especially as Christian persecution took on monstrous proportions during the Second World War. He is reminding his readers that, as all men are Jews, so all Jews are men. This is an important principle within the

eighteenth-century Christian/Enlightenment humanism that Malamud self-consciously inherits throughout his fiction, especially as
that humanism was expressed by such philosemitic German intellectuals as Gotthold Ephraim Lessing. Malamud may be recalling Lessing in the name of his major protagonist, while Lessing's close association with Moses Mendelssohn may form the basis of Harry
Lesser's fantasy of himself as Moses (p. 184). At the same time,
Malamud is also, in portraying all men as Jews and all Jews as Christs,
recalling the important fact of Christianity's origins within Judaism.
In both respects, Malamud is asserting the affinities between Jewish
culture and Christian culture. He is constructing his portrait of the
Jew as universal suffering human being through the Jew's relation
to the Christian philosophical and theological tradition. In relation
both to Christ and to Lessing, the Christian position reflects and
internalizes Jewish content, and Malamud would expressly remind
us of this. But for Malamud, the Jew as he or she exists today is no
longer the Jew in any identifiable religious or ethnic sense. Rather
the Jew is a symbol: a symbol of the suffering Christ.

In *The Tenants* Malamud does more than turn to one of the most
troubling public issues of his time: he also implicates his own universalist, Enlightenment, Christian assumptions concerning the Jew
as Christ figure. For this reason, *The Tenants* is as much about the
relationship between Jewish tenant and Jewish landlord as it is about
Jewish and black writer. Levenspiel's last word, the painful stutter of
mercy on which the novel falters and concludes, harmonizes with
the message of most of Malamud's fiction. But the *rachmones* for
which Levenspiel pleads, in a Jewish language, is, as he has insisted
earlier, *for me,* for the Jew.

Although it may be slightly overstating the case, I would argue
that the story of the Jewish writer, whose Jewish identity extends no
further than his identifying himself as genetically Jewish and taking
offense at the occasional anti-Semitic utterance, is an allegory of
Malamud's own career as a nominally Jewish writer.[13] This writer
finally comes to realize the importance of Jewish ethnic identity
within the work of art and the real endangerment, in America, as
once in Europe, both of literal, physical Jews and of their culture.
"If it's news to you," Lesser says to Spearmint, who has just uttered
an anti-Semitic slur, "I'm Jewish myself" (p. 41). We might almost
say that while this is likely not news to Willie, it is news to Harry, who
just a short time earlier in the story did not respond to a similarly
anti-Semitic statement (p. 30). And it may well be that no one is
more surprised in all this than Malamud himself, who had earlier

imagined the possibility of black Jewish angels and black Jewish Christs.

The Tenants expresses the worry that the fertility and vitality of the American Jewish imagination may be doomed to sterility, not because blacks (as the final vivid image of the book would seem to suggest) would violently castrate or murder either Jews or Jewish culture, but because the Jewish American achievement may have programmed itself for disappearance. Hence a major feature of the novel: Lesser's astounding writer's block. The book that Lesser cannot write is aptly named *The Promised End.* Lesser's "end" in sterility (both within the fantasy ending of mutual murder and castration at the end of the book, and in his refusal to marry Irene and have a family) has to do with the perhaps inevitable consequences of his substituting for the biblical land promised to the Jews another land. This land, in the imaginations of generations of Americans, from Puritan tracts and treatises to more recent productions such as Mary Antin's autobiographical *Promised Land,* or Claude Brown's fictional autobiography, *Manchild in the Promised Land,* had also come to seem a promised land, as much for Jews as for white Christians and African Americans.

Like a series of American protagonists before him, from Hawthorne's Reuben Bourne and Melville's Captain Vere to Hemingway's Jake Barnes, Fitzgerald's Jay Gatsby, and Faulkner's Isaac McCaslin, Harry Lesser is locked in the past, desperately attempting to *re*write an already written story rather than to create one of his own. Like his other predecessors in the American line, Harry Lesser refuses to marry. He prefers to remain a bachelor in a decaying house rather than move on into sexuality and the future. For him, as for them, the future is already in the past, so that the present can only be an attempt to recoup what has already been. It is not surprising, then, that Harry's greatest literary effort, which is the focus of the tense culminating sections of Malamud's text, is the rewriting of "the manuscript of blessed memory" (p. 197). This is the manuscript that Willie Spearmint, now named Bill Spear, has destroyed in the fire. It is also, however, the manuscript of which that original manuscript (which also existed in duplicate) was also only a version: the Holy Bible. The consequence of all this, for Harry as in the whole tradition of texts that Malamud's carries on, is sterility and death – precisely the linked, culminating events of *The Tenants.*[14]

Nor is the American-ness of Harry's projected *Promised* [Land] *End* its only problem. The text is also archetypically Christian. "For Christ's sake," the landlord Levenspiel rails at Harry, "what are you writing, the Holy Bible?" to which Lesser (who would, in his own fantasy of himself, be at least the equivalent of a psalmist like King David – p. 49) responds, "Who can say? Who really knows?" (p. 22). "I have to redeem myself," Lesser explains to Levenspiel; "I don't write on Sundays. . . . It's just this last section I have left. . . . I've been working on it the better part of a year and it's still not right. Something essential is missing that it takes time to find. But I'm closing in – I can feel it in my blood. I'm proceeding within a mystery to its revelation. . . . When you read it . . . even you will love me. It will help you understand and endure your life as the writing of it has helped me sustain mine" (pp. 17–22). Lesser, we are told later on, fantasizes his text as "diaphanous, radiance, fire, Moses himself climbing down the burning rock, Ten lit Commandments tucked under his arm. The writer wants his pen to turn stone into sunlight, language into fire. It's an extraordinary thing to want by a man his size and shape, given all he hasn't got" (p. 184). Lesser's language will indeed, by the end of the story, turn into fire. The fire, however, will illuminate nothing. And it will realize the promised end in the most apocalyptic, catastrophic terms: *the fire next time.*

I return to this idea shortly, and to the James Baldwin essay that stands behind Malamud's novel as it stands behind the exchange between Ellison and Howe that Malamud's book calls to mind. For now what concerns me is that Lesser is producing a recognizably Christian and American, as opposed to Jewish, text. Lesser's failure as a writer, therefore, may be understood as having to do with his lack of something significant and new to write about. "Something essential is missing," we are told concerning Harry's stalled manuscript.

Throughout the novel, Harry is represented as a reflection of someone or something else, a coil of self-reflexivities with nothing substantial at center to provide meaning to the still other insubstantial reflections he generates. Our first view of Lesser in the opening line of the novel is of him "catching sight of himself in his lonely glass," as he "wakes to finish his book," which, we soon learn, is itself only a distant reflection of another text. This book, *The Promised End*, is itself thinly veiled autobiography, about a writer "who is often afflicted by the thought that he has wasted more of his life than he was entitled to, or essence thereof [and who] night after night wakes in sweaty fright of himself, stricken by anxiety because he finds it hard to give love" (p. 192). The name of this alter-Lesser is, in the first draft, Lazar Cohen (p. 192), who is, we recall, a real-life friend of Lesser's (the name spelled with a "K" rather than a "C"), a painter who (like Lesser himself) "became successful too soon" and whose "portrait of the woman . . . had never been completed":

> Kohn had worked on it for years and then given up. Lesser had learned this from the model, Kohn's one-time mistress. Kohn, in defeat, after all his labor, doubt, despair he was not making it, nor ever would, had turned the unfinished canvas to the wall; she had eluded him. (p. 110)

Although Kohn becomes a success in spite of himself, he dies young, struck dead by a huge moving van (p. 110). No wonder Harry is afraid to move.

As if this coil of repetition were not sufficiently tense, the self-reflexivity of Lesser's text (about an artist who is a version of himself) is replicated in the repetition and self-reflexivity this produces in Malamud's text. Malamud not only repeats Kohn in Lesser (not to mention himself in Kohn and Lesser both; another Cohn reappears as the major protagonist in *God's Grace*), but, insofar as it is Malamud who is producing this entire text (including Lesser's), he uses the same character twice: Cohn and Kohn. Does the name "Lazar" suggest that Cohn resurrects something of Malamud's own earlier, youthful, perhaps Lesser, but more (as the term Cohn suggests) priestly, self? Can, then, Lesser's scrounging in the garbage can for Spearmint's refuse be taken as an image for *The Tenants* itself, which constructs itself less out of Jewish materials than the leavings of African Americans?[15]

For if the major subject of *The Tenants* is the competition between African and Jewish American writers, the novel itself, as Jewish-authored text, mirrors the problem it reveals. One could, of course, take the shared occupancy of Malamud's text by blacks and Jews as affirming the need in America for full integration among the nation's ethnic communities. Black and Jew in this novel are "brothers" (p. 54). " 'I am not my brother's brother.' Who says?" asks Lesser, who "for an odd minute played with the thought he had left himself hard at work somewhere" (p. 26); and Spearmint "remarked there might be a diddle of black in Lesser's blood" (p. 100). Throughout the novel, each is the "presence" (p. 28) that defines the other.

And yet the situation is not so simple. Lesser and Spearmint do not occupy symmetrical positions in the novel, vis-à-vis each other or American culture. Harry is no temporary resident in a decaying world, efficiently, cleverly, subversively utilizing the resources of a racist society to his own advantage (like Willie or like the protagonist whose existence stands firmly behind Willie's: Ellison's invisible man). Rather, he is "the legal paying tenant" (p. 201) of the condemned apartment building. Harry remains stuck in a decaying past because he can imagine no alternative to being there. Importantly, neither money nor opportunity is the issue for Lesser. Not only has he profited by his earlier writings (in particular, in the bastion of Jewish success, Hollywood), but the landlord of the building is willing to buy him out at a sum that becomes increasingly lucrative. Harry's resistance, then, to moving on figures the absence in his imagination of a place for him to move on to. Spearmint's art is (in the American vein of individualistic fiction) as self-concerned as Lesser's. Nonetheless, the African American writer in Malamud's text does have a story to tell, which is not the same old story America and Western civilization have been telling themselves for centuries. And while Spearmint is having no better a time than Lesser producing his text, nonetheless he is at the beginning of a career. Lesser – like Malamud, perhaps – is at the end.

It may be significant in this context that, according to James A. McPherson, Malamud actually did not write certain portions of the book, which were composed instead by McPherson himself. (This claim is still under investigation by Malamud scholars, raising yet another specter of black–Jewish competition.)[16] In other words, to produce a viable, vital text, Malamud literally imports into his writing culturally different, African American, materials. For the American Jew, Malamud is suggesting, it may already be too late to return to cultural origins. He stands in danger either of telling the story of some other community or of having absolutely nothing whatsoever to say.

"Knowing Negro Writer" and "Presuming White Intellectual": The Terms of the Black–Jewish Cultural Debate (Ralph Ellison, Irving Howe, and Stanley Edgar Hyman)[17]

Just one year after the publication of *The Tenants*, Cynthia Ozick read Malamud's novel as the bloody 1970s realization of the black–Jewish conflict that had begun more quietly and with greater civility in the 1960s. "It took the narrowest blink of time," writes Ozick, "for Malamud, who more than any other American writer seeks to make a noble literature founded on personal compassion, to come from 'Believe me, there are Jews everywhere,' " in "Angel Levine," to "the passionate bloodletting" of *The Tenants* (pp. 91–92). In particular, Ozick hears behind the anger and violence that characterize the relationship between Lesser and Spearmint, an earlier, more civilized, friendlier debate in American culture, between two highly successful intellectuals, Irving Howe and Ralph Ellison. What this exchange reveals, according to Ozick, is that from the black perspective, as expressed by Ellison, " 'Angel Levine' never *was* true: impossible for black man and Jew to share the same skin and the same pair of eyes out of which to assess reality. . . . [B]lack and Jew are not, will never be seen to be, mutually salvational. . . . This is perhaps why Malamud went forward from the failed dream of 'Angel Levine' to the warlike actualities of *The Tenants*" (p. 101). For Ozick, *The Tenants*, like one of Willie's projected fictions, is nothing less than a novel of pogrom (p. 109).

For Ozick the fundamental issue in the Howe–Ellison exchange is the sincerity of Jewish concern for blacks. By this Ozick does not mean, narrowly, as figured in Malamud's novel or in the literary exchange it recalls, intellectual conversation between scholars and academics. Rather, it means the politics of Jewish involvement in the 1950s Civil Rights movement. It is this involvement that Ozick defends (quite rightly) and that Ellison, she argues, calls into question. But while the question of sincerity hovers over the Howe–Ellison materials, sincerity is not a major issue in *The Tenants*. Malamud presents us with one Jewish protagonist who is totally apolitical and unconcerned with black rights, and another who is a slum landlord and a racist.

What does it mean that, in what is otherwise an astute, insightful, reading of Howe–Ellison and Malamud, back-to-back, Ozick focuses on a subject not taken up in the novel, at least not in the form in which it existed either in 1950s and 1960s political reality or, in more attenuated form, in the Howe–Ellison materials? The Civil Rights activism and socialist/communist/labor context of African–Jewish American relations is not ignored in several other books of the 1960s concerning blacks and Jews, including Jo Sinclair's *Wasteland,* Jay Neugeboren's *Big Man,* Nat Hentoff's *Call the Keeper,* and Lorraine Hansberry's *Sign in Sidney Brustein's Window,* as in some earlier books, such as Chester Himes's *If He Hollers Let Him Go* and *The Lonely Crusade*. It does not, however, feature in Malamud's *Tenants*.[18]

Let me put forward the Ellison–Howe debate itself, which, as Ozick describes it, is "a collision rich in felt honesty and therefore somehow strange, hurtful and agonizing, eluding decent summarization" (p. 96). The debate took place in 1963–64 over four separate installments in *Dissent* (the journal Howe edited) and *The New Leader*. Howe's part of the exchange was republished the same year in *A World More Attractive,* while Ellison's appeared a year later in *Shadow and Act.* Significantly for the study of black–Jewish literary relations, both parts of the exchange are reproduced for future readers of Howe and Ellison in isolation of each other, and therefore without the context of the debate in which the statements appeared. Furthermore, while Ellison's part of the discussion refers to Howe, Howe's (which probably appeared simultaneous with its appearance in *Dissent*) does not mention Ellison's.[19] Although I personally believe that Malamud was aware of the exchange, if not from its original publication, then from subsequent reprintings, it does not matter to my argument if Malamud is less responding to this particular conversation than crystallizing a moment of transformation in Jewish–black dialogue.

In very cursory form, this is how the Howe–Ellison exchange proceeds, or, at least, how it seems to proceed. In the first document, Howe writes a very typical literary-critical essay, such as characterized literary scholarship at the time, defending Richard Wright as the quintessential black writer against James Baldwin and Ralph Ellison. Both Ellison and Baldwin, Howe acknowledges, are great writers. Neither, however, from Howe's point of view, adequately understands Wright, or perpetuates his legacy. At issue here, or so it appears, is a Marxist idea of literature, which, in Howe's view, Wright embodies, and which neither Baldwin nor Ellison (in part for reasons of oedipal tension) pursues.

Ellison responds to Howe by saying three things. The first is, on the surface of it, purely formalistic and anti-Marxist: that literature may have political impact without being overtly political. The second is more ethnically freighted, though still literary: that black writers in America are as much a part of the Western literary tradition as of any more local, black tradition. And the third, which is still more ethnic and yet also literary: that the black community is not monolithic, and therefore no one has the right to say who most defends or realizes its cultural interests. By strong implication Ellison means as well that no one from outside the community has any right to impose his or her perspective, of which Marxism itself, and not simply a Marxist critic like Howe, is an example.

In Howe's response to Ellison, Howe accuses Ellison of not having understood what he, Howe, was saying, and Ellison, in the final volley, angrily defends himself as follows:

I did not intend to take the stance of the "knowing Negro writer" against the "presuming white intellectual." While I am without a doubt a Negro, and a writer, I am also an *American* writer, and while I am more knowing than Howe where my own life and its influences are concerned, I took the time to question his presumptions as one responsible for contributing as much as he is capable to the clear perception of American social reality. . . . Whatever my role as "race man" . . . I am as writer no less a custodian of the American language than is Irving Howe. . . . So let me emphasize that my reply to Howe was neither motivated by racial defensiveness nor addressed to his own racial identity.

It is fortunate that it was not, for considering how Howe identifies himself in this instance, I would have missed the target, which would have been embarrassing. Yet it would have been an innocent mistake because in situations such as this many Negroes, like myself, make a positive distinction between "whites" and "Jews." . . . I feel uncomfortable whenever I discover Jewish intellectuals writing as though *they* were guilty of enslaving my grandparents, or as though the *Jews* were responsible for the system of segregation. Not only do they have enough troubles of their own, as the saying goes, but Negroes know this only too well.

The real guilt of such Jewish intellectuals lies in their facile, perhaps unconscious, but certainly unrealistic, identification with the "power structure." Negroes call this "passing for white." Speaking personally . . . I would like to see the more positive distinctions between whites and Jewish Americans maintained. Not only does it make for a necessary bit of historical and social clarity, . . . but I consider the United States freer politically and richer culturally because there are Jewish Americans to bring it the benefit of their special forms of dissent, their humor and their gift for ideas. (pp. 125–26)

Given the recent publication by the Nation of Islam of *The Secret Relationship Between the Blacks and Jews,* Ellison's final exoneration of the Jews here might seem to be something Jews would like to have blacks say. Still, we cannot avoid the fact that Ellison introduces into a discussion of black literature in white America the subject of the *Jew,* and that he does so at a moment when he is less than pleased with his literary adversary, who happens to be Jewish and whom Ellison identifies as such.

Implicit in Ellison's comment is an important criticism of the American Jew, which I, at any rate, had thought more recent in

African American scholarship. This is simply that in assuming positions of guilt within American society, Jews were assuming as well positions of power. They were identifying with the power structure, passing for white, as Ellison puts it. By accusing Howe of putting on blackface, Ellison alludes to the same minstrel tradition that recent criticism of *The Jazz Singer* has used to accuse Jews in the movie industry of exploiting black materials to their own assimilationist ends.[20]

Is Ellison's reference to the Jew a legitimate defense against Howe's accusations against him personally and against nonpolitical black writing generally? And how does it help define the argument between Ellison and Howe? Does it turn a literary, aesthetic, cultural debate into a racist clash? Or does it discover, in Howe's discourse, a prior racial assumption presenting itself as aesthetic argumentation?

Before even beginning to answer these very loaded questions, let me present all of the relevant Ellison passages from his final rebuttal of Howe. Ellison's culminating judgment of the Jews is not in the least unprepared for in his text:

> Of course, Irving, I know that you haven't believed in final words for twenty years — not even your own — and I know, too, that the line from Marx to Howe is as complex and as dialectical as that from Wright to Ellison. (p. 127)

And the following:

> Being a Negro American has to do with the memory of slavery and the hope of emancipation and the betrayal by allies. . . . It involves, too, a special attitude toward the waves of immigrants who have come later and passed us by. (p. 131)

And this:

> Being a Negro American involves a *willed* . . . affirmation of self . . . which rejects all possibilities of escape that do not involve a basic resuscitation of the original American ideals of social and political justice. And those white Negroes (and I do not mean Norman Mailer's dream creatures) are Negroes too – if they wish to be. (p. 132)

And finally, in the essay's concluding words:

> You will recall what the Talmud has to say about the trees of the forest and the making of books, etc. But then, Irving, they

recognize what you have not allowed yourself to see; namely, that my reply to your essay is in itself a small though necessary action in the Negro struggle for freedom. . . . I hope . . . you will come to see this exchange as an act of, shall we say, "antagonistic cooperation." (pp. 142–43)

The word "Jew" does not appear in any one of these passages. Nonetheless, by posing the question of who is the guardian of the American "language" through noting the appearance of waves of "immigrants" who have passed the black population by, and concluding that the "white Negro" is as much an affirmation of quintessential American values as anyone else (though not, Ellison specifies, the white Negro as invented by the Jewish Norman Mailer), Ellison produces an extensive, albeit oblique, commentary on African–Jewish American relations. At the very least Ellison is reminding the Jewish, immigrant, Yiddish-speaking Howe that he is indeed Jewish, and that American Jews have entered rather late into the American cultural scene, certainly in comparison with Negroes (whether they are black Negroes or white). For this reason Ellison insists that Howe should take off his "black"-face, which Ellison reveals is also his "white" face, and admit that he is neither black nor white but Jewish.[21] But Ellison's desire to produce from Howe a confession of his Jewishness (if it's news to you, Lesser says to Willie, I'm Jewish myself) goes deeper than this.

Howe, of course, is Jewishly identified elsewhere; and Ellison, as well as the readers of this exchange, are not likely to be under any misconceptions about this. Also, Ellison's insistence seems to be self-contradictory, given that Ellison is resisting Howe's demand that he, Ellison, speak as a black. We may be dealing with a simple tit for tat here: You want me to speak as a black? Well, then, you speak as a Jew. But if we are, Ellison's evening of the score between himself and the Jewish critic is no simple or superficial matter.

Let me continue to read backward and get the range and depth of Ellison's indictment of Howe (and, perhaps, of American Jewish intellectuals) on the table before I tease out of Howe's discourse its silent accusations and assumptions, which prompt Ellison's responses. Howe, I think, is right in his initial rejoinder to Ellison, that Ellison is distorting what Howe is saying. But Howe is being ingenuous in his response to Ellison in not admitting outright that he understands exactly what Ellison is getting at in his reply to Howe, thus provoking the anger of Ellison's final response.

Until the direct statement concerning Howe as Jew in the second of Ellison's replies, the word "Jew" has appeared only twice in the exchange (it also does not reappear, except by implication). Both occasions are so slight as almost to escape the reader's attention, until Ellison's outburst later makes one reconsider what those references are doing there. The first time is in Howe's original article, where it is spoken not by Howe himself, but by James Baldwin, whose critique of Richard Wright's *Native Son*, "Everybody's Protest Novel," is the direct impetus to Howe's article. "Baldwin," Howe has to admit, does "score a major point" against Wright when he objects to Wright's failure to represent " 'the relationship that Negroes bear to one another' . . . the climate of the book, 'common to most Negro protest novels . . . has led us all to believe that in Negro life there exists no tradition, no field of manners, no possibility of ritual or intercourse, such as may, for example, sustain the Jew even after he has left his father's house' " (pp. 109–10; the quotation is from Baldwin's "Many Thousands Gone," the second essay in *Notes of a Native Son*, which continues the argument of "Everybody's Protest Novel," pp. 35–36). The second time occurs in Ellison's initial rejoinder to Howe:

> I understand a bit more about myself as Negro because literature has taught me something of my identity as Western man, as political being. . . . It requires real poverty of the imagination to think that this can come to a Negro *only* through the example of *other Negroes,* especially after the performance of the slaves in recreating themselves, in good part, out of the images and myths of the Old Testament Jews. (p. 117)

We might miss the thrust of the Ellison passage, and its relation to Howe's original quotation from Baldwin, but Howe does not. Ellison is reminding Howe, rather sharply, that the "Negro" as he exists today, both to Howe and to Ellison, is already constituted by a reference to Western, indeed to Jewish, culture; and Howe, who quotes Baldwin making use of such Western, Jewish reference, can be expected to know this. Howe's quotation of Baldwin's statement concerning the Jew and his father's house identifies Howe's own cultural position. Not only is he a direct descendant of those Old Testament Jews whom blacks have already incorporated into their own identity, but, as a Jew, he is sustained (as Wright, in Baldwin's view, will not acknowledge blacks to be) by the density, however implicit and unstated, of Jewish history and heritage. So why won't Howe say this directly? Ellison prompts us to ask. Why won't Howe identify that he speaks from within a Jewish context, which is to say, from within a context that has also already imposed itself to some great degree on black life and culture?

In the final paragraph of his reply to Ellison, Howe gives clear evidence that he understands what Ellison is getting at. But rather than directly acknowledge his understanding, he responds with an indirection matching Ellison's. Howe's move replicates and worsens the indirection, to which Ellison is objecting, of his initial reference to Jews through the voice of Baldwin. "It is not, after all, as if these problems [i.e., of social discrimination and the conflict between aesthetics and politics] were unique to the Negro writers," says Howe, and he then launches into the final paragraph of his essay, which concerns, with no introduction or transition or any personal reference concerning Howe himself, Yiddish writers, both in America and in Europe (p. 14).

In this way Howe evidences what Ellison is holding against him: his unwillingness, at the moment of his commenting on the American and Western literary traditions, to engage directly and as a Jew his own cultural background, even though that background is clearly implicit in his responses and constructs his sense of what ethnic identity is and means. This interpretation of Howe's strategy is confirmed by a 1993 postscript to the reprinting of her "Literary Blacks and Jews," in which Ozick indicates that Howe himself insisted that "in his exchange with Ellison he was not approaching their discussion from any Jewish standpoint."[22]

Howe also, however, indicates that he has understood Ellison quite correctly to be saying two additional, even more problematical, things about Jews and American culture. In citing the "literature [that] has taught me something of my identity as Western man, as political being," Ellison is directly setting in opposition the Western tradition and Howe's particular kind of Jewish, Marxist, literary aesthetic. This has the effect of moving the Jews out of the mainstream of Western literature and anticipating what he will say more directly in his final response to Howe: that the Jews are not whites but Jews. Simultaneously, however, Ellison is acknowledging that Jewish culture has nonetheless to a considerable extent structured the formation of black culture in America (and white Western culture as well). This is the case both in the example Jews have provided to writers like Baldwin (which Howe quotes) and in terms of Old Testament refrains that have come to be intrinsic parts of black as of Christian religion – a subject that Ellison and Baldwin both take up in their respective essays. But Jews, although they know this, will not say this;

and that makes their influence secretive, something verging on conspiracy.

This seems to be what Ellison is getting at as he himself evidences the Old Testament influence on him, when he begins his rejoinder to Howe by casting it in the following terms:

> [I]n his zeal to champion Wright, it is as though he felt it necessary to stage a modern version of the Biblical myth of Noah, Ham, Shem and Japheth (based originally, I'm told, on a castration ritual), with first Baldwin and then Ellison acting out the impious role of Ham. (p. 109)

As we shall see shortly, this myth is fundamental as well to Baldwin's *Fire Next Time* (to which Howe refers in his initial essay). *The Fire Next Time* begins and ends with a quotation from Noah. The same reference is imported into *The Tenants,* replete with the threat of castration (which hovers as well over Ellison's *Invisible Man*).[23] References to Ham and Noah continue to punctuate Ellison's response. The Noah text evidences Ellison's recognition of the importance of Jewish within Western and African American culture. However, insofar as Ellison is arguing against black culture forming itself in an Old Testament (white, Jewish, Howesque) image (this is the whole point of Ellison's response: to prevent white and Jewish critics from saying what black culture ought to be), and insofar as the issue between him and Howe is the Jew's unwillingness to articulate the Jewish role in Western culture, the Noah text also constitutes an accusation against the Jews of a kind of conspiracy against Western civilization, here mounted on cultural as opposed to economic or political grounds. Insofar as Marxism was an important basis of black–Jewish relations during the 1930s and 1940s, the political grounds are not far from Ellison's thinking, as they are directly pertinent to the thinking of a black intellectual like Harold Cruse or in writers like Wright, Baldwin, and Chester Himes.

Ellison's charge against the Jews, anticipating by a good decade the arguments of black aestheticists in the 1970s and on, is that they have, in some important way, "enslaved" the American black, albeit intellectually and imaginatively rather than literally (it will take the Nation of Islam to produce the literal charge). Thus, to carry forward the argument, which is to carry it backward again, through the documents, when Ellison, in his first letter, writes, "[Wright] had his memories and I have mine, just as I suppose Irving Howe has his – or has Marx spoken the final word for him?" we think Ellison is doing no more than marking the literary critical or even political dimensions of the disagreement between them (p. 118). But in the company of Ellison's Old Testament references, the names "Marx" and "Freud" (Ellison is also accusing Howe of a primitive Freudian analysis of Baldwin's and his own relationship to Wright) shade into code words for "Jew." Howe knows this, even before Ellison shows his hand in his final reply. As elsewhere Ellison is reminding Howe of his Jewishness. More pertinent, Ellison is probing what it means that his Jewishness remains unstated, unidentified, in Howe's literary, cultural, and political statements, as in Western and American culture generally.

As the passages moving from Noah and Ham through Old Testament Jews to Marx begin to construct a pattern within Ellison's second essay, we realize that he is charting a very large (if subtle) pattern of Jewish intellectual influence, in which black people, in his view, have become enmeshed. Although Ellison seems to be striking out for universal humanism in his essays, he is in fact garnering the forces of black cultural autonomy – thus making some of the 1960s and 1970s African Americanist attacks on him quite misplaced. He is also, however, ironically, paradoxically, proving the validity of Howe's oedipal interpretation, as Ellison invokes the patriarchal text in order to rebel against it, like Ham against Noah – but with Howe (or at least Old Testament Judaism) and not Wright in the role of the (Jewish) father. As we shall see, Ellison's move here exactly imitates a major feature of Baldwin's *Fire Next Time.*

But this is to anticipate, if only a moment too soon, where I am going in terms of these writers' mutual constructions of their ethnic identities. Therefore, before I turn the argument around and produce from within Ellison's text his repetition of what he is objecting to in Howe's article, let me interpret just a few more elements in Ellison's replies to Howe concerning what Ellison later (apparently seeming to praise American Jews) calls their special forms of dissent (a somewhat slighting reference, I take it, to Howe's journal). These are Ellison's notations, only two paragraphs into his first reply, to "Hannah Arendt's 'Reflections on Little Rock' in the Winter 1959 *Dissent* (a dark foreshadowing of the Eichmann blowup)" (p. 108) and, in his second, to Norman Mailer's "White Negro," also published in *Dissent* (p. 132).

As I have already suggested, at very least Ellison is once more reminding Howe of his Jewishness. More important, however, Ellison is calling attention to the tendency of American Jews to assume what he calls Howe's "Olympian" tone, as they presume, from positions of cultural and religious authority, to comment on African Americans. Howe's quotations in his original essay from Alfred Kazin and Isaac Rosenfeld support Ellison's sense of a virtual Jewish obsession with the American black; did no one outside the black community but Jews, one wants to ask, write about blacks? Jews in America, in Ellison's view, have tended to concern themselves with everything but Jewish history, and where they have dealt with Jewish history, as in Arendt's piece, they have tended to be highly intellectualized and almost anti-Jewish in their criticism of it. Just a few months later both Howe and Norman Podhoretz take Hannah Arendt to task for her *Eichmann in Jerusalem,* which initially appeared as a series of articles in the *New Yorker* only months after it had published Baldwin's "A Letter from a Region in My Mind" (which later came out in book form as *The Fire Next Time*).

That both Howe and Podhoretz take note of what may amount to no more than a publishing coincidence confirms Ellison's sense that Jewish intellectuals are specially tuned to black–Jewish convergence.[24] More to the point, however, what Howe and Podhoretz witness in their responses to this odd publishing fact is what Ellison is in fact claiming in his essays: that even though Jews see similarities between black and Jewish concerns, nonetheless they are involved in Jewish issues in ways different from their involvement in black history. Therefore, they apply to black writing a set of demands they do not require of Jews. At the same time, they tolerate, in condescending ways, a lack of standards on which they do insist in Jewish-authored texts.

Howe states directly that the publication of Baldwin's "Letter" in the *New Yorker* did not trouble him until Arendt's piece appeared. Then his sensitivity to decorum, to publishing serious and complex discussions in a commercial magazine, replete with advertisements and with no possibility of rebuttal, is roused. He feels compelled to respond, as indeed he does. Similarly, Norman Podhoretz, in his even lengthier response to Arendt's piece, is provoked only after the appearance of Arendt's "Eichmann" to take note of the facility with which the popular media bandy around serious intellectual issues.

Podhoretz's treatment of the relationship between the Baldwin and Arendt documents supports Ellison's complaints against "Black Boys and Native Sons." Podhoretz is not at all distressed by the "black and white account" that Baldwin provides, but he takes Arendt sternly to task for underlining "every trace of moral ambiguity" in what is, for Podhoretz, an illegitimate desire on her part to make her argument "appeal to the sophisticated modern sensibility"

(p. 201). Podhoretz may well be right about Arendt as well as about the necessity (evidenced in the Baldwin text) to see evil as evil and good as good. Nonetheless, what he manages to do in his coupling of Baldwin and Arendt is to produce a simplistic black and a complex Jew. Given Arendt's earlier philosophical effort in "Reflections on Little Rock" (offensive to many black intellectuals), this strategy could only serve to perpetuate, within the African American community, a sense that Jews held themselves intellectually superior to blacks.

And this is at least one aspect of what Ellison is getting at in Howe's discussion of Wright, Baldwin, and Ellison. It is what he means, in part, by Howe's Olympian tone. Even Howe's refusal to engage directly the potentially anti-Semitic implication of Ellison's comments represents a form of condescension on Howe's part: he is above racial or religious engagement, but he allows Ellison the liberty, as a person in a presumably lesser cultural position, to engage in vindictive retort. Does Malamud encode this presumption in Lesser's quotation of Lear's "Who is it that can tell me who I am?" The quotation can be understood to represent Lear's genuine uncertainty as to who he is. Or it can articulate his, and thus Lesser's, challenge exactly to remember, without his having to say it, who he is.

Stanley Edgar Hyman, in another dialogue with Ellison in *Partisan Review* a few years earlier, was similarly willing to absorb the force of Ellison's attack against him. Like his response to Howe, Ellison's critique of Hyman goes to Hyman's presumption as a white Jewish critic. As I have already begun to suggest, Malamud may be aware of this exchange (Ellison's part of the discussion is also reprinted in *Shadow and Act*). He may be encoding it in the novel in the title and epigraph of Lesser's novel, which, like Hyman's title, derive from *King Lear*. Malamud would have found particularly congenial Hyman's belief in "literature as secular salvation and redemption." Like Malamud, Hyman "substantially repudiated" "Jewish culture and religious training."[25] And Malamud may well have taken from Hyman's essay his information concerning the black blues tradition and his knowledge of the game called "the dozens" that Willie has Lesser play (Hyman, p. 305; Malamud, p. 131). As I have already noted, Malamud uses "I got to make it, I got to find the end – Bessie Smith" as an epigraph to his novel (further emphasizing the "end" motif of Malamud's, Lesser's, and Hyman's productions). He provides Lesser with a large Bessie Smith collection; Smith is one of the musicians to whom Hyman makes constant reference in the essay.[26]

Like his argument with Howe, Ellison's objection to Hyman's discussion of black folklore seems to hinge on Ellison's belief "that the Negro American writer is also the heir of the human experience which is literature" (p. 58). This is the feature of black experience that, in Ellison's view, Hyman, like Howe, forgets. "Hyman's fascination with folk tradition and the pleasure of archetype-hunting," argues Ellison, "leads to a critical game that ignores the specificity of literary works. And it also causes him to blur the distinction between various archetypes and different currents of American folklore, and, generally, to oversimplify the American tradition" (p. 46).

In his republication in *The Promised End* of his segment of the exchange with Ellison, Hyman notes that "when I finished the manuscript I sent it to my friend Ralph Ellison for an opinion. He replied with a long eloquent letter arguing the other half of the truth, the indebtedness of American Negro literature to the European literary tradition" (pp. 314–15). But Hyman's essay, like Howe's, is a very careful work of appreciative scholarship (Ellison acknowledges this: p. 46). In no way does it deny the influence of European on black literature. Indeed, Hyman begins by acknowledging varieties of African American literature, some of them "indistinguishable from white writing" (p. 296). He chooses, however, to focus on "the half-dozen or so Negro writers who seem to [him] largely to have gone beyond any sort of mimicry or naturalism," and who, "in their use of literary form as an act of the moral imagination," have "joined the mainstream of modern literature" (p. 296).

Of these the major figure is Ralph Ellison, whose *Invisible Man* is Hyman's major text, and whose enactment of the "darky act" and "trickster" figure represents, for Hyman, the "fullest development" of these archetypes, not only in black fiction, but in fiction generally (pp. 297–99). Thus, writes Hyman,

> If Wright, Fisher, and Ellison get the darky act from the realities (and travesties) of Negro life in America, from folk tales of Buh Rabbit and John, and ultimately from West African mythology, those are still not the only sources. The same mocking figure dances through Western literature. . . . In other words, when the Negro writer retreats furthest from white models and deepest into Negro folk tradition, back in fact to African myth, he is paradoxically not furthest from Western literature but finds himself sharing a timeless archetype with Aristophanes, Shakespeare, and St. Paul, who in turn derived it from *their* folk sources in myth and ritual. High Western culture and the

Negro folk tradition thus do not appear to pull the writer in opposite directions, but to say the same thing in their different vocabularies, to come together and reinforce insight with insight. (pp. 300–301)

Given Hyman's statements, it is not possible, I think, to claim in defense of Ellison, as does Robert O'Meally, that "troubled by the 'segregated' idea that black writers strictly depend on black sources, and angered by even the dimmest suggestion that as a black writer he himself performed the obscene function of a blackface minstrel man, Ellison threw Hyman a hyperbole" when, seeming to "contradict [his own] belief that folklore provides a secure base for great literature," he took Hyman to task for his reading of the novel.[27] Ellison's response, I suggest, is not hyperbole. It is motivated, as in the exchange with Howe, not by what Hyman says but by what Hyman does not say.

We miss the point of the Hyman–Ellison exchange if we imagine the issue between them to be only whether or not black writers write out of the Western tradition. For inclusion within Western civilization is *not* Ellison's only or primary objective here. It is also not his goal in the debate with Howe. Rather, his purpose is something utterly different, more profound, more difficult of achievement, and more likely to mark exactly where blacks and Jews move from cooperation to antagonism.

Strangers in the Promised Land (James Baldwin and Cynthia Ozick)

It must certainly be one of the ironies of African American literary scholarship that Ellison's reclamation as a seminal figure occurred when critics like Houston Baker in *Blues, Ideology, and Afro-American Literature* and Henry Louis Gates in *The Signifying Monkey* discovered in Ellison not the relation to Western humanism that Ellison claimed for himself, but his encoding of a secret trickster, double-talk aesthetic, such as Hyman was already describing in Ellison's work in the 1950s.

As Kerry McSweeney notes, the celebration of Ellison's novel as universal and "dealing with timeless difficulties that are everywhere and always the same, rather than with particular, historically and culturally conditioned problems rooted in the contradictions of a white capitalist society" began "to take a lambasting in the later 1960s with the rise of black power, black aesthetics, and ideologically motivated criticism."[28] Typical of this criticism of Ellison, and touching exactly the issue that apparently constitutes the sore spot of contention between him and Hyman, Susan L. Blake accuses Ellison of a "ritualization of black folklore." This ritualization, according to Blake, removes black folklore from the sociohistorical conditions of black people in America and thus rationalizes white racism:

> By denying the need for real change, broadening the context of black folklore perpetuates the oppressive relationship on which it is based. Thus the definition of black experience achieved by Ellison's ritualization of black folklore is ultimately not black but white – white not only because the 'larger' con texts into which ritual fits the folklore are those of predominantly white American and Western societies but also because the very idea that a change in mental context can change social reality supports the interests of white society by implicitly denying those of the black. Ellison's adaptation of black folklore, however involuntarily, exchanges the self-definition of the folk for the definition of the masters – an effect it would not have if it did not undertake to define black identity.[29]

When Baker and Gates come in to defend Ellison as producing folklore and not its ritualization, neither mentions Hyman, even though they both cite the Ellison essay that refers to Hyman's part of the exchange between them. Part of the problem here is, of course, that neither Hyman's nor Ellison's portions of the exchanges are, after their initial appearance in *Partisan Review*, published together. Read together, the dialogue reveals the ways in which Ellison's position was taken, not absolutely nor even in response to white racism, but in direct contradistinction to an implication within what was probably, in his own view of the matter as well, the most generous of white criticisms of black texts.

This implication is, I think, the major discovery of Ellison's critique of Howe. It is his reason for taunting Howe to declare his Jewishness, and it defines his objection to Hyman's reading of him. As Ellison understood it, the critical establishment in America, of which Jewish intellectuals like Howe and Hyman were key representatives, did not really have trouble listening to blacks speak as blacks. Rather, they had trouble with listening to blacks speak as Americans. Baldwin's resistance to Wright's *Native Son,* like his resistance to Harriet Beecher Stowe's *Uncle Tom's Cabin,* has to do with the ways in which these novels functioned in American culture, not to undermine basic assumptions about who or what constituted that culture but, rather, in protesting injustice, to affirm America's best view of itself. In other words, in Baldwin's view, and Ellison's, protest fiction was too easy. It was too white. It didn't assert the hard truth, which Baldwin and Ellison state over and over again in their essays and fiction, that America is not white but interracial. "The 'protest' novel," Baldwin argues against Wright, "so far from being disturbing, is an accepted and comforting aspect of the American scene, ramifying that framework we believe to be so necessary. . . . [T]he oppressed and the oppressor are bound together within the same society; they accept the same criteria, they share the same beliefs. . . . Below the surface of this novel [*Native Son*] lies . . . a continuation, a complement of that monstrous legend it was written to destroy" ("Everybody's Protest Novel," pp. 19–22).[30] Ironically, a similar logic can be (and indeed has been) applied to Baldwin's and Ellison's own successes within the white world.

This is not to say that Baldwin and Ellison, in fact Wright himself, do not write subversive novels and essays. It is, however, to claim that since the American readership did not necessarily hear the subversive note in any of these writers (as Ellison and Baldwin fail to hear this note in Wright, as Wright has been interpreted, for example, by Paul Gilroy), these texts could be assimilated into a comfortable and comforting notion of black–white relations.[31] The intentions of these texts are, however, entirely different. Consider, for example, Ellison's figure of invisibility in *Invisible Man,* a figure prominent as well in the title essay in Baldwin's collection "Notes of a Native Son" (pp. 95–97). To be black in America is not literally to be invisible. From more than one perspective, blacks might seem too visible, too much the object of media and public interest. Rather, blacks are invisible as human beings. Even more important for the cultural argument I wish to bring into focus here, they are invisible as Americans. They are (as the opening and closing scenes of Ellison's novel vividly suggest) the unseen users of American services. They are also the unseen contributors to American culture. For this reason the name of the protagonist/author of Ellison's novel goes unspoken, while the name of *Emerson* is overspoken. What Ellison realizes is that in 1950s American culture, the name "Ellison" or "Negro" can be spoken only in its silence, indeed in its being displaced by the name Emerson, which is one of America's names for itself. But in speaking this way – and this is both the great insight of Ellison's novel and the source of its tremendous artistic power – he imitates nothing so much as the way in which American culture, indeed all culture, speaks to itself. Cultural speaking, Ellison knows, is always conducted with absolute casualness and disregard (such as Howe exhibits) for having to identify who (ethnically, religiously, racially) is doing the speaking.

As Baldwin puts it in "The Discovery of What It Means to Be an American," again anticipating what have become commonplaces of our literary-critical vocabulary, "every society is really governed by hidden laws, by unspoken but profound assumptions on the part of the people, and ours is no exception. It is up to the American writer to find out what these laws and assumptions are" (*Nobody Knows My Name*, p. 11). By forcing the reader to produce the name Ellison/ Emerson, Ellison achieves an American voice. He produces the voice that the American reader will acknowledge to be his or her own. Ellison's invisible man is his white Negro; his black man as American, since America, Ellison realizes, is not white culture but interracial, black-white, culture. In other words, Ellison as invisible man speaks in his lack of explicit cultural identification as America speaks to itself: as America.

In Ellison's view, white America (Jewish America included) not only tolerated black speaking, it welcomed it. But it welcomed it exactly because such speaking was not, in their view, the voice of America itself. Rather, it was the voice of the tried-and-true tradition of American dissent and protest by the margins of American society, whose challenge to the culture was a necessary part of the cultural construct. The American reading public could listen to a genuine black voice speaking genuine black protest. It could not hear the very different kind of voice spoken by Baldwin and Ellison in their essays and novels – the voice of the African *American*. What white America, its Jews included, had trouble with, Ellison understood, was listening to blacks speaking, not on the margins, challenging and thus reenforcing an American status quo, but as the central players in the American culture game.

This recognition of the centrality of the American black, and of the African American voice as the voice of America itself, is, I suggest, exactly what Howe cannot hear in Ellison or in his retort to Howe, which Ellison disentangles from the Marxist rhetoric and other literary-critical and social concerns of Howe's discourse. It is as well what Hyman misses in Ellison's response to his essay. Hyman does not, as Ellison accuses him, cordon off African American literature as separate from the Western tradition. Thus, Hyman misreads Ellison's response to his essay as presenting the "other half of the truth," which in Hyman's view is the degree to which black texts are a part of the Western tradition. Hyman has already acknowledged this truth. What Hyman doesn't respond to is Ellison's real complaint, which is that Hyman (like Howe and others) imagines black literature as controlled by, as opposed to itself participating in the creation of, Western culture. Especially problematic, therefore, from Ellison's point of view, is "Hyman's favorite archetypical figure . . . the trickster," which Hyman expressly tells us is a feature of Western tradition itself. This trickster, suggests Ellison, does not "grow out of the Negro American sense of the comic . . . but out of the white American's Manichean fascination with the symbolism of blackness and whiteness expressed in such contradictions as the conflict between the white American's Judeo-Christian morality, his democratic political ideals and his daily conduct – indeed in his general anti-tragic approach to experience" (pp. 46–48; cf. "A Very Stern Discipline," in *Going to the Territory,* pp. 280–81).

In other words, the trickster in white literature is already a reference to African American culture. Anticipating by several decades the point made by Toni Morrison, first in "Unspeakable Things Unspoken," subsequently in *Playing in the Dark,* Ellison is directing the white critic, in this case the white Jewish critic, to do three things. The first is to examine his or her own tradition to see how it is constructed by racist attitudes and assumptions rather than to examine the Negro tradition, to which the white (Jewish) critic has little access (*Judeo*-Christian morality, Ellison says, in an era when recalling Christianity's origins in Judaism is not the dominant mode and in contradistinction to the claim he makes in his rejoinder to Howe that he would like to see a positive distinction made between white Americans and Jews).[32] The second is to recognize that American culture already incorporates and reflects, and thus is constituted by, black culture. And the last – the claim that is most problematical of all for white (and Jewish) audiences, and that had already been made, and similarly went unheard, as Michael Kramer has pointed out, by W. E. B. Du Bois (and also in relation to the Jews): that American culture *is* African American culture.[33]

This is how Ellison explained it in a 1976 interview:

American literature is partially an expression of a society in which the race problem has always been at the core of its moral concerns. . . . The American vernacular culture out of which what we identify as American writing arose was very much influenced by the oral lore, the oral literature of the Afro-American. This appears in Mark Twain; it appears in the music. It appeared in a great, original musical art form which was the minstrel show. It appeared in popular songs, the folk songs of the cowboys, the boatmen, the raftsmen along the Mississippi. All this is accounted for in the memoirs of travelers and is recognized by such people as Mark Twain, whose *Huckleberry Finn* is very much concerned with Afro-American speech, superstition, humanity.[34]

Similar comments appear throughout Ellison's essays, for example, when he says that

> the spoken idiom of Negro Americans . . . , its flexibility, its musicality, its rhythms, freewheeling diction, and metaphors, as projected in Negro American folklore, were absorbed by the creators of our great nineteenth-century literature even when the majority of blacks were still enslaved. Mark Twain celebrated it in the prose of *Huckleberry Finn:* without the presence of blacks, the book could not have been written. No Huck and Jim, no American novel as we know it.[35]

As Shelley Fisher Fishkin notes, Ellison's "stunningly correct . . . comment sank like a stone, leaving barely a ripple on the placid surface of American literary criticism."[36] The question Ellison is raising, which Baldwin is raising as well, is: Who is America, and who speaks in its name, and how?

For American Jewish intellectuals like Howe and Hyman, speaking as America meant, for them as Jews, speaking in a universalist discourse. In "Metaphor and Memory" (1986), Cynthia Ozick defines the ethic that, I think, characterizes both Howe's and Hyman's positions in their exchanges with Ralph Ellison. And she links it to the very word that identifies both what Jews and blacks share in their historical experiences and what distinguishes the one group from the other. In her essay Ozick notes the appearance, no fewer than thirty-six times, of the verse that, in Ozick's account, marks the special moral genius of the Old Testament, "history as metaphor, memory raised to parable: *The stranger that sojourneth with you shall be unto you as the homeborn among you, and you shall love him as yourself; because you were strangers in the land of Egypt*" (p. 279). According to Ozick, this injunction to love the stranger far exceeds, in its moral depth and power, the admonition that precedes it by sixteen verses, the imperative taken up so prominently by Christianity, to "love thy neighbor as thyself." To love thy neighbor, notes Ozick, is "a glorious, civilizing, unifying sentence, an exhortation of consummate moral beauty, difficult of performance, difficult *in* performance. And it reveals at once the little seed of parable: the phrase 'as thyself.' 'Thyself' – that universe of feeling – is the model. '*As thyself*' becomes the commanding metaphor." But, Ozick continues, "we are still, with our neighbor, in Our Town. We are still, with the self, in psychology. We have not yet penetrated to history and memory. . . . Without the metaphor of memory and history, we cannot imagine the life of the Other. We cannot imagine what it is to be someone else. Metaphor is the reciprocal agent, the universalizing force: it makes possible the power to envision the stranger's heart" (p. 279).

The experience to which the phrase "because you were strangers in the land of Egypt" refers is specifically the experience of slavery. It is the imagination of the slave, of the stranger, that Ozick wishes to claim for Jewish culture. And she wants to put that mind-set into opposition to classical culture. The contemporary world, Ozick remarks, has romanticized and exalted the Greeks. But the Greeks, unlike the Jews, Ozick argues, were

> not universalists. . . . They were proud of despising the stranger. . . . [T]hey never undertook to imagine what it was to be the Other: the outsider; the alien; the slave; the oppressed; the sufferer; the outcast; the opponent; the barbarian who owns feelings and deserves rights. And that is because they did not, as a society, cultivate memory, or search out any historical metaphor to contain memory. . . . A nation of slaves is different from a nation of philosophers. Out of that slavery a new thing was made [and] this new thing [was] "metaphor." (pp. 277–78)

What is more, such metaphor was not mere aesthetic description. It was moral imperative, injunction, a commandment (not a suggestion) to love, not one's neighbor, but the stranger, as oneself.

Whether Jewish culture conforms as completely as Ozick suggests to the biblical commandment, I want to claim Ozick's interpretation of the stranger as fundamental to one important American Jewish intellectual position, the universalism of Ozick, Howe, and Hyman. Of course, Jews were never strangers in the land of America in the technical definition offered by Ozick's Old Testament text, though they were, at first, foreigners, come from the pogrom-shattered ghettos of eastern Europe and later from the devastation of the German death camps. Nor did the nation to which they arrived any longer contain strangers in the biblical sense, although it contained many of their descendants, who had also suffered massive abuse and annihilation, and whose lives both before and after slavery were often as impoverished, degraded, and threatened as those of European Jews. So, while America has not, for over a century, been a land of "strangers" exactly, it has been a land occupied by strangers of sorts, the descendants of strangers, who have shared not only the memory of slavery (at various generational removes and in different forms) but its basic text as well; or at least they seem to share this text. For a question that must be asked concerning blacks and Jews is whether the Old Testament from which both derive the tropes and ethics of exodus and freedom is the same Old Testament; and whether when blacks and Jews speak of the stranger they mean "stranger" in the same sense.

Given the history of both African American experience in general and religion in particular, it is not in the least surprising that the culminating essay in Baldwin's *Notes of a Native Son* should be entitled "Stranger in the Village," or that it should resonate so powerfully with Ozick's "Metaphor and Memory," written three decades later. As Baldwin puts it in an earlier essay in the volume, "the hymns, the texts, and the most favored legends of the devout Negro are all Old Testament and therefore Jewish in origin: the flight from Egypt, the Hebrew children in the fiery furnace, the terrible jubilee songs of deliverance" ("The Harlem Ghetto," p. 67). Ralph Ellison also develops this idea in several of his essays. But if Ozick's point is that the Jews preserve the memory of their having been strangers as what enables their moral relationship to others, Baldwin's point in this essay, as in the major essays of *Notes of a Native Son,* is quite the opposite. Baldwin may well be a "stranger" (albeit not in the biblical sense) in the little village in Switzerland where he is writing his essay. He is "not," however, "a stranger in America" (p. 168), "not a visitor to the West, but a citizen there, an American as American as the Americans who despise him, the Americans who fear him, the Americans who love him" (p. 173).

The major point of Baldwin's essay is to describe the mutual creation of African American and white American identity, each by the other, and therefore the joint construction, by blacks and whites as equal participants, of what we think of as American culture. In this Baldwin, like Ralph Waldo Ellison, is nothing less than prophetic of contemporary Americanist discourse. African Americans are already arguing in the 1950s what will become the major thesis of multicultural studies in the 1980s and 1990s: that there is no such thing as white American culture; that there is only the interracially determined culture that blacks and whites (and Native Americans and others) mutually constructed in the United States. There is an even more radical and aggressive claim contained within this one, which Baldwin, Ellison, and others inherit from W. E. B. Du Bois, but let me delay, for a while, putting this up front.

In order to assert the idea of the mutual black–white construction of American culture, Baldwin retrieves an idea of blacks and whites equally as "strangers," each equally implicated in the fate and identity of the other: "this village [in Switzerland]," writes Baldwin, "brings home to me this fact: that there was a day, and not really a very distant day, when Americans were scarcely Americans at all but discontented Europeans, facing a great unconquered continent and strolling, say, into a marketplace and seeing black men for the first time" (p. 168). The consequence for blacks and whites of the founding of America on the institution of slavery was that for both of them – for the black whose "past was taken from him" (p. 169), and for the white who had removed to the new continent – the task was the same. They had to construct a native American identity, where such construction was linked, from the beginning, to their shared occupation of the American continent: "The identity of the American Negro comes out of [the] extreme situation" of (in Franklin Frazier's words) finding

> a "motive for living under American culture" [while] the question of [the American Negro's] humanity, and of his rights therefore as a human being, became a burning one for several generations of Americans . . . the black man, *as a man,* did not exist for Europe. But in America, even as a slave, he was an inescapable part of the general social fabric and no American could escape having an attitude toward him. . . . The ideas on which American beliefs are based are not, though Americans often seem to think so, ideas which originated in America. They came out of Europe. And the establishment of democracy on the American continent was scarcely as radical a break with the past as was the necessity, which Americans faced, of broadening this concept to include black men. (pp. 169–71)

And Baldwin concludes:

> The time has come to realize that the interracial drama acted out on the American continent has not only created a new black man, it has created a new white man, too. No road whatever will lead Americans back to the simplicity of this European village where white men still have the luxury of looking on me as a stranger. I am not, really, a stranger any longer for any

American alive. . . . This world is white no longer, and it will never be white again. (p. 175)

What Wright's *Native Son,* in Baldwin's view, fails to present to the American reader is the "we"-ness of this already interracial American culture. From the initial publication of the essay entitled "Notes of a Native Son," and later the volume that bears that title, which is of course an allusion to and, insofar as it argues against Wright, a displacement of Wright's *Native Son,* Baldwin puts this claim of his American nativism up front; and he repeats the gesture in 1961 in *Nobody Knows My Name: More Notes of a Native Son.* "The root function of language is to control the universe by describing it," Baldwin suggests in "Stranger in the Village" (p. 166). In a distinctly Emersonian fashion, he transforms the sting of the pejorative word "native" into a claim of nativism and cultural centrality. The African American is neither a native in the sense of an African primitive, as some white Americans would understand the term to mean; nor is he or she a native like the Native Americans. Rather the African American is America's truest native son: no stranger in the village but one of its original inhabitants.

"I am not a ward of America," Baldwin announces in no uncertain terms in *The Fire Next Time,* "I am one of the first Americans to arrive on these shores" (p. 132). Thus in "Many Thousands Gone" Baldwin speaks in the first-person plural, not as a black man defending himself against his exclusion within white society, but as fully participant in American democracy as those who would keep him out: "Our dehumanization of the Negro then is indivisible from our dehumanization of ourself: the loss of our own identity is the price we pay for our annulment of his" (p. 25). For Baldwin, one of the most painful aspects of Wright's *Native Son* is that blacks, not only whites, will understand Bigger Thomas to represent the "dark and unloved stranger" that is the African American, not only in his disenfranchisement by whites, but in his or her own acceptance of this exclusion from what is the American blacks' own, and only, culture (p. 42).

Christians, Sun-baked Hebrews, and Sons of Ham: Jews in the Crossfire Next Time (James Baldwin) [37]

Let me put as clearly as possible the difference between Baldwin's and Ozick's application to the idea of the stranger. Ozick uses the formula of the stranger to set the Jew, who is, by the time Ozick is writing, centrally within American culture, outside that culture. She places the Jew in a larger, antecedent cultural arena, going back to the Old Testament itself. And she defines a certain Jewish moral relation to the world in which a sense of strangeness functions as the basis for a universal ethical philosophy. Baldwin's stranger, on the other hand, serves to identify, in order to condemn, the internal dynamics of American culture itself. In America, the African American, though once literally a stranger in America and considered by many Americans (including black Americans) still to be a stranger of sorts, constitutes as foundational an element in the construction of that culture as the American white (who in the not so distant past was also a stranger of sorts). The African American, therefore, must make his fellow Americans see him not as a stranger, but as an American.

Baldwin's protest against the protest novel does not, as Howe imagines, have to do either with Wright's political position or with the fact that Wright has a political position. Rather, as Howe almost gets to but cannot quite articulate, it has do with Wright's willingness to speak as Americans would have him speak, as the stranger. He speaks as the outsider whose challenge to American culture can be absorbed (even if it is to be acted upon rather than deflected) because it is a challenge from outside. Bigger Thomas, for Baldwin, is (like Uncle Tom) "the incarnation of a [white, racist] myth." Wright's novel omits "the relationship that Negroes bear to one another, that depth of involvement and unspoken recognition of shared experience which creates a way of life." The protest novel, Baldwin argues – and Howe quotes him on it without quite taking the depth and range of Baldwin's point – leads us

> to believe that in Negro life there exists no tradition, no field of manners, no possibility of ritual or intercourse, such as may, for example, sustain the Jew even after he has left his family's house. But the fact is not that the Negro has no tradition but that there has yet arrived no sensibility sufficiently profound or tough to make this tradition articulate. For a tradition expresses, after all, nothing more than the long and painful experience of a people; it comes out of the battle waged to maintain their integrity or, to put it more simply, out of their struggle to survive. When we speak of the Jewish tradition we are speaking of centuries of exile and persecution, of the strength which endured and the sensibility which discovered in it the high possibility of the moral victory. ("Many Thousands Gone," pp. 35–36)

It is in terms of conveying a black sensibility, predicated on their integrity and survival and the high possibility of the moral victory, that, in Baldwin's view, Wright's novel does not succeed. Therefore, Wright's book can also not do the political work that he, no less than Howe, would demand of black fiction. This is the work of racially integrating America, not in the sense that most Americans (including many American blacks and Jews, too) erroneously understood, by accepting the black stranger into white society. Rather, as Baldwin makes lucidly clear in his much later, much angrier *The Fire Next Time*, he means by integration enabling Americans to recognize that America is already integrated and always has been. Making Americans see this, and act on it, will not only constitute the moral victory of the black experience in America for blacks but, in keeping with Baldwin's insistence that America is as much his country as anyone's, it will constitute the high moral victory for America itself: "There is no reason for you to try to become like white people and there is no basis whatever for their impertinent assumption that they must accept *you*," Baldwin writes to his nephew James, to whom the volume is addressed, saying further that

> the really terrible thing, old buddy, is that *you* must accept *them*. And I mean that very seriously. You must accept them and accept them with love. For these innocent people have no other hope. They are, in effect, still trapped in a history which they do not understand; and unless they understand it, they cannot be released from it. . . . But these men are your brothers. . . . And if the word *integration* means anything, this is what it means: that we, with love, shall force our brothers to see themselves as they are, to cease fleeing from reality and begin to change it. For this is your home . . . do not be driven from it . . . and we can make America what America must become. (pp. 19–21)[38]

In thus formulating his project, the aptly named James, writing to his namesake James, produces nothing so much as a new African Americanist gospel, one of many such in the African American literary tradition, as we shall see.

Writing gospel directly affects the relationship of the black text to Jewish tradition.[39] In a move recognizable as both supersessionist and antitypological, Baldwin establishes the apocalyptic text of his African Americanism as a last new work of scripture. This African American gospel supersedes Old and New Testament both. It reveals to the white Christian majority of America (and its Jewish minority as well) the underlying truths that have, in the Western religious tradition, as once within Judaism, become obscured and falsified and are thus in need of revision. In this process of supersessionist intervention, Baldwin cannot help but confront the American Jew, with troubling, if highly familiar, consequences. The problem between blacks and Jews is not simply sociological, the two groups (as both Baldwin and Malamud make clear) competing for urban space. It is also theological.

Part of the problem is, simply, as Baldwin himself confesses, that black Christians partake of a Christian view of the Jews. The conflict between blacks and Jews may be more fraught because of the ways in which black Christians are also in opposition to white Christians, but, on its way to a new specificity, the black relationship to the Jews reconstructs the essential disagreement between Christianity and Judaism. In other words, even as they need to disentangle the white church from the black church, so blacks must also wrestle their Christianity free of its Judaic origins. And they must do this without causing an out-and-out rupture between themselves and Judeo-Christian culture. This means discovering both the place of black Africa within Judaism and Christianity and of Judaism and Christianity within African American religion and culture.

This is the cultural, theological work done by *The Fire Next Time*. The essay is a stunning document just in terms of its statements concerning America's race problem. But the *Fire* is more stunning still if one takes seriously its rhetorical strategy, which is to embed the race issue within the more personal drama of a young man's rebellion against his father. Ellison's charge against Howe, that he stages Baldwin's and his own relation to Wright as the rebellion of Ham against Noah, has a subtext beyond (indeed behind) Howe: Baldwin's staging of this rebellion in the *Fire,* to which Howe may or may not, consciously or unconsciously, also be responding and in which the rebellion has nothing to do with Richard Wright and everything, perhaps, to do with Jews.

As in *Notes of a Native Son,* Baldwin turns in the *Fire* to the subject of black–Jewish relations, even though it is not a subject necessarily dictated by the larger purposes of his essay. He sees this relationship as the consequence of a series of interwoven and mutually complicating factors, some of which he had cited earlier in "The Harlem Ghetto." One set of factors is sociological. Jewish sympathy toward blacks, especially during the Civil Rights movement, produced a philo-Semitism in blacks, as did Jewish persecution and the Holocaust. Nonetheless, living in close quarters in the major city ghettoes, where Jews began to function as slumlords and shopkeepers, produced a native and natural black "anti-Semitism" among the black community.[40] This lived relationship to the Jews reproduces the complexity of a prior theological relation between the two groups. On the one hand, blacks first encounter Jews through a Christian interpretation of the Old Testament. In other words, they confront Jews through at least some measure of institutional anti-Semitism.[41] On the other hand, blacks, as themselves victims of white Christian racism, identify with the Old Testament Israelites and their suffering. Although Baldwin implies that these Old Testament Israelites and contemporary Jewry are one and the same, it is not at all clear that the Jew he puts center stage of his narrative is not more Israelite than contemporary Jew.

It may be a mere desire for comprehensiveness that draws Baldwin to the subject of black–Jewish relations or a realization that Jews number profusely in his audience. Most of the original essays published in *Notes of a Native Son* were originally published in Jewish journals like *Commentary, Partisan Review,* and the *New Leader,* and the Jewish journals remained committed to reviewing and publishing Baldwin throughout his career. Nonetheless, the richness of Baldwin's *Fire* vis-à-vis its relationship to Jewish culture does not lie in its analysis of Jewish–black affinities and tensions, even though these passages in the *Fire,* as earlier passages in *Notes of a Native Son,* were clearly taken up this way by later African and Jewish American scholars. Rather, the key moment in the *Fire's* thinking about Jews and Jewish culture is far more personal and far more fraught:

My best friend in high school was a Jew. He came to our house once, and afterward my father asked, as he asked about everyone, "Is he a Christian?" – by which he meant "Is he saved?" I really do not know whether my answer came out of innocence or venom, but I said, coldly, "No. He's Jewish." My father slammed me across the face with his great palm, and in that moment everything flooded back – all the hatred and all the fear and the depth of a merciless resolve to kill my father rather than allow my father to kill me – and I knew that all those sermons and tears and all that repentance and rejoicing had changed nothing. I wondered if I was expected to be glad that a friend of mine, or anyone, was to be tormented forever in Hell, and I also thought, suddenly, of the Jews in another Christian nation, Germany. They were not so far from the fiery furnace after all, and my best friend might have been one of them. I told my father, "He's a better Christian than you are," and walked out of the house. The battle between us was in the open, but that was all right; it was almost a relief. A more deadly struggle had begun. (pp. 54–55)

This battle, I would suggest, rages not only between Baldwin and his father, but, in some sense at least, between Baldwin and the Jews.

The passage divides painfully along the lines of its two subjects. The first is Baldwin's rejection of Christianity as a white racist religion designed to keep black people in their place, in heaven as well as on earth. The second is his rebellion against his father, who, though he is represented in this passage and elsewhere in the essay as a trope of Christianity (with its specifically black fears and repressions), is also, of course, Baldwin's simple, ordinary (albeit not biological) father. The slap of the father's great palm may be nothing more than an expression of the anti-Semitism/racism of Christianity, as Baldwin's immediate reference to the Holocaust would suggest. Still, it may also, or even primarily, function as a recognizable paternal response to the son's arrogance and presumption, in spitting in his father's face the word "Jew." Indeed, we might well be entitled to reverse the ostensible dynamics of the scene and understand the father's response as itself containing a sense of the son's irreverence, not only to Christianity and himself, but to the Jew, who is thus appropriated, the father understands, by the son in his very private warfare with his father. Given what Baldwin has already said about Christianity, it doesn't seem much like a compliment on Baldwin's part to say that the Jew is the better Christian. And Baldwin's father's slap may be very aptly interpreting an aspect of Baldwin's procedure, not only in the argument with his father but in his argument with white culture.

I leave psychoanalytic, Freudian interpretations of Baldwin's relationship to his stepfather to other critics.[42] What interests me here is the black–Jewish narrative that *The Fire Next Time* is unraveling in terms of its race argument. This argument takes Baldwin to the Nation of Islam and its position vis-à-vis the Jews and Israel, and then away from it again, though not away from the issue of Jewish–black relations. Howe's sense of Baldwin's rejection of Wright as something of an oedipal rejection or Ellison's revision of that paradigm from an oedipal to a biblical setting are not without warrant in terms of the relationship that Baldwin sketches between himself and his father. This is the same relationship that exists between Christianity and Judaism, black and white Christianity, and Christianity, Judaism, and Islam.

In part, the literary strategy at work here is archetypically American. It is the same impulse we see at work in Malamud's Harry Lesser: the desire for autonomous self-birth, in complete dissociation from any real ancestry. Baldwin's essay opens in a moment in his adolescence. It narrates his entry into the Christian ministry as a "Young Minister" (p. 48), which he represents as a "seduction" (45) and a desire to find his appropriate parentage or lineage. "Whose little boy are you?" asks the woman pastor, in "precisely the phrase used by pimps and racketeers on the Avenue when they suggested, both humorously and intensely, that I 'hang out' with them." Baldwin would like nothing so much as to find an answer to this question ("I unquestionably wanted to be *somebody's* little boy"), which he then repeats and answers: "Why, yours" (pp. 43–44). He repeats the question again to himself many years later, when he meets the fatherly (p. 88) Elijah Muhammad: "Now he turned toward me . . . and carried me back nearly twenty-four years, to that moment when the pastor had smiled at me and said, 'Whose little boy are you?' I did not respond now as I had responded then, because there are some things (not many, alas!) that one cannot do twice. . . . He made me think of my father and me as we might have been if we had been friends" (pp. 88–89). This feeling finally yields to the more somber realization that "my weak, deluded scruples could avail nothing against the iron word of the prophet. I felt that I was back in my father's house – as, indeed, in a way, I was" (p. 98). Baldwin's rejection of Elijah Muhammad reenforces his rejection of his father, his rejection of Islam as of Christianity, thus establishing a major motif in this essay: "the American Negro [is] a unique creation" with "no counterpart anywhere, and no predecessors" (p. 139). Therefore, the "black boy" (to adapt Wright's title) is nobody's little boy but his own. Baldwin must give birth to himself.

For this reason, Baldwin almost reflexively includes his Jewish friend at the scene of his break from his father. In unraveling backward out of an indebtedness that comes to seem a form of enslavement, Baldwin has to push back out of the originating conceits of Christianity and Islam, even in Islam's more purely African American form as the Nation of Islam. This means finally backing up into Old Testament Judaism, and then out of it as well, in an attempt to discover the anteriority or priority that Toni Morrison superbly, if problematically, manages in *Song of Solomon* (as we shall see). But whereas Morrison will discover origins in African history, Baldwin (like Ellison and Malamud) will find them more purely in himself, making the motion of his supersessionism like no one's so much as that of Emerson and Whitman before him. Baldwin, like Ellison, is not Afrocentrist. He is Emersonian. Baldwin is not deceiving us when, in the scene of his rebellion in the *Fire,* he indicts his father and his father's Christianity for anti-Semitism. Nor is there any reason to discount the sincerity of his statements concerning the Holocaust. Nonetheless, Baldwin's relationship to the Jews has fundamentally to do with his struggle for autonomy and self-generation, and therefore with his love–hate relationship to the idea that something precedes and produces him, personally and culturally. Confusing Israelites and Jews, Baldwin finds himself, perhaps inevitably and even inadvertently, on a collision course with contemporary Jewish history.

In this confusion between Israelites and Jews, Baldwin has no lesser a predecessor in the tradition than W. E. B. Du Bois. Like Baldwin later, Du Bois locates black culture as centrally and integrally part and parcel of American culture. Indeed, he goes further and claims the origins of American culture in the black experience. "We the darker ones," writes Du Bois in *Souls of Black Folk,* "come even now not altogether empty-handed: there are to-day no truer exponents of the pure human spirit of the Declaration of Independence than the American Negroes; there is no true American music but the wild sweet melodies of the Negro slave; the American fairy tales and folklore are Indian and African; and, all in all, we black men seem the sole oasis of simple faith and reverence in a dusty desert of dollars and smartness" (pp. 11–12). As the word "desert" suggests, an Old Testament type is not far from Du Bois's thinking here. "Few men ever worshipped Freedom with half such unquestioning faith as did the American Negro," writes Du Bois. "Emancipation was the key to a promised land of sweeter beauty than ever stretched before the eyes of wearied Israelites" (pp. 6–7).[43] Or: "Here at last seemed to have been discovered the mountain path to Canaan; longer than the highway of Emancipation and law, steep and rugged, but straight, leading to heights high enough to overlook life" (p. 8).

These are not isolated instances of Old Testament imagery in *Souls of Black Folk.* Of the fourteen epigraphs to the book's chapters, one of the only two that do not come from contemporary literature comes from the Old Testament. Not coincidentally, it is the same text from which Toni Morrison takes the title for her novel *Song of Solomon* (p. 91). Also not coincidentally, this chapter contains both significant Old Testament allusions and statements on literal Jews. Although the first of the chapter's references to Jews is completely neutral (noting how a once prosperous plantation has been broken apart and divided among "Jews and Negroes" – p. 95), the others, as Michael Kramer has noted, are extremely problematical. As Kramer observes, they were changed after the Holocaust made apparent to Du Bois "how even unconscious repetition of current folklore such as the concept of Jews as more guilty of exploitation than others, had helped the Hitlers of the world."[44] Writes Du Bois in *Souls of Black Folk*, it is "the Jew [who] is the heir of the slave-baron" (p. 103); "nearly all the lands belong to Russian Jews" (p. 109) (another plantation is "owned now by a Russian Jew" – pp. 104–05). These Jews, furthermore, are presented stereotypically. "Only a Yankee or a Jew," we are told, "could squeeze more blood from debt-cursed tenants" (p. 105).

Putting aside both potential and actual anti-Semitism, Du Bois's interest in the Jews is significant in that, as Kramer argues, it is coupled with a definition of the black as the American folk. Equally important, the claim for black culture as the quintessential American culture proceeds through a competition for the Old Testament text, which would bestow on the American black the status of Israelite within the new American promised land – the status once maintained by those original Christian founding fathers of America, the Puritans. In this one-time "Egypt of the Confederacy" (pp. 100 and 102), now become a "Land of Canaan" (p. 103), the savior who will lead the people to freedom is a "tall and powerful black Moses" (p. 109). For Du Bois, as for Baldwin later, the story of the Jews is now the story of the American Negro, as Baldwin's concluding sentence and the title of his essay remind us:[45]

> If we – and now I mean the relatively conscious whites and the relatively conscious blacks, who must, like lovers, insist on, or create, the consciousness of the others – do not falter in our duty now, we may be able, handful that we are, to end the racial nightmare, and achieve our country, and change the history of the world. If we do not now dare everything, the fulfillment of that prophecy, recreated from the Bible in song by a slave, is upon us: *God gave Noah the rainbow sign, No more water, the fire next time!* (p. 141)

Baldwin's concluding words do more than issue a political challenge to his readership of relatively conscious blacks and whites. They do more than warn the nation, in fairly dramatic apocalyptic terms, of the consequences of its failure to act now on the race issue. Rather, they remind us that this text is as much scripture as historical or cultural narrative. Like the tradition of scriptures preceding it – the Old Testament of Noah and the New Testament of Revelation – so the African American slave song not only incorporates and supersedes the prior texts (their words now becoming its words), it also realizes their underlying logic or meaning. It presents scriptural history as always moving toward this revelation of the biracial brotherhood of humankind, which the biblical story was, from the start, constructed to reveal. As Alice Walker has one of her characters in *The Temple of My Familiar* say of her fantasy of "a new tribe of our own," this fantasy "is also the fantasy upon which the Old Testament rests . . . but without any mention of our intimacy with the other animals or of the brown and black colors of the rest of my folks."[46] "I am black but comely," Du Bois quotes the Song of Songs. Toni Morrison will produce an entire novel named *Song of Solomon* to remind the Judeo-Christian world of its own buried knowledge of the origins of white Judeo-Christian culture, in black, African culture.

In bringing this knowledge to consciousness, the adherents of this new last book of scripture will do no more than fulfill the original intentions of prophecy. They will write the text that will proclaim these truths to the world as the originary truths of Western culture. For this reason Baldwin prefaces the book publication of his *New Yorker* essay with a letter to his nephew and namesake, James. James Baldwin the nephew is the disciple or apostle of James Baldwin the writer. As the son of Baldwin's younger brother, whom Baldwin "carried . . . in my arms and on my shoulders, kissed and spanked . . . and watched him learn to walk" (p. 14), the nephew is inheritor and son. He is also the reincarnation of Baldwin's father, whom the nephew strongly resembles and who dies before the nephew is born (p. 13). In this way, he becomes a figure of origination and redemption. "Know whence you came," Baldwin tells his nephew (pp. 18–19):

> I said that it was intended that you should perish in the ghetto, perish by never being allowed to go behind the white man's definitions, by never being allowed to spell your proper name. You have, and many of us have, defeated this intention; and by a terrible law, a terrible paradox, those innocents who believed that your imprisonment made them safe are losing their grasp of reality. But these men are your brothers – your lost, younger brothers. And if the word *integration* means anything, this is what it means: that we, with love, shall force our brothers to see themselves as they are, to cease fleeing from reality and begin to change it. (pp. 20–21)

A type of Moses (or, more accurately, perhaps, an antitype) who was to have perished and never to have known his proper name or whence he came, the younger James Baldwin is instructed by the older James Baldwin in the doctrine of love. This is the doctrine to be preached to the innocents, who are also his brothers. "Younger" brothers: for, as in the manner of all such scriptural revisions, later becomes earlier, and younger becomes older, and the new last final book of scripture displaces everything that has come before it. This "legacy" is not only the injunction of the biblical text, to serve the Lord, but the text itself, which becomes now black scripture as much as white, Christian as much as Jewish. For all its rage, the point of Baldwin's *Fire Next Time* is that the fire next time is still not come. Its not coming has to do with pushing the flow of biblical and Western history backward, to undo and recover in order properly to realize the right direction of human history, which has horribly, painfully, gone astray.

"As for me and my house, we will serve the Lord": The Competition for the American House of Fiction

In order to produce great art, the Jewish artist of Malamud's *Tenants,* who is unable to write his book, tells Willie, in true universalist, humanist fashion, that he will have "to make black more than color or culture, and outrage larger than protest or ideology" (p. 67). "There has to be more emphasis on technique, form, though I know it's not stylish to say that," he goes on. "You've got to build more carefully" (p. 72). Black power culturalist Willie responds as follows:

> Black ain't white and never can be. It is once and for only black. It ain't universal if that's what yo are hintin up to. What I feel you feel different. You can't write about black because you don't have the least idea what we are or how we feel. . . . I'm writin the soul writin of black people cryin out we are still slaves in this fuckn country and we ain't gonna stay slaves any longer. How can you understand it, Lesser, if your brain is white? (pp. 74–75)

Lesser's response to Willie's tirade exposes not only Lesser's underlying aesthetic assumptions, but those of Malamud, Howe, Hyman, and others as well. This is not simply the claim of universal humanism but the largely unexamined belief that such universalism is synonymous with a nonracial but for that reason white, Western culture: "So is your brain white. But if the experience is about being human and moves me then you've made it my experience. You created it for me. You can deny universality, Willie, but you can't abolish it" (p. 75). The problem that Malamud's *Tenants* and the other texts that stand behind it raise is whether universalism includes or excludes, expresses or denies, the different ethnic groups it would subsume.

A fascinating feature of Malamud's novel, as Ozick notes in "Literary Blacks and Jews," is that it reverses the Ellison–Howe positions. It is the black writer who articulates Howe's politics, the white writer who insists on Ellison's Western humanism (Baldwin's image of himself arriving in Paris "armed with two Bessie Smith records and a typewriter" would seem to be incorporated in both Lesser and Spearmint).[47] The reversal, however, is not complete. As a Jew completely uninterested in his Jewish identity, Lesser is an extreme version of Howe, Hyman, and Malamud. Willie Spearmint is not, however, Ellison in this reversal of the reversal, but, rather, Wright and Baldwin, whom Ellison (in the exchange at least) rejects and Howe promotes. (It is, of course, the manuscript of Ellison's long-awaited second book that is reputed to have been burned, not a manuscript by Irving Howe.)

One reason for this reversal and blending of the Ellison–Howe positions is that for Malamud, Jews more than blacks are the culprits in black–Jewish relations. Howe, not Ellison, promoted the militant black aesthetic that might well have been predicted to swing out of control – as, indeed, Marxism itself swung out of control irrespective of American race politics and also in relation to Jews. Nathan Glazer makes a point very similar to this in a 1969 *Commentary* article in which he blames a "white, predominantly Jewish intelligentsia" for "the expansion and inflammation of anti-Semitism among blacks."[48] Furthermore, and also consistent with the intra-Jewish message of Malamud's book, as well as in tandem with Ellison's argument, Howe is guilty of the failure to make explicit his Jewish identity. Howe creates the cultural vacuum that has necessitated that America's Jews look elsewhere for their cultural materials, putting them into direct confrontation with blacks. Malamud's fiction reveals Ellison's rebuke to Howe to capture not only the essence of a Jewish hubris vis-à-vis blacks but its relation to Jewish self-denial vis-à-vis Jews. Jewish Americans, Malamud realizes, construct their ethnic identity in such a way as to make the ethnic component of that identity all but disappear. In dramatizing this condition of Jewish sterility in America, Malamud may be confessing his own culpability.

But the partial reversal of Ellison and Howe in Lesser and Spearmint also gets at the major issue both in the Ellison-Howe debate and in the Baldwin essays. These are the high stakes for Malamud, Howe, Ellison, Baldwin, and Ozick as well of the black–Jewish exchange that Howe and Ellison and Lesser and Spearmint rehearse: nothing less than who will occupy the central places of American (and Western) culture, and as owners rather than as tenants: blacks or Jews?[49] Who will speak not the critique of American culture from outside that culture, but the cultural *self*-critique? This cultural self-critique can only be articulated by the true voice of America, which has no need to identify itself as such because it is already recognized for what it is. Are we all, as Americans, white, so that integration becomes the expansion of white culture to incorporate black culture (or, for that matter, Jewish culture)? Or are we all, as Americans, blacks, or, as Malamud once imagined it, Jews: outsiders, individuals, so that the black voice (as once the Jewish voice) is America's own truest representation of itself? And if so, where did that voice come from? From the white culture that enslaved black people? Or from the eruptions within white culture of the souls of black folk ("I'm writin the soul of black people cryin out," says Willie), which white culture attempted to silence but could not? In other words, what is the universal in American culture? white culture, as if white culture existed separate from black culture and could make room for it? or black culture? And where are the Jews in all this?

As Baldwin puts the question that Malamud's book also asks:

> What it comes to is that if we, who can scarcely be considered a white nation, persist in thinking of ourselves as one, we condemn ourselves, with the truly white nations, to sterility and decay, whereas if we could accept ourselves *as we are,* we might bring new life to the Western achievements, and transform them. The price of this transformation is the unconditional freedom of the Negro; it is not too much to say that he, who has been so long rejected must now be embraced, and at no matter what psychic or social risk. He is *the* key figure in his country, and the American future is precisely as bright or as dark as his. And the Negro recognizes this, in a negative way. Hence the question: Do I really *want* to be integrated into a burning house? (*The Fire Next Time,* pp. 126–27)

Willie's advocacy of a black power aesthetics goes beyond a claim for a place within American culture. It claims Western tradition for itself. "You want to know what's really art? *I* am art. Willie Spearmint, *black man. My form is myself"* (p. 75). Willie's words recall the earlier announcement of Ralph Ellison's *Invisible Man:* "I yam what I am." As I have argued elsewhere, in this statement Ellison inherits Emerson's own inheritance of Descartes and the Western philosophical tradition, not to mention the tetragrammaton and thus the religious tradition as well.[50]

Like the invisible man, and like Baldwin in *The Fire Next Time,* Spearmint produces the self-affirmation that is inseparably part of one dominant American literary tradition. Malamud also turns us to this feature of Willie's African Americanism through his name, Willie Spearmint, later called Bill Spear, which evokes Walt Whitman's spears of grass and their own Emersonian claims, thus producing in Malamud's African American text, as in Ellison's, the unnamed name *Emerson.* "I could suppress the name of my namesake out of respect for the achievements of its original bearer," writes Ellison in "Hidden Name and Complex Fate," "but I cannot escape the obligation of attempting to achieve some of the things which he asked of the American writer." As Ellison quotes Henry James as having said, "being an American is an arduous task, and for most of us, I suspect, the difficulty begins with the name" (*Shadow and Act,* p. 166).[51] *Invisible Man* is Ellison, is Emerson, is the American text, is America: the greatest of poems, as Whitman called it.

For this reason, as representatives of two minority cultures in America, Lesser and Spearmint are in competition to occupy the American house of fiction. Not for naught does Malamud have Lesser remark that Mark Twain is rumored to have inhabited the house next door (p. 7) or gives one of the black characters the name Sam Clemens; in *Invisible Man* Ellison also alludes to *Huckleberry Finn,* which Ellison reveals in his essays to be one of his most important predecessor texts. Lesser and Spearmint would be Emerson and Whitman and Twain. They would, further, be the American Shakespeare (recalling Melville's aspirations), Lesser by writing *The Promised End,* Willie Spearmint/Bill Spear through the very articulation of his being as contained in his name ("Willie Shakespear," Lesser calls him – p. 76).

King Lear, which is about nothing so much as family dissension and division, about who, if anyone, will inherit the kingdom after the two fathers in the play are left without legitimate heirs, is exactly the right Shakespearean text for Malamud to produce from behind his own novel of cultural conflict. A source here may be Chester Himes's *Primitive* (1955), in which a black writer, who is being denied publication because his book is too violent, comes back at his publisher with: "What about Hamlet? Shakespeare destroyed every-body and killed everybody in that one." Nor are the theological implications of *Lear* irrelevant to Malamud's statement concerning black–Jewish relations. This is the first of the many endings of Mal-amud's *Tenants,* a mere twenty pages into the story: "Up goes the place in roaring flames. . . . Nobody says no, so the fire surges its inevitable way upwards and with a convulsive roar flings open Les-ser's door. END OF NOVEL" (p. 23). "You ought to burn up both of these yourself, Willie," says an unidentified voice of vengeance, "on account of this cat stole your white bitch and pissed up your black book. Deprived you of your normal sex life and lifelong occu-pation according to the choice you made. Must feel like you been castrated, don't it? You got to take an eye for a ball it says in the Good Book" (pp. 177–78).

The threat of the "fire next time," with its theological as well as its social implications, hovers over, and virtually consumes, this text. But this reference to Baldwin's essay reminds us that the competi-tion between Lesser and Spearmint is even more fierce than mere authorial rivalry, however ethnically and religiously freighted. Rather, Jew and black in Malamud's novel vie for the position of legitimate heir. In terms of the scriptural and cultural models they are all adapting, they vie to be antitypical representatives of the souls of the American folk.

In *The Fire Next Time,* Baldwin links urban violence with a typolog-ical reminder about the relationship between Old Testament and New, Jews and Christians, and now, in the new turn of events, be-tween the American black, who is both Christian and (later) Mos-lem, and his predecessors. "You think you are the Chosen People," Willie says to Harry. "Well, you are wrong on that. *We* are the Chosen People from as of now on. You gonna find that out soon enough, you gonna lose your fuckn pride" (p. 224), by which Willie will come to mean nothing less than Harry's sexual organ. Ellison's invisible man's "I yam what I am," as I suggested, has similar theological aspirations. Already in "The Harlem Ghetto" (in *Notes of a Native Son*), Baldwin, like Malamud in stories such as "Angel Levine," had set up the terms of this new supersessionism, producing the black as the Jewish Christ of the modern world:

> The hymns, the texts, and the most favored legends of the devout Negro are all Old Testament and therefore Jewish in origin. . . . The covenant God made in the beginning with Abraham and which was to extend to his children and to his

children's children forever is a covenant made with these lat-
ter-day exiles also: as Israel was chosen, so are they. The birth
and death of Jesus, which adds a non-Judaic element, also im-
plements this identification. It is the covenant made with Abraham again, renewed, signed with his blood. (p. 67)

Or as Ellison puts it,

"Go Down, Moses" is an absorption of certain Jewish religious
traditions and that's my possession; no one can take that away
from me. It's been taken through that identification with universal human conditions, and when my people as slaves began
to fashion their particular kind of American music what was
there as poetry, what was there as part of the Christian doctrine
but the story of the Israelites? So it's that sort of opportunity to
create and recreate one's background that is most American.[52]

As I have already begun to suggest and will develop more fully in
Chapters Four and Five, Toni Morrison's *Song of Solomon* has both
Baldwin's essays and Malamud's novel in mind, in its apocalyptic
non-ending of suspended animation and in its supersessionist play
in relation to Christian and Jewish culture (a feature of Morrison's
Beloved as well). Malamud will tackle this subject of typology and
supersessionism one final time in *God's Grace* (appropriately enough
his last novel before his death), which, containing both the fire and
the flood, might well be subtitled "The Flood Next Time." What the
mutual interaction of these texts amounts to is a bid for cultural
dominance, much like the foundationalist/supersessionist tension
between Judaism and Christianity, white Christianity and black
Christianity, and thus Judaism and black Christianity. For what black
culture resists, as did Christian culture before it, is the idea of inheriting a model in which it is nowhere included. Thus, Christianity
would not only supersede but antitype Judaism. African Americanism would supersede and antitype Christianity and Judaism both.
And Judaism would insist on its priority in relation to both Christianity and the African American black, as will white Christians in
relation to black Christians.

And yet, just because Judaism and Christianity and white and
black American culture have shared so much common ground for
so many centuries, they find themselves, both in affirming and resisting each other, drawn into patterns of mutual self-construction.
Each uses the other's materials. Each formulates positions (whether
in approval or disaffection) in terms of the other. It is this mutually

self-constructing cultural competition that the debate among Baldwin, Howe, Hyman, Ellison, Malamud, and Ozick epitomizes, as all of these individuals find themselves involved in a pattern of paradoxical, ironic repetition. Each shadows the cultural strategies of the other, their defenses and rebuttals becoming displacements and appropriations of each other's cultural materials. This produces a mutuality of cultural construction, which is not the ostensible intention of any of the interacting parties, but which is, nonetheless, the result of their attempting to define themselves through their resistance to each other.

In opposition to Howe's insistence that he speak as a black, or Hyman's reading of him as a folklorist, Ellison insists on his right to speak as a Western man and an American. In so doing, Ellison replicates Howe's and Hyman's universalist assumptions, of which their Marxism is one form. He imitates as well their cultural assimilation, of which, as for many leftist socialist Jews of the 1930s and 1940s, Marxism is also already an expression. Similarly, in trying to trace the secret, subversive, Jewish underpinnings of Western society that necessitate that Jews acknowledge and take responsibility for their role in contemporary civilization, Ellison proceeds, against Howe's and Hyman's absolute refusal to say anything concrete about their Jewishness, as secretively and subversively as he accuses the Jewish critic of proceeding. Throughout the exchange between them Ellison, like Baldwin before him, produces a Jewish, Old Testament–centered response rather than an Afrocentric one, even though or, rather, precisely because his objective is to deliver black culture from Jewish (and white and Christian) hands.

By imaging his own identity as a black writer through the position of the Jewish intellectual, whom he opposes, and through the Jewish intellectual's thinking of black culture, Ellison (like Baldwin) gets locked into a position not autonomous and not even distinctly his own. Ellison becomes Ham to Howe's (or even Hyman's) Noah, even as he denies the relevance of the biblical terms that he and Baldwin (and not the Jewish critics) introduce into the discussion. In the process of competing for places of American essentialism, black and Jew both, in these exchanges, lose the specificity of ethnic identity that makes such competition comprehensible in the first place and that legitimates strategies of cultural confrontation. Willing to assume neither Jew-face nor blackface, Howe, Hyman, and Ellison evidence a facelessness that becomes a silencing voicelessness, as the final confrontation in Malamud's *Tenants* clearly reveals.

But in taking on the guilt and responsibility, not for black oppression but for Jewish self-denial, and in realizing the dangers of this self-denial for Jews and blacks both, Malamud still constructs his own, new, Jewish identity in *The Tenants* (as does Howe in his essay) as a response to the American black, who is now cast (for both Howe and Malamud) as black activist rather than as black victim. "In plucking Willie out of the black writing that made him," Malamud, observes Ozick, "has not invented the politicization of fiction. And in inventing *The Tenants,* Malamud ironically follows Willie – he has written a tragic fiction soaked in the still mainly unshed blood of the urban body politic" (p. 112).

In other words, Malamud gets caught in the same process of repetition he exposes (through Lesser) as being Ellison's predicament. So, for that matter, does Ozick. For if Malamud's confessional reads as a Jewish protest novel, more typical of a Wright than either an Ellison or a Howe, Ozick's essay is protest criticism, such as James Baldwin produced in texts like *The Fire Next Time.* If Howe's original mistake in the exchange with Ellison is not putting his Jewishness up front, Ozick corrects for Howe in her forthright insistence that she speaks as a Jew in defense of Jews, as had Baldwin for blacks in the *Fire.* But when she does so, she repeats the black move to which she objects in her essay, the "literature and politics of the black movement" that, in her view, produced Willie Spearmint (p. 108). Thus, Ozick also misreads Malamud's acknowledgment (implicit in his reversal of the Ellison–Howe positions) of the degree to which Jewish intellectuals are responsible for having had their sincerity misunderstood; or the degree to which Jews understood the culture to which they were welcoming blacks as their culture, and not that of the African American. The problem in Malamud's view is not with the Jews' "special forms of dissent," which took the form of apparent presumption in statements like Malamud's own "All men are Jews." (This statement can certainly be read as a Jewish reclamation of chosenness against Christian supersessionism.) Rather, the problem, as revealed by Malamud's casting the Jew as an assimilated intellectual uninvolved in Civil Rights, is the Jewish disregard for self-identification and affiliation within their Americanism. The problem is also their not recognizing that the problem of black rights was not purely legal and civil but (like their own relationship to America) cultural as well. Blacks might want what Jews seem quite unwilling to forfeit in their integration into America: a sense of specialness, of chosenness, of priority or anteriority or even essentialism beyond their fair share in America, such as can, in Baldwin's words as quoted by Howe, "sustain the Jew even after he has left his father's house."

Howe, I suggest, does not declare his ethnic identity in his correspondence with Ellison, but not because he thinks Jews have made it in America. Howe and Hyman both write beautifully and well on the Jewish experience elsewhere. Nor is it because he has to some large degree delivered his Jewish identity to larger callings, like Marxism and Civil Rights, though this is closer to the truth. Rather, Howe does not declare himself a Jew because, in part (like Malamud and like the reductive version of both of them, Harry Lesser), he experiences his Jewishness as a form of chosenness (like, perhaps, his Americanness as well), so that saying the word "Jew" would amount to Howe, not to a confession or sympathetic identification or a mode of cultural sharing, but to a form of cultural bragging. And Ellison knows this.

Hence Ellison's references in his reply to Howe to language and immigrancy and the internal Jewish conflict over the state of Israel; hence his quotation from the Talmud; and hence Malamud's image of tenancy and *The Promised End.* You, Irving, Ellison is saying to Howe, are the stranger in this land; for you America cannot be the promised land; and therefore I, not you, speak for America and for its inheritance of Western culture; I am the truly hyphenated American, thus the American: you are the Jew in America. And Howe, not exactly contradicting Ellison, is saying back what he has been saying all along: such concept of promise as exists and as matters originates with my culture, and therefore when I speak, I speak not only for America, which comes late into the culture game, but for all of Western culture. Howe's international cast of Yiddish writers comes as evidence that Jewish experience transcends and incorporates, even as it precedes, the American and Western experiences.

Nor would these cooperative antagonists in America contend only for the position of American, or even Western, culture. They would also speak from above culture, and beyond it, virtually in the voice of God. Ellison quite rightly identifies Howe's tone as Olympian; but so is Ellison's and so, for that matter, is Baldwin's (the review of *Notes of a Native Son* by the *Library Journal,* quoted in the Beacon Press edition of the text, calls Baldwin's "Olympian detachment . . . almost frightening"). Ellison and Howe are both (like Lesser and Willie) writing the Holy Writ, as if they were gods, not men.

In this multiparty exchange, the only people who speak the pride of ethnic identity directly and unabashedly are Baldwin and Ozick.

But declaring her own pride up front, Ozick misses the degree to which Howe and Malamud and Ellison are unwilling to express racial/religious pride, making them less cooperative antagonists than mirrors of mutual self- and other-denial. Nor does she recognize her affinity to Baldwin, who is the quintessential Old Testament prophet of the fire next time dramatized in Malamud's novel. In this Ozick follows Baldwin himself, whose *Fire Next Time* is determined by the logic of the tradition he resists. The *Fire* reproduces his own accusation against the protest novel – that it mirrors the tradition it rejects. The Baldwin men (father–son–nephew) produce a lineage like nothing so much as the New Testament's inheritance of the Old, including even the genealogical gap whereby the son is not, biologically speaking, the father's son. So, too, Ozick becomes antiprotest Jewish protester, arguing an essentialist line of Jewish morality with the antiprotest black activist.

What these mutual constructions of black and Jewish identity miss about themselves and each other, and what they nonetheless brilliantly succeed in producing, constitutes the substructure of much of the African and Jewish American intertext that pervades a large part of black–Jewish dialogue and writing.

2

Crisis and Commentary in African–Jewish American Relations

> He was no longer a Negro or a Christian but had become a Jew.
>
> Nella Larsen, *Passing*[1]

In Chapters Three, Four, and Five I discuss a series of mutually constructing African and Jewish American fictions. Like Malamud's *Tenants,* these short stories and novels produce portraits of ethnic identity by utilizing materials of the other ethnic group. Now, however, I want to pursue a few more nonfictional conversations in the mutual construction of African and Jewish American identity. These conversations appear in a series of journal articles and books, most of them from the 1950s through the early 1970s. My focus is on the post–Second World War period, for several reasons. First of all, this is the period when Jews started to move into positions of power within American society. It is also the period when, possibly because of their newly gained strength but very likely also because of the questions of Jewish survival raised both by the Holocaust and the precarious existence of the State of Israel, they participated in large numbers in black movements.

The war was equally decisive for blacks. As the pages of *The Crisis* make exceedingly, bitterly, clear, American blacks had pinned their hopes for integration and social justice on their record in the war. The painfully disappointing experiences of demobilized black soldiers and their families directly fed the passions of Civil Rights activism in the postwar decades. They also set blacks and Jews on a collision course concerning their respective places and their mutual relations within American society.

In the multiperson, multilevel conversation I now want to record, as in the conversation among Baldwin, Ellison, Howe, Hyman, Malamud, and Ozick, a certain mishearing and consequent misrepresentation, both of the self and of the other, occur. As in the preceding dialogues, the cause of such misunderstanding is neither racism nor anti-Semitism. Almost every participant to this black–Jewish dialogue, as to the earlier one, is dedicated to promoting civil and human rights. Nonetheless, what produces in these conversations more antagonism than cooperation is the same phenomenon I have already begun to trace. The participants to the dialogue fail to hear what is actually being said, not only in the discourse of the other but within their own language as well. Just as important, unintended distortions occur as ethnic materials and goals become entangled within one another.

Plantations and Pogroms, Slavery and the Holocaust: Disentangling Black and Jewish History (Stanley Elkins, Ralph Waldo Ellison, and Hannah Arendt)

In 1975, in the Jewish journal *Commentary*, Stanley Elkins published an essay entitled "The Slavery Debate." In this article, Elkins reviewed a series of recent books in the field of slave history. He also defended his own earlier study, *Slavery*, against the storm of protest it had engendered.[2] As important as the subject of the essay is the fact of its appearance in *Commentary*. Inaugurated in November 1945, explicitly in response to the Holocaust, as "an act of faith in our possibilities in America," *Commentary* distinguished itself during the 1950s and 1960s and well into the 1970s with an uninterrupted flow of articles concerning race prejudice, Civil Rights, and black–Jewish relations in the United States.[3] No other topic, aside from the Jewish concerns that the journal ostensibly was founded to represent, received the same kind of extensive treatment as the situation of the American black.[4]

From its founding through 1970, *Commentary* published more than seventy full-length features, book reviews, and symposia, written by blacks, Jews, and other Americans, on a range of race-related subjects, including sociological analyses of race prejudice, black history, segregation in the South, black housing and economics, education, and (increasingly as one moves into and out of the 1960s) black power and black–Jewish relations, especially as these are complicated by that decade's crisis in the New York City school system and by affirmative action. Until the period of black–Jewish tensions in the 1960s, most of these articles refer very little, if at all, to Jews. This is not to say that Jewish self-interest did not motivate some, perhaps most, of the concern with black Civil Rights. Nonetheless, for the decade from the time of its founding, *Commentary* expressed a direct intellectual and moral engagement with the issue of black rights. Its focus, moreover, was overwhelmingly sociological and legal. How are we to understand this Jewish *Commentary* on the African American experience? And, more to the point perhaps, how were African Americans to respond to this overwhelming Jewish involvement, both material and intellectual, in the struggle for black Civil Rights?

The African American journal *The Crisis: A Record of the Darker Races* is a much older journal than *Commentary,* producing its first issue under the editorship of W. E. Burghardt Du Bois in November 1911 as the official organ of the newly founded NAACP. The trauma that precipitated its founding, although neither more nor less vile than the Holocaust, was certainly of longer duration, and much more inherently American. Hence, perhaps, the difference between the journals' titles. The catastrophe in Europe had resulted in the horrific deaths of six million Jews. Nonetheless, it had left Jewish culture in America intact. American Jewry, furthermore, was only indirectly affected by the killing in Europe. By and large it was a stranger to the extreme anti-Semitism that had precipitated Nazi genocide. It is an exaggeration and an affront to claim, as does Harold Cruse, that "what European Jews suffered in Europe has had very little bearing on the American experience." Nonetheless, it is probably true, as Cruse continues, that "for all practical purposes (political, economic and cultural) as far as Negroes are concerned, *Jews have not suffered in the United States.* They have, in fact, done exceptionally well."[5]

Therefore, perhaps, American Jews felt after the war that they were able to enter into serious but leisured commentary concerning Jewish affairs, including the newly founded State of Israel, with all the questions that the new nation raised about Jewish identity, American and otherwise.[6] African Americans, however, in the first decade of the twentieth century, were, as they had been and would continue to be for some decades to come, in deep crisis. They still had to mount the effective campaign that would bring to an end the disabling and often murderous consequences of racism (lynchings of blacks in the South are a major recurring theme in the *Crisis*). They had yet to gain acceptance of their cultural heritage and identity, and recognition of what was increasingly for them the most fundamental fact about American culture: its biracialism.

No two journals could seem more different.

Yet the subject of Jews, both in America and abroad, while not nearly as extensively treated as the subject of African Americans in *Commentary,* is hardly absent from the journal's pages. During the years preceding and during the Second World War, the *Crisis* unrelentingly covers, first, the disenfranchisement of the Jews in Germany, including the violence perpetrated against them (so like the lynchings with which southern blacks were all too familiar), and finally their extermination. Nor is the fact of the Jewish experience in America or American Jewish participation in the NAACP and in other Civil Rights organizations ignored. Certainly this interest in Jews has something to do with Jewish moneys and legal support, which helped to found and sustain the nascent NAACP. An important element in black–Jewish relations must be the individuals who fostered those relations, such as the Spingarn brothers, Joel and Arthur (who served as presidents of the NAACP from 1930 to 1965; Du Bois dedicates *Dusk of Dawn* to Joel Spingarn); and Julius Rosenwald, whose foundation supported the work of such figures as Ralph Waldo Ellison. But the reference to Jews in the *Crisis,* which is subtitled *A Record of the Darker Races,* of which, in Du Bois's view, the Jews were one, exceeds the debt.[7] Like the Jewish interest in blacks, it represents a phenomenon quite apart from the material concerns it might also express. And yet, something goes wrong in Jewish speaking about blacks, and black speaking about Jews. And it begins almost at the beginning of the dialogue itself, in the mid-twentieth century.

In addition to the ways I've already mentioned, the Second World War was decisive both for African and Jewish Americans and for their relationship to each other in still one additional aspect. Although black history was hardly invented in the postwar years, nonetheless the field experienced an explosion of interest on the parts not only of African American scholars, but of white scholars as well. Many of these white scholars were Jews, recently demobilized soldiers, going to college on the GI Bill, and making their careers not in the study of Jewish culture, but in fields such as English and American literature and American history. Stanley Elkins's *Slavery* is one such example of a Jewish-authored text that took as its subject not Jewish, but black history. At the center of Elkins's study, and producing a violent backlash on the part of the African American community (including no lesser a figure than Ellison himself), was Elkins's Jewishly accented perception of blacks as he forged his famous (some would say infamous) analogy between the Nazi death camps and the southern slave plantations.

As even his sharpest critics realized, Elkins's purposes in writing *Slavery* were above reproach. Published in 1959, *Slavery* can be said to have intended nothing less than a major address to the issue of black Civil Rights.[8] Elkins set out to lay to rest, once and for all, any romantic defenses of plantation slavery. He strove to isolate, scientifically, the absolute differences between American slavery and all other slave systems. Those other slave systems, in Central and South America, had, in his view, allowed for both the regular manumission of slaves and their successful integration into their host societies. This was not permitted by the American system, which was a "closed" and therefore much more oppressive system, with consequences that endured much longer.

In an effort to make clear these consequences and to hammer a final nail into the coffin of white American romanticizations of the slave experience, Elkins recovered the "Sambo" myth of the black personality. "Sambo," he attempted to show, was not a feature either of African American biology or, arguing against some of the theories of Franz Boas and Melville Herskovitz, even of African culture. Rather, it was the direct result of the dehumanizing, infantilizing effects of the "peculiar institution" itself, as Kenneth Stampp (in his own effort to overturn more benign representations of slavery) had three years earlier entitled his book.[9]

Elkins proceeds cautiously. He realizes that even to call the "Sambo" figure a stereotype is to lend to it a certain unwarranted and distasteful legitimacy. Nonetheless, he maintains that the figure is too widespread in black as well as in white culture for us to imagine it a "conspiracy." For this reason, he argues, it must be taken seriously. Its origins, within the brutalizing reality of plantation life, must be brought forward.[10] Elkins does this through his meticulously documented analogy to the Nazi death camps of the Second World War. And this, of course, is what sparks the controversy that turns the motives of Elkins's study virtually on their head. Instead of producing a voice allied with blacks in a struggle against oppression, it comes to signify one more white, intellectual, Jewish assault against blacks. How can one scholar's good intentions go so totally astray?

Had Elkins's thesis remained purely academic, perhaps the backlash against his work might not have been so severe. But in March 1965, a mere six years after the publication of Elkins's book, Daniel

Patrick Moynihan, then assistant secretary of labor, produced "The Negro Family: The Case for National Action," commonly known as "The Moynihan Report."[11] The report, which was intended as a confidential document, solely for use in planning governmental assistance to black people, hit the public eye in June 1965, when President Johnson, speaking at Howard University, cited, in an eloquent pro–Civil Rights address, the breakdown of the Negro family as one of the major issues confronting the African American population. For many blacks, the speech, and the report on which it was based, crossed a critical line between legitimate governmental concerns and an indecorous critique of the African American community. And at the center of this public insult to African Americans was the very image of the dehumanizing and infantilizing consequences of slavery that informed Elkins's study.

In a chapter entitled "The Roots of the Problem: Slavery," the report summarized Elkins as follows:

> Stanley M. Elkins, drawing on the aberrant behavior of the prisoners in Nazi concentration camps, drew an elaborate parallel between the two institutions. This thesis has been summarized as follows by Thomas F. Pettigrew:
>
>> Both were closed systems, with little chance of manumission, emphasis on survival, and a single omnipresent authority. The profound personality change created by Nazi internment . . . was toward childishness and total acceptance of the SS guards as father-figures – a syndrome strikingly similar to the "Sambo" caricature of the Southern slave.
>
> . . .
>
> Unquestionably, these events worked against the emergence of a strong father figure. . . . In this situation, the Negro family made but little progress toward the middle-class pattern of the present time.

The report entitles one of its later chapters "The Tangle of Pathology."[12]

Responses to the report came fast and furious, with statements in leading journals and newspapers by individuals such as James Farmer, Whitney Young, Jr., and Bayard Rustin. The argument between these leaders of the black community and the government, like the debate between Elkins and (among others) Ralph Waldo Ellison, returns us to the issues already raised in relation to Ellison, Howe, Hyman, et al.: what could be perceived of, by blacks, as condescension, even specifically Jewish condescension, and what white people, Jews included, might well see as black ingratitude and even malice. As Kenneth Clark aptly remarks, what would "Jews and others . . . think if a conference of Negro leaders were to devote a roundtable to the problem of 'The Jew in the United States'?"[13] Clark's statement exposes as a major problem in black–Jewish relations the same issue we have already seen emerging in the Ellison/ Baldwin/ Howe/ Elkins debates: who is and speaks for/as America. Had blacks during the Second World War organized a roundtable on the subject of the Jew in *Germany,* I suspect American Jewry would have greeted this with tremendous gratitude. Although American Jews themselves barely woke up in time to the catastrophe in Europe, nonetheless, when they did, they wanted nothing more than the support of the American people, and their material assistance. From the American Jewish perspective, the "Negro problem" (as it got so unfortunately labeled) was exactly like the "Jewish Question" (an equally unpalatable description) in Germany. Their lending support to Civil Rights was therefore, as they saw it, analogous to blacks (and others) lending their support to German and European Jewry. But if the "Negro problem" was an American problem, the "Jewish Question" was not. Thus, American Jews, even those as recently arrived as the war refugees, could speak as Americans. African Americans, in their view – and this was the problem to which they were directing themselves in *Commentary* and elsewhere – as yet could not.

Of course, American Jews saw parallels between their minority status in the United States and that of blacks. Nor were they insensible to the discrimination against Jews earlier in the century, especially in the period surrounding the First World War. But fundamentally, for them, anti-Semitism was a European problem, racism was an American one, and Jews did not suffer from racism. Thus, they could address the problem of racism as Americans, and not from a specifically Jewish or even American Jewish perspective. This is why, as Clark suggests, Jews would likely have resented an African American roundtable on the subject of the Jewish Question.

The confusion for Jewish Americans between European Jewish history and Jewish American history goes to the heart of the complexity of Jewish American self-identity, especially as that self-identity dissolved into non-Jewish forms, such as Marxism, Stalinism, socialism, universal humanism, and so on. The history of Jewish assimilation is a long one. It begins well before the exodus from Europe to the United States, many American Jewish socialists being products of assimilation, not to America but to the European societies of their origin. But no host society provided Jews with as perfect an environment for their integration as the United States. America, for the Jews, was the final, grand solution to the problem of prejudice and disenfranchisement, and not, as it was for blacks, the source of the problem. *Commentary*, we recall, was founded on this basis.

Nonetheless, American Jews did suffer in the United States from some residual anti-Semitism, in the form of social restrictions and university quotas. They were well aware, in the 1940s and 1950s, that they had not completely made it in the United States. Furthermore, if American Jews retained a memory of their European experience during the first half of their sojourn in America, and if native American anti-Semitism helped keep that memory alive, the catastrophe that took six million Jewish lives during the Second World War produced in Jewish Americans a renewed sensitivity to the potential threat to themselves, even in the United States. And that directly affected Jewish thinking about the race issue.

One must note immediately that the Holocaust also influenced non-Jewish considerations of racism after the war. John Higham, for example – who, as he makes abundantly clear, is not Jewish – notes in his preface to the second edition of *Strangers in the Land* (1966) what he does not say in the first, 1955, edition, that

> I began work on this book in 1948 in an effort to understand historically the interplay of two aspects of contemporary life that concerned me deeply. One was nationalism, that essential cement of modern societies that has so frightfully disrupted the modern world. The other was ethnic prejudice, the older and deeper repulsion between peoples of dissimilar cultures. I wanted to know how, and under what conditions, these protean impulses had interacted in America. So I embarked on an investigation of American attitudes and policies toward foreign-born minorities.[14]

Although Higham does not name the Holocaust as such, and although his study deals with many different ethnic and religious communities (some of them, like blacks, *not* foreign-born), nonetheless his dating of the work and his associating his subject with the nationalism that recently disrupted the modern world suggest that the extermination of the Jews is not far from his thinking. That Higham would not allude to the Holocaust in the original publication of his book is wholly in keeping with the way in which most intellectuals in the late 1940s and throughout the 1950s – and even beyond – did not name the Holocaust or enter into direct discussion of it. Nonetheless, the title of his book, which is an allusion to the same text in Leviticus so important to Ozick's discussion of memory and metaphor, and to Baldwin's assertion of his Americanism, serves to identify the particular occasion for Higham's work.

Higham's almost silent inscription of the Holocaust in his groundbreaking work on "ethnic prejudice" has parallels in other midcentury publications on race and ethnicity, at least two of them by Jews. In 1945 Ernst Boas posthumously published a selection of his father's more popular writings on race prejudice in the United States. Some of them concerned Jews. The overwhelming majority of them, however, had to do with blacks (Boas, one recalls, was a major influence on the life and writings of Zora Neale Hurston, as was his student Melville Herskovits, who was also Jewish).[15] Franz Boas, notes his son, had little desire to print these essays, having as recently as 1940 produced a "volume of his collected scientific papers." But "during his last years, largely as a result of the impact of Fascist and Nazi ideology, he became convinced of the urgent need for popular education, of the vital importance of explaining to the man in the street the basis of our culture, and the roots of democracy; and of demonstrating the scientific falsity of much of our thinking and of many of our prejudices."[16]

The Holocaust is similarly cited by Oscar Handlin as being the occasion for the 1957 publication of *Race and Nationality in American Life,* in which he republished many of his earlier essays:

> In the brief span of the past quarter century we have seen a tragic succession of horrors challenge the assumption, upon which modern civilization rests, that personal dignity is inherent in the condition of human beings.
>
> A blind fury that welled up into indiscriminate destruction animated the Turks in Smyrna in 1922. Ten years thereafter in the Ukraine the rulers of the Soviet Union undertook a systematic extermination of millions in the interests of high policy. And in little more than a decade later the Nazis had set their extermination camps in operation.
>
> These tragic holocausts were all shocking in their indecency. But the cremation ovens evoke a peculiar horror. They revealed that the men who built them were moved by ideas and preconceptions and emotions that negated the oneness of humankind and affirmed the ineradicable differences among people.

The first essay in the volume is entitled "The Origins of Negro Slavery." The race issue, not anti-Semitism, remains the dominant chord in the collection.[17]

There is, of course, nothing unusual or unique or wrong in one historical event transforming our perceptions of other historical realities, even wholly different events. Nonetheless, the Higham, Boas, and Handlin publishing decisions affirm African American accusations that events in Jewish history often overshadowed interest in black history, even as they prompted concern with the issue of Civil Rights. Without in any way failing to register the horror of Nazi Germany in the 1930s and 1940s, editorials in the *Crisis* noted with bitter irony that Americans could express outrage at what was happening in Germany without the least concern for similar horrors happening in the American South. German anti-Semitism, the *Crisis* made clear, was to be condemned. But America's moral sympathies, the journal insisted, might better be focused on the United States than on Europe.

This is from one editorial in April 1938 (the editor at this point is Roy Wilkins):

> The President's proposal to have the nations of the world united in a plan to extend aid to the refugees from Hitler's wrath in Central Europe has all the earmarks of the fine, generous, impulsiveness and sympathy which are so typically American. It has, also, the American trait of sweeping aside consistency.
>
> With this plan we have no quarrel . . . But, we ask, how about relief for the oppressed Negro citizens of our own land? An examination of their plight will show that they suffer practically the same persecution visited upon the Jews in Central Europe.

Or in September 1938:

> Nothing ought to be done to impede the necessary and human efforts being made by our government and by organizations and individuals to rescue the victims of Nazi terror and provide a place for them in our great country. But while THE CRISIS would not suggest a cessation of this work, we reiterate the sentiments expressed here some months ago: that there are millions of Negro American citizens – not under Hitler's heel – who need and are entitled to amelioration of the prejudices against them, and the opportunity to achieve independence and happiness in their own nation.

Similar editorials appear in October and December 1938, January, February, and March 1939, April, May, and June 1941; and January 1942, with editorials as late as February and October 1947 still treating the similarities between the Nazi assault against the Jews and American racism.[18]

One must hasten to say that while the Nazi death camps had already begun to implement the Final Solution by the late 1930s, nonetheless world consciousness of the extent of the catastrophe was not yet in place. The *Crisis* is responding in its editorials to anti-Semitism, not genocide. Nonetheless, the editorials suggest the degree to which blacks, even during the war years, perceived concern for the Nazi Holocaust both as deflecting attention from American racism and as evidencing the degree to which the existence of such domestic racism did not even remotely figure in American moral conscience and consciousness. Certainly, after the war, with the large influx of Jewish refugees, simultaneous with the nation's flagrant disregard for returning black soldiers, African Americans could not have welcomed either American or American Jewish concern with the Holocaust.

Hence, perhaps, one source of the fierce opposition, so many years later, to Elkins's depiction of blacks as camp survivors (which intensifies a component of postwar publication on the race issue, such as the Higham, Boas, and Handlin volumes). During the war, Americans could see only Germany and Jews. After the war, Americans finally began to look at American blacks, but only through the prism of the Holocaust. Although critics like Boas and Handlin prove the black assertion wrong, they also verify it. Realizing, quite intelligently, that the Holocaust can become instrumental in the rethinking of domestic racism, they nonetheless confirm the greater significance, for Americans, of the Jewish example.

This comes out, somewhat differently, in the following anecdote in the introduction to *Black Anti-Semitism and Jewish Racism*, edited jointly by Nat Hentoff and James Baldwin. The incident occurs at a meeting of the New York Civil Liberties Union during the city school crisis (1968):

> The debate was fierce, and at one point, an elderly man stood up. His accent was unmistakably Yiddish, and he started by saying: "I am making my statement as one who grew up in Germany under Hitler, who spent four years in Nazi concentration camps in Poland during World War II, whose parents, relatives, and almost all friends were murdered by the Nazis,

and as one who came to this country to find freedom and justice for myself and my children."

A black woman seated before me grimaced. I expect I know what she was thinking: "Oh God, we're going to hear about the six million murdered Jews again."

Hentoff's story, however, has a twist to it:

> The speaker went on, telling of how he had become frightened as the battle between the United Federation of Teachers and the blacks in charge of the Ocean Hill–Brownsville school district grew harsher. He finally went to see for himself, he told us. The black woman in front of me sighed in anticipatory exasperation. "I found," the speaker continued, "a black community whose schools were surrounded by barricades and by thousands and thousands of helmeted white policemen who were enforcing a city government's policy against the wishes of the people there. It was a sight which I had not seen since the days when Germany and Ukrainian police would take over a Jewish ghetto in eastern Poland.

" 'The black man is, in truth, the American Jew,' " Hentoff informs us. " 'In America,' says African American Julius Lester, who later converts to Judaism, 'it is we who are the Jews.' "[19] Jewish terrorism in Israel, Hentoff reminds us at the end of his statement, "was born in the concentration camps of Europe. We are, all of us who are white, the *goyim* in America. The further question is: Which among us are the Germans?"[20]

In Hentoff's story the Jew emerges not only as victim, but as potential victimizer, an idea that would resurface in relation to Israeli politics in the 1980s. In seeing the Jew this way, Hentoff is following the lead of one of the contributors to his volume. Writes Harold Cruse, in a statement I have already quoted in part:

> What European Jews suffered in Europe has very little bearing on the American experience, excepting that many of the Jewish intellectuals here tend to adopt as their own, the martyr's mantle of those who were nailed to the German Iron Cross. One cannot deny the horror of the European Jewish holocaust, but for all practical purposes . . . *Jews have not suffered in the United States.* . . . But the fact remains that the European experience shows that when it comes to playing the role of the Chosen People in history, the danger is that *two* can play this game as well as one. When that happens, woe be to the side that is short on numbers.[21]

In Cruse's analogizing, the Jews become sacrificial Christs as a consequence of a metaphor – that of the chosen people – which they themselves have launched. As we shall see in a moment, Elkins's analogy between slaves and camp survivors will similarly implicate Jews in their victimization, making his description, like Hentoff's, as problematical for Jews as it is for blacks.

I do not intend in any way to condemn the impulse on the part of scholars, Jewish or non-Jewish, to focus their attention on racism. That such an impulse may have had something to do with historical anti-Semitism and, later, with the Holocaust hardly detracts from the moral dedication of individuals like Boas and Handlin and others. Nonetheless, to blacks, the Jewish backgrounds of such thought necessarily had to compromise Jewish commitment. At the same time, the model of the Holocaust produced, within Jewish thinking about racism, and in black responses to such Jewish thinking, certain real distortions.

One problem with imagining a people's horror through the lens of another people's tragedy is, quite simply, that it may introduce counterproductive misinterpretations (in both directions) that undercut the purpose of the analogy. This is very dramatically the case, for example, with Hannah Arendt's "Reflections on Little Rock," which appeared in Howe's journal *Dissent* in 1959, along with a set of rejoinders, to which Arendt then responded in the next issue of the journal. In a box prominently placed right above the article's title, the editors of *Dissent* (read: Howe) state unequivocally that they do not agree with the essay's content, and they direct the reader's attention to the replies published along with the essay.[22] Following this pattern of contextualization, Arendt notes in her own preliminary comments prefacing the article that the essay "was written more than a year ago upon the suggestion of one of the editors of *Commentary*." It was not published "because of the controversial nature of my reflections, which, obviously, were at variance with the magazine's stand on matters of discrimination and segregation." She also, in advance of putting forward her position, already defends that position against some of the attack against it. Thus comes into print, deeply contextualized and couched, a most complicated and troubling comment on the problem of American racism by a world-renowned German-Jewish philosopher, who had come to the United States as a refugee from Nazi Germany, rawly sensitive to the Final Solution, yet also deeply German and secular in her intellectual attitudes and assumptions.[23]

As Arendt acknowledges in her prefatory comments, she writes her essay as an "outsider." What she produces is a powerful, dispassionate, complexly philosophical text concerning the rights of free association within democratic societies. "Discrimination," she writes, "is as indispensable a social right as equality is a political right. The question is not how to abolish discrimination, but how to keep it confined within the social sphere, where it is legitimate, and prevent its trespassing on the political and the personal sphere, where it is destructive." If, for example, Jews want to associate solely with Jews, even at hotels and country clubs, they have every right to do so. This does not mean, Arendt hurries to add, that movie theaters or museums can be restricted, since these are not places where people go to associate with each other. Nor is there any legitimacy to such things as segregated seating on buses, which clearly perform public services and function within the public realm.

What all of this is leading toward, which sets off a furor of protest against Arendt's article, is her position on school integration. In Arendt's view, education exists on a delicate border between the public and the private. Therefore, although the government is required to provide education, it does not, she maintains, have either the right or the responsibility to compel school integration. "To force parents to send their children to an integrated school against their will," argues Arendt, "means to deprive them of rights which clearly belong to them in all free societies – the private right over their children and the social right to free association. As for the children, forced integration means a very serious conflict between home and school, between their private and their social life, and while such conflicts are common in adult life, children cannot be expected to handle them and therefore should not be exposed to them."[24]

Preceding the conclusion toward which her argument is moving Arendt makes the following important clarifying but also revealing comment:

> It has been said, I think . . . by Mr. Faulkner, that enforced integration is no better than enforced segregation, and this is perfectly true. The only reason that the Supreme Court was able to address itself to the matter of desegregation in the first place was that segregation has been a legal, and not just a social, issue in the South for many generations. For the crucial point to remember is that it is not the social custom of segregation that is unconstitutional, but its *legal enforcement*. To abolish this legislation is of great and obvious importance and in the case of that part of the Civil Rights bill regarding the right

to vote, no Southern state in fact dared to offer strong opposition. Indeed, with respect to unconstitutional legislation, the Civil Rights bill did not go far enough, for it left untouched the most outrageous law of Southern states – the law which makes mixed marriage a criminal offense. The right to marry whoever one wishes is an elementary human right . . . Even political rights, like the right to vote, and nearly all other rights enumerated in the Constitution, are secondary to the inalienable human rights to "life, liberty, and the pursuit of happiness."[25]

As in her much more extended treatment of the Eichmann trial, Arendt is not the passionate partisan of one cause or another. Rather, she is an impartial philosopher. She stakes her confidence in the operations of the law rather than in human emotions. But, as in her analysis of Eichmann, something goes terribly wrong in Arendt's position on school desegregation.

By her own account, Arendt is an outsider on the scene of American race politics. She is also by her own account without race prejudice. "Like most people of European origin," she writes, "I have difficulty in understanding, let alone sharing, the common prejudices of Americans in this area . . . as a Jew I take my sympathy for the cause of the Negroes as for all oppressed or underprivileged peoples for granted and should appreciate it if the reader did likewise."[26] Nonetheless, whether goodwilled or not, her approach to school integration could not have been more out of tune with American passions, both black and white, as evidenced by the two responses that *Dissent* printed immediately following Arendt's piece. The piece by Melvin Tumin is so fierce that, in her "Reply to Critics" in the next issue, Arendt refuses even to answer it.[27] Still, to ask the question that Tumin asks, "Granted her moral convictions. . . . Granted her sympathy with the Negro. Granted her self-imposed special responsibilities in virtue of being a Jew": "How could she have written this?"

The answer to Tumin's well-put question is contained in Arendt's attentiveness to the rights of personal association in no area so prominently as in the right to marry. Before she even begins her essay, Arendt asserts her "contention that the marriage laws in 29 of the 49 states constitute a much more flagrant breach of the letter and spirit of the Constitution than segregation of schools." She even finds it necessary to contradict Sidney Hook's reply to this proposition (*New Leader*, April 13; I gather Hook read the essay originally submitted to *Commentary*) that "Negroes were 'profoundly uninterested' in these laws."[28] Profoundly uninterested may be an understatement, as Tumin reveals in his response, when he takes Arendt's concern with these laws to evidence her inherent racism. "A little touch of miscegenation or of that intermarriage of which Miss Arendt is such an ardent champion," he responds, and suddenly all those "visible differences" Arendt is so intent on maintaining disappear.[29]

The misunderstanding between Arendt and Tumin is absolute and total. It reflects the different sociopolitical places from which they speak. For the Jewish German refugee, the Nuremberg-like laws of proscribed marriages sound a warning bell much more fiercely than the possibility of segregated schools. Arendt would have experienced Jewish schooling in Germany with no particular anxiety. Indeed, Jewish Germans (like many Jewish Americans today) often reveled in the possibility of having their own school systems, in which they could perpetuate their Jewish culture and remain affiliated as Jews, without forfeiting participation in the larger social realm. Nor would this outsider to American culture have thought much about the issue of miscegenation. She would not have understood the degree to which the black and white American populations had already interbred and intermarried, the degree to which, within the black population at least, there could be no separation between black and white. Arendt's "racism" is nothing more than her unexamined application of her own racial sensitivities as a German Jew to the quite different circumstances of the African American – at least in the 1950s, for in the manner of many such historical reversals, black power advocates of the 1960s implicitly affirm exactly Arendt's argument in favor of segregation in the *private realm*. No less relevant in this context is that for African Americans earlier in the century, the proscription against interracial marriage seemed as central an issue as it did to Arendt. In Charles Chesnutt's 1901 novel, *The Marrow of Tradition,* for example, the plot hinges on the legality of an interracial marriage, while the black editorial manipulated by the white press to produce the race riot at the end of the book has specifically to do with "the miscegenation laws by which it was sought, in all the Southern States, to destroy liberty of contact, and, for the purpose of maintaining a fanciful purity of race, to make crimes of marriages to which neither nature nor religion nor the laws of other states interposed any insurmountable barrier."[30]

Still, Arendt's essay offends, and oddly enough it is Howe himself, having consented to publish Arendt's piece (albeit with a disclaimer), who isolates one major source of this offensiveness. Ironically – or maybe predictably – Howe exposes this source of the essay's problem, not in relation to Arendt's "Reflections on Little Rock," but in relation to her *Eichmann in Jerusalem*. In so doing, Howe produces an additional offense of his own, the same offense to which Ellison is pointing in his conversation with Howe concerning Richard Wright. Addressing himself to the "resentment I had had upon first seeing [the publication of *Eichmann in Jerusalem*] in the pages of the *New Yorker*," Howe (following Marie Syrkin's own objections to this publication event) locates the problem in the fact that most Americans would never read any statement other than Arendt's. Thus: "Hundreds of thousands of good middle-class Americans will have learned from those articles that the Jewish leadership in Europe was cowardly, inept, and even collaborationist; that the Jewish community helped the Nazis achieve their goal of racial genocide; and that if the Jews had not 'cooperated' with the Nazis, fewer than five to six million Jews would have been killed."[31] The very same logic could be adapted to impute Arendt's statement concerning blacks. In Arendt's philosophically detached statements, the actual condition of blacks in the South is woefully obscured.

Of course, not that many people were likely to read Arendt in the pages of *Dissent*, which was hardly a popular journal. Still and all, as Tumin points out in his retort to Arendt, her statement, however well intentioned and philosophically sound, not only gave aid and comfort to the enemy but reenforced many of the most objectionable of popular southern prejudices against black people. It certainly activated the most central and visceral fear of southerners – that blacks wanted to intermarry with whites and thus dissolve white into black. A philosophical mind as astute as Arendt's ought to have been able to anticipate and adjust for the popular reception of her words. She ought to have been able to grasp the centrality of miscegenation in American racial thought.

But then again, Howe might also, like the editors of *Commentary*, have held back the publication of Arendt's essay. The rights of free speech dictate that Arendt be entitled to her say. Nonetheless, *Dissent*, like *Commentary*, was under no obligation to print Arendt's essay. Therefore, when Howe objects to the publication of *Eichmann in Jerusalem* in the *New Yorker*, as he had not to "Reflections on Little Rock" in *Dissent* or to Baldwin's "A Letter from a Region in My Mind," also in the *New Yorker*, he compounds an already complicated publishing decision. And Ellison, in his exchange with Howe in *Dis-*

sent and the *New Leader,* is right on top of Howe's double standard. Already at the beginning of the second paragraph of his initial response to Howe, Ellison, we remember, recalls the appearance of Arendt's essay in Howe's journal, which is where Howe's own essay on "Black Boys and Native Sons" also appears. He also links the publication of "Reflections on Little Rock" and "Black Boys and Native Sons" to the later Arendt publication (and perhaps, implicitly, to Howe's statement at that time concerning the *Eichmann* essays). "Black Boys and Native Sons," Ellison says, "is a lively piece, written with something of the Olympian authority that characterized Hannah Arendt's 'Reflections on Little Rock,' in the Winter 1959 *Dissent* (a dark foreshadowing of the Eichmann blowup)."

That "Olympian authority," which I've spoken of earlier, returns us to the subject with which this discussion of slavery and the Holocaust began: Elkins's concentration camp analogy and the black protest it engendered. The link between Arendt (and Howe) and Elkins can be brought into further focus through a slender and, one would have to say, uncharacteristically thoughtless moment in Elkins's otherwise very cautious study. The moment occurs as Elkins is trying, quite valiantly, to counter arguments that either racial or even African cultural inferiority accounts for the American "Sambo." He is attempting as well to quell the incredulity of his readers that a mere institution (even as horrible a one as slavery) could produce such personality-transforming consequences as he is observing in African Americans. Therefore, Elkins produces the image of the camp Jews to testify to the possibility of such dehumanization and infantilization. The Jews of Europe, Elkins asserts by way of explanation, were "people in a full state of complex civilization, . . . men and women who were not black and not savages."[32]

At this moment Elkins lays bare the assumption that the example of the Jews can productively be brought to bear on the problem of race prejudice because it is a stronger, clearer case of the problem, involving (presumably) a more literate, more sophisticated, more civilized, population. As James Baldwin puts it,

> The Jew's suffering is recognized as part of the moral history of the world and the Jew is recognized as a contributor to the world's history: this is not true for blacks. . . . The Jew is a white man, and when white men rise up against oppression they are heroes: when black men rise they have reverted to their native savagery. The uprising in the Warsaw ghetto was not described as a riot, nor were the participants maligned as hoodlums.[33]

The Jewish position vis-à-vis history, both from their own perspective and from that of others, coupled with a Jewish inattentiveness to the concealed assumptions of their own discourse, emerges vividly in a heated exchange between Baldwin and Shlomo Katz, which once again engages blacks and Jews in a scramble over the Holocaust. In this exchange Katz objects to the Holocaust analogizing of Baldwin's "Open Letter to 'My Sister, Miss Angela Davis,'" which had appeared in the *New York Review of Books* in January 1971. In his response to Katz, Baldwin both reproduces his original (and from Katz's perspective, offensive) statement and notes as well what Katz leaves out in his reply:

> "You look exceedingly alone – as alone, say, as the Jewish house-wife in the box-car headed for Dachau, or as any one of our ancestors, chained together in the name of Jesus, headed for a Christian land." Apparently, the second part of this sentence neither impresses nor convinces you. Perhaps it is because you have forgotten the name of *my* sister and *my* mother: their name is Hagar.

Katz's response reveals neither bad faith nor the inappropriateness of his objection but, rather, a certain assumption of Jewish innocence. Writes Katz:

> What call was there for me to invoke Hagar? Now that he brings up her name, I wish to assure him that I have never forgotten her name. How could I? Were Mr. Baldwin familiar with traditional Jewish education of children, how the Bible is drilled into their heads, he would have realized that Hagar's name is part of my earlier confrontation with my history. Hagar is, in a sense, my aunt and Ishmael is my first cousin. In fact, Jews in eastern Europe – when there still were Jews there – invariably referred to Arabs and Turks – and sometimes to all Moslems – as Uncle Ishmael, an affectionate appellation, to distinguish them from Christian countries and what they had done to us in the name of Jesus.

Katz's answer misses both the thrust of Baldwin's comment and the position of Hagar in the Old Testament story. In other words, he misses the position of Hagar within traditional Jewish thinking about the other nations, including Christianity and Islam. Uncle Ishmael emerges as the Jewish equivalent of Uncle Tom: well meant and extremely offensive.[34]

Not only is Katz's tone, like Elkins's, Olympian, but his view of the

Jews corresponds to the feature within white and Jewish thinking about the differences between white/Jewish and black history and about Jewish attitudes toward blacks, to which Baldwin points us: that the Jewish example is more primary, more basic. But Katz, in engaging Baldwin's example, also exposes Jewish guilt within historical racism: almost from the beginning, Jewish history separated between Jews and others and identified those others racially. In similar fashion, Elkins's analogizing between black "Sambos" and infantilized survivors implicates not only blacks but Jews, his view of the Jews corresponding to no one's more closely than Hannah Arendt's. Like Arendt in *Eichmann,* Elkins puts before his American public (in a place and form not likely to cause the reader to investigate the subject further) the fact of *Jewish* nonresistance. Furthermore, he portrays the Jews as one dominant stereotype even preceding the war: as "Sambos," helpless, childlike, brutalized. That view of Jews was as much a part of the logic of the Final Solution as the similar attitudes that constituted the bases and justifications for plantation slavery. Indeed, as one traces the image of the Jew emerging through Elkins's study of slavery, one cannot here help but wonder whether thinking through black history didn't produce the "Sambo" view of Jews rather than the other way around.

It is relevant in this context that the 1943 article by Bruno Bettelheim on which Elkins heavily bases his argument is itself the consequence of some mutually constructing thought concerning blacks and Jews. During the years he was writing "Individual and Mass Behavior in Extreme Situations," Bettelheim was employed by the American Jewish Committee in studying anti-Semitism in the United States. This study involved Bettelheim in making his own numerous comparisons between blacks and Jews.[35] Furthermore, in his own judgment of it, Bettelheim's article was private therapy. This not only calls into question the applicability of Bettelheim's theory to blacks and Jews both, but it also exposes as a possible feature of Elkins's own relationship to the theory his desire, as a Jew, to explain what many people after the war perceived as Jewish acquiescence in their slaughter. As it turns out, Bettelheim's own credentials, as a psychologist and as an interpreter of the Holocaust, were none too solid, and Bettelheim's work itself has emerged as evidence of (rather than evidence concerning) Jewish dysfunction.[36]

And this brings me back to the Elkins essay with which I began. His 1975 piece on "The Slavery Debate" produces one final turn in the mutual construction of black and Jewish history, which is similarly compromising both for African Americans and for Jews.

In that essay Elkins answers objections to his book, which he understands as part of a larger movement within African American studies. This was the movement from the "damage" theory of slavery, with its stress on the brutality of slavery and its brutalization of blacks, to the "resistance" theory, which, in Elkins's view, gave "legitimate" expression to "the search for black culture."[37] A key spokesperson for this shift was Ralph Waldo Ellison, whose position on the subject, Elkins notes, is consistent with many other of his statements from the 1940s on.

As in so many things, Ellison anticipated the issues that came to dominate the scene in the following decades. Elkins cites three illustrative Ellison essays in this context: his review of Gunnar Myrdal's *An American Dilemma,* which Ellison faults for presenting blacks as if the three hundred years of their history in America amounted to nothing more than a reaction to white culture; his review of Howard Zinn's *Southern Mystique* with its Elkins-inspired suggestion that with integration into white American society, black history will no longer matter; and a 1965 interview in *Harper's* magazine, later reprinted in revised form in *Going to the Territory,* in which Ellison specifically responds again to Elkins.[38]

In this last document, Ellison penetrates to the source of the problem vis-à-vis Jewish history, while launching the countermove that will characterize one equally problematical line of black response to the positioning of black history within Jewish-authored texts. "I get damned tired of critics writing of me as though I don't know how hard it is to be a Negro American," complains Ellison, as if Howe's "Black Boys and Native Sons" were still painfully rattling around in his head. "My point is that it isn't *only* hard, that there are many, many good things about it. But they don't want you to say that. This is especially true of some of our Jewish critics. They get quite upset when I say: *I like this particular aspect of Negro life and would not surrender it. What I want is something else to go along with it.*" And he continues,

> Contrary to some, I feel that our experience as a people involves a great deal of heroism. From one perspective, slavery was horrible and brutalizing. . . . And the Negro writer is tempted to agree. "Yes! God damn it, wasn't that a horrible thing!" And he sometimes agrees to the next step, which holds that slaves had very little humanity because slavery destroyed it for them and their descendants. That's what the Stanley M. Elkins "Sambo" argument implies. But despite the historical

past and the injustices of the present, there is from *my* perspective something further to say. I have to *affirm* my forefathers and I *must* affirm my parents or be reduced in my own mind to a white man's inadequate – even if unprejudiced – conception of human complexity.

   . . . Any people who could endure all of that brutalization and keep together, who could undergo such dismemberment and resuscitate itself, and endure until it could take the initiative in achieving its own freedom is obviously more than the sum of its brutalization. Seen in this perspective, theirs had been one of the great human experiences and one of the great triumphs of the human spirit in modern times. In fact, in the history of the world.[39]

Carefully separating between the brutality of the slave system and "the next step" – its brutalization of blacks, in which, despite its best attempts, slavery, in Ellison's view, did not succeed – Ellison argues against the notion that African Americans created themselves in the image of someone else's distorted view of them. But Ellison in his essay does more than overturn the Holocaust analogy. He inverts its implied claims concerning Jewish history. Although Jews may have been brutalized (dehumanized, infantilized, destroyed) by their historical experience, Ellison implies, blacks were not. While the Jewish example has to do with the death of the human spirit, black history has to do with its triumph. Therefore it is the blacks' experience (not the Jews') which is the great human experience, and not only in modern times, but in the "history of the world."

   Ellison's victory, however, is not total; and the resistance theory that he articulates, like the damage theory he resists, has negative implications, as Elkins quite accurately argues. As they emerge in Elkins's rhetoric these implications turn out to be as serious for Jews as for blacks. Jews, Elkins realizes, have developed their own resistance theory of the Holocaust. "Judging from what others have published over the last few years," Elkins admits, "Ralph Ellison . . . has clearly carried his point on black culture." This is not, however, Elkins's last word. "It seems equally clear," he insists, "that the culture argument is at something of a crossroads. . . . Culture, under such conditions as those of slavery, is not acquired without a price; the social and individual experience of any group with as little power, and enduring such insistent assaults . . . is bound to contain more than the normal residue of pathology. Any theory that is worth anything must allow for this. It must allow, that is, for damage."[40]

Leading into this point, and to lend his sympathy once more to the black cause, even as he refutes African Americanist claims such as Ellison's, Elkins turns again to the example of the Jews. Reviewing Orlando Patterson's recent lament on the failure of the slave insurrection, he suggests that Patterson, "rather like a young Israeli tank sergeant of a decade ago commenting on the Holocaust, is demanding to know why they capitulated, why they were not more heroic."[41] From Elkins's point of view, this desire, though understandable, threatens severe consequences for the understanding of black and, one must now add, Jewish history.

As in Elkins's earlier example of the camps, it is not at all clear whether thinking about Jewish history produces the examples by which Elkins understands black history or, vice versa, whether thinking through African American history inevitably, irresistibly, provides the perspective on the Jewish experience. For truth to tell, whether in imitation of black power moves of the 1960s or in response to statements such as Ellison's or in an independent parallel to features of black historical revisionism, Jewish historians in the 1970s and 1980s produced their own resistance theory of the Holocaust. Like Ellison's, these theories addressed serious deficiencies in previous interpretations. They also, however, created problems of their own, such as Elkins aptly describes in relation to Ellison.

In 1976, for example, in *The Survivor: An Anatomy of Life in the Death Camps,* Terrence Des Pres, referring directly to Bettelheim and Elkins, refutes both Bettelheim's original thesis and Elkins's adaptation of it. He portrays the behavior of camp inmates not as childlike but as highly focused on maximizing the possibilities of survival.[42] Des Pres's study is part of a larger movement within Jewish historiography, which stressed resistance (even in the very slender and partial forms in which such resistance was enacted in the camps), and which paid more attention to such events as the activities of the Jewish underground and the ghetto uprisings.

In relation to Jews as to blacks, it is not by any means clear that such resistance theory, when it emerges, does not, as Elkins had argued, compromise the moral condemnation of slavery and genocide. If some Jews could have resisted, then all of them could have, and if they didn't, isn't their extermination their own fault? Such lack of Jewish resistance forms a cornerstone of accusation in Hannah Arendt's *Eichmann in Jerusalem,* and the Jewish critics who oppose Arendt are quite aware of this.

In a reply as angry and indignant as Tumin's five years earlier to Arendt's "Reflections on Little Rock," Norman Podhoretz puts the case concerning *Eichmann* as follows: "Whenever [the Nazis] encountered determined opposition, she says, they backed down . . . one can readily agree that the determining factor in the number of Jews murdered was the amount of resistance (either active or passive) offered to the Final Solution. The important question to be decided, however, is: resistance by *whom?* Miss Arendt knows, of course, that it was the attitude of the local populace that made the main difference," and not, as she suggests, of the Jews. And once more producing that inevitable linkage between black and Jewish texts, Podhoretz states that "if Baldwin is all eloquence and no cleverness, Miss Arendt is all cleverness and no eloquence; and if Baldwin brings his story unexpectedly to life through the bold tactic of heightening and playing exquisitely on every bit of melodrama it contains, Miss Arendt with an equally surprising boldness rids her story of melodrama altogether and heavily underlines every trace of moral ambiguity she can wring out of it"[43] – as, we might add, she had done in her "Reflections on Little Rock."

In linking Arendt and Baldwin, Podhoretz reaffirms Elkins's point concerning the dangers of the resistance theory and its galling accusation against the victims of atrocities such as slavery and genocide. For Jews and blacks both, in the aftermaths of Holocaust and slavery, the apparent failures of their groups to take action had to feel so painful as to require some comment, explanation, or even refutation. But this is to say that both the "Sambo" theory and the "resistance" theory that refutes it, whether concerning blacks or Jews, represent theories under conditions of extremity as compelling as the conditions of extremity they attempt to interpret. Both, therefore, are suspect. Both bring into play defensive reactions on the parts of interpreters who are also members of the group whose history is being discussed; or on the parts of interpreters of members of another group, who bring to bear on the history they are analyzing an unrelated, personal, psychological burden.

As Laurence Thomas has pointed out, the comparison between plantation slavery and the Holocaust falters in many places, and Elkins's reference to the Israeli tank commander can, I think, help to isolate the chief of these. The slave experience, Thomas notes, lasted over centuries and had as its primary objective the eradication of black cultural solidarity rather than the extermination of the population itself. The Holocaust transpired over less than a decade. Its purpose was to destroy the Jewish people, along with the culture they had already evolved.[44] Elkins's recurrence to the example of the Israeli tank commander implicitly recognizes that the issue for the

Jews was one of survival (not, as Ellison is arguing for blacks, of culture). The issue is armed resistance. Zionism, needless to say, had other origins within Judaism and Jewish history. But the immediate precondition for the founding of Israel was the extermination of the six million. Armed insurrection is very much to the point of the Zionist response to the Holocaust. It is Patterson's subject vis-à-vis slavery. It is not, however, what Ellison is talking about.

The more plausible analogy to plantation slavery in Jewish history, which Ellison's comment suggests, would be the centuries-long experience of persecution, expulsion, and pogroms. This experience was not genocidal. More like plantation slavery than the Holocaust, Christian anti-Semitism intended to "convert" Jews into something else, even to employ them (as moneylenders and international couriers) within the larger non-Jewish economy.[45] But once this view of Jewish history has been put alongside African American history, then what can be said of blacks concerning "damage" can and, indeed, once the analogy has been released, must be said concerning the Jews as well: that centuries of pogroms and dispersions cannot but have had an effect on the Jewish personality.

And it has been said. In a very recent response to Norman Podhoretz's "My Negro Problem – and Ours," Joe Wood reads Podhoretz's confession of racism as covering for "the problem of his Jewishness," his hatred of "his weakness, his Jewishness."[46] Wood is not alone in arguing this point. But if Jews were already, at the time of the camps, the victims of the "pathology" of their history – and how could they not be? – then the example of the Jews as a people in a more "complex state of civilization" either falls away or must be made to yield its implicit affirmation of Ellison's contention: that culture happens, and happens brilliantly and without brutalization, even under the most horrific and brutalizing of human circumstances.

Elkins's original example of the camps and his later recurrence to the Israeli military lend themselves more to an explanation of black power in the 1960s and 1970s than to an exposé of the black personality. By the same token, Ellison's reply, falling too readily into the mode of accepting the analogy between slavery and the Holocaust, which then necessitates his refuting its implications, fails to take into account the triumph of Jewish civilization over Christian persecution. When writers such as Alice Walker and Toni Morrison inherit Ellison's insights, they will continue his problematical distortion of the relationship between blacks and Jews. They will complete the swerve away from kinship to alienation, their own positions as

African Americans incorporating an unacknowledged response to Jewish forays into black–Jewish analogies.

I do not impugn Elkins's motives, or Ellison's, in relation either to blacks or to Jews. Nor do I wish to psychoanalyze any one of these players in the culture game. All of us argue through our historical moment. We are all implicated in and constructed by the worldviews that we both share and shape. Elkins is, I think, right, in relation to both black and Jewish history regarding resistance theory. Potentially, at least, it converts victims into collaborators in their victimization. And Ellison is surely as right about the existence of a nonbrutalized, resistant culture as Des Pres is concerning Jewish survival. Nonetheless, in bringing together such vastly different events as slavery and the Holocaust, the Jewish and black critic further complicate what are already highly fraught negotiations between the historical record and the contemporary psychological needs of a civilization to understand its past. And they set blacks and Jews on a collision course from which they may well not yet have recovered.

Assimilation, Miscegenation, Black Nationalism, and Jewish Zionism (Norman Podhoretz and Harold Cruse)[47]

Given the nature of Ellison's objections to Hyman's, Elkins's, and Howe's forays into black culture and history, he could not have been any happier with the appearance of an even earlier document, which also fashioned its theory of the African American in relation to the Holocaust. This document is by a black, not a Jewish, writer. The Holocaust-inflected text on which Anatole Broyard bases his argument in "Portrait of the Inauthentic Negro" (*Commentary*, 1950) was as unpalatable to Jews as the later document was to blacks. As the note accompanying the essay makes sure to point out, "Portrait of an Inauthentic Negro" is an "analysis of the situation of the American Negro" "similar" to that of Jean-Paul Sartre's of the Jews. Before its publication as a book, *Anti-Semite and Jew* also appeared in the pages of *Commentary* "as a series of articles . . . in the April, May, and June issues of 1948."[48] That both of these studies appear in a Jewish journal is itself significant to our thinking about black–Jewish relations.

Both Sartre and Broyard, it should be stressed, are writing directly after the war. They are writing in the immediate wake of the Jewish devastation and at the moment when returning black GIs are beginning to confront (again) the realities of American racism. For this reason, there is something at least mildly indecorous in the focus of both Broyard's and Sartre's essays. To Broyard, "as to Sartre, the ultimate horror of discrimination is the victim's unconscious re-molding of his own personality into something untrue to himself." Broyard's piece, which is a weak copy of Sartre's, delivers the same offense to blacks that Sartre's does to Jews. It leads to the same extremely problematical conclusions. "It is not the Jewish character that provokes anti-Semitism," writes Sartre as he nears his conclu-sion, "but, rather, it is the anti-Semite who creates the Jew." Simi-larly, Broyard: "Today the anti-Negro is a secondary problem; their first problem is their individual selves, their own authenticity. Their personalities have been lost in the shuffle, a shuffle with marked cards, dealt from the bottom of the deck."

Of course, the internality of both Jewish and black cultural iden-tity forms a legitimate concern in the writings of many Jewish and African American critics. Nonetheless, there is something inappro-priate, even offensive, in both Sartre's and Broyard's foci, in partic-ular in their assumption that blacks and Jews as they exist in the middle of the twentieth century are only reflections of someone else's distorted view of them. African Americans ride in seating-segregated buses, use segregated facilities, and are being lynched throughout the South, and Broyard's major concern is not with the "anti-Negro" but with the authenticity of the black personality. In the case of *Anti-Semite and Jew,* Sartre draws the implications even further, toward what must offend both blacks and Jews in both Sar-tre's and Broyard's portraits. "With the problem thus stated, what are we to do about it?" asks Sartre. "In short, what can we seek? Assimilation? That is a dream; the true opponent of assimilation is not the Jew but the anti-Semite."[49]

It is difficult to find the right words to pose the objection to this, especially since whatever offense the essay offers is even further ag-gravated by the fact that Sartre is not himself a Jew. This is as much the case when Sartre's solution to the "Jewish Question" is presented by Broyard as the solution to the Negro problem, even though Bro-yard is himself African American, albeit one who spent most of his life passing as white.[50] To complicate matters even further, the au-dience for his comments is not the African American population but American Jewry. Six million Jews have been exterminated in Europe, and Sartre is advocating the further disappearance of the Jews as Jews. Black people are being segregated and hanged and Broyard's solution is that blacks as blacks disappear.

Norman Podhoretz proposes a very similar and similarly offensive argument in an article that, as Podhoretz, in a later postscript to the essay, quotes one reader as observing, had "something in it to offend everyone."[51] "My Negro Problem – and Ours" appeared in *Commentary* in February 1963, shortly after Baldwin's "Letter" appeared in the *New Yorker*. Podhoretz's piece is a direct response to Baldwin, whose essay was meant to have appeared in *Commentary* and who dealt in his essay (as elsewhere) not only with white culture but, as I have already noted, with the relationship between blacks and Jews.[52] It also leads forward to two writings by Harold Cruse – *Crisis of the Negro Intellectual* and "My Jewish Problem and Theirs" – both of which are constructed in relation to Jewish texts, in particular Podhoretz's own Baldwin-inspired essay, and both of which, even though Cruse goes to the heart of the misreading in Podhoretz's piece, seriously misread Jewish moves and motives. For Cruse, the basic confusion, forced upon him by his eagerness to engage the impressive success of Jews in America, has to do with the difference, which he cannot quite grasp, between American Jewish assimilation and Zionism. This confusion is set into motion by Podhoretz's own earlier blurring of the difference between integration for blacks, assimilation for Jews, and what he means, in his essay, by the term "miscegenation."

Guiding Podhoretz's thinking in his essay is Baldwin's openness, in the "Letter" as earlier in *Notes of a Native Son*, concerning his negative feelings toward Jews. Equally important to Podhoretz are Baldwin's instructions (which he quotes as an epigraph to his essay) to those "relatively conscious whites and . . . relatively conscious blacks, who must, like lovers, insist on, or create, the consciousness of others." "Baldwin's demand," writes Podhoretz, is that "color," which in Podhoretz's (mis)interpretation of Baldwin is "not a human or personal reality, [but] a political reality," "must be forgotten." This can happen, Podhoretz continues, still representing Baldwin's point of view, only in "the transcendence of color through love." This idea leads Podhoretz into his startling and, to many, offensive conclusion:

> In thinking about the Jews I have often wondered whether their survival as a distinct group was worth one hair on the head of a single infant. . . . It is a terrible question and no one, not God Himself, could ever answer it to my satisfaction. And when I think about the Negroes in America and about the image of integration as a state in which the Negroes would take their rightful place as another of the protected minorities in a pluralistic society, I wonder whether they really believe in their hearts that such a state can actually be attained, and if so *why*

they should wish to survive as a distinct group. I think I know why the Jews once wished to survive (though I am less certain as to why we still do): they not only believed that God had given them no choice, but they were tied to a memory of past glory and a dream of imminent redemption. What does the American Negro have that might correspond to this? His past is a stigma, his color is a stigma. . . .

. . . I cannot see how [integration] will ever be realized unless color does *in fact* disappear: and that means not integration, it means assimilation, it means – let the brutal word come out – miscegenation.[53]

Like Hannah Arendt before him, Podhoretz doesn't quite take in the power of that brutal word, not so much from the white perspective as from the black.

Some critics, like Harold Cruse, chose deliberately to misread Podhoretz's article and attacked it as primarily an occasion for his confessing his "hatred . . . for Negroes." This line of thinking has recently been revived, albeit with the purpose of furthering rather than hindering black–Jewish relations, in an essay by Joe Wood.[54] In Cruse's "My Jewish Problem and Theirs," where the word "theirs" is as much an accusation against philo-Semitic blacks as against Jews, the Jews emerge as virtually demonic, as Cruse produces a litany of anti-Semitic stereotypes concerning Jewish power, money, superiority, and so on.

Nonetheless, Cruse quite accurately locates a central defect in Podhoretz's essay, which hinges on the word "miscegenation." Cruse's objective, both in "My Jewish Problem and Theirs" and in his earlier chapters on Negroes and Jews in *The Crisis of the Negro Intellectual,* is to wean blacks from their philo-Semitism. In Cruse's view, black affection for Jews has only worked to their disadvantage. It has prevented them from assuming control over their own destinies and from recognizing the degree to which black and Jewish interests do not converge. His purpose in writing his critique of the Negro intellectual is to produce, as he puts it in "My Jewish Problem": "a genuine black American intellectual point of view."[55] Thus, Cruse writes in *The Crisis of the Negro Intellectual* that, because blacks believed that "Jewish liberalism was different from white liberalism proper"

it must have been quite a shock . . . when Norman Podhoretz, the editor of *Commentary,* made public his considerable phobias toward the Negro, in his article "My Negro Problem and Ours."

Lorraine Hansberry, one of the most convinced exponents of Negro-Jewish unity, retorted indignantly that Podhoretz had to "hold his nose" when contemplating Negroes at close range. But after all, Podhoretz only expressed honestly what many other Jews who had intimate dealings with Negroes, had intimated in random conversations.

Cruse's next sentence is crucial: "What lay behind Podhoretz's avowals, however, was the fact that the Jewish community was in the process of reevaluating the position of Jews in American society."[56] This reevaluation, Cruse realizes, has to do with the meaning of the term "assimilation" as Podhoretz uses it in his essay and as an idea of assimilation informs American Jewish intellectual thought.

Although Cruse takes his arguments to objectionable and mistaken conclusions in *The Crisis of the Negro Intellectual,* still and all, Cruse is, I think, right about what lies behind Podhoretz's avowals. This is so, despite the fact that Podhoretz later comments about his essay that, "even though I spoke explicitly as a Jew throughout, and even though in the concluding section I drew a comparison between blacks and Jews, I was writing not as a Jew but as a white liberal." Podhoretz's remark recalls Irving Howe's similar disclaimer concerning the position from which he wrote "Black Boys and Native Sons."[57] Podhoretz's later confession goes directly to what I will be arguing about his essay, though not for the reasons Podhoretz imagines. In the course of proposing the disappearance of blacks, Podhoretz finds himself of necessity perilously close to advocating something very similar for Jews. He pulls back, however, from a full endorsement of that position. Both Podhoretz's willingness to imagine the disappearance of the Jews and his inability, finally, to see that argument through go to the heart of the black–Jewish entanglement that produces the essay in the first place. And both features problematize the essay's relationship to its two constituencies and the relationship of its two constituencies to each other.

Before interrogating Podhoretz's essay along these lines, and examining Cruse in the light of Podhoretz, let me present Podhoretz's undertaking on its own merits and failings. Most of Podhoretz's readers praised the honest courage of his confession (as of Baldwin's before him), registering as well, at least implicitly, the strategic function of both Podhoretz's and Baldwin's autobiographical narratives.[58] In order to make the call for the transcendence of hate meaningful, readers understood, both Podhoretz and Baldwin had to establish the power of the resistance to it, on their parts as well as on the parts of their audiences. And yet, even this gainsaid, Podhoretz's essay seemed to many of his readers painfully to miss something about the race problem.

Many of the responses solicited by Podhoretz's piece, which *Commentary* (to its credit) printed over the next several issues of the journal, indicate that "My Negro Problem – and Ours" was as offensive to Jews as it was to blacks, and in relation to Jewish as much as to black culture. The essay's misstep, readers wrote in to explain, had to do with what one such respondent isolated as the "same old story of asking the Negro to do it all." The comment recalls the objections to both the Sartre and the Broyard essays:

> This is asking the Negro, who has been thwarted and denied in every endeavor *because* he is a Negro, to give over the drive to succeed, to count, while at the same time remaining a Negro. Podhoretz can understand why Jews want to survive: they are tied to a memory of past glory. But not the Negroes. Their past is stigma, their color is a stigma, their "vision of the future is the hope of erasing the stigma by making color irrelevant."[59]

This position, as one Jewish reader points out, is as intolerable to Jews as to blacks:

> The article is offensive to any Jew who has had any association with Jewish tradition. Such a Jew is told in effect that because he helped to keep Jewish identity alive, he must bear part of the responsibility for the annihilation of six million Jews ... The article is offensive to any Negro. In effect, the Negro is told he has no past worth looking back at and no future, except his escape from his past by intermarriage.[60]

Or another response (Jewish):

> The solution is so easy I wonder how no one else ever thought of it. If we had no Negroes or Jews we would have no minority problems. . . . To eliminate persecution, bigotry, prejudice, and the like we just remove the victim.[61]

As another reader recognizes, Podhoretz fails to recognize the rights of groups as of individuals to their survival.[62] "The Negro demand," writes Lorraine Hansberry, "is for equality for *Negroes; the biological and sociological reality of Negroes as they presently exist.*"[63]

What leads Podhoretz into his denial of the rights of survival to ethnic and religious culture, and what accounts, therefore, for his willingness to see Jews and blacks disappear as Jews and blacks, is the same analogy that produces the misperceptions and distortions in Elkins's and Arendt's positions: the importation into the center of his thinking about race of the example of the Jews in Nazi Germany. Given the absolute alternatives of life and death – which are not the alternatives for African Americans in the 1960s (nor, for that matter, for Jews after the war) – Podhoretz chooses life, even if such survival on the individual level means the death of the group as a religious or racial entity. Just as Elkins is drawn to his black-as-Sambo/Jew-as-Sambo image by the two-directional pressures of his analogy, so Podhoretz, both in his conclusions concerning blacks and in his question concerning Jews, is forced by his mutual entanglement of the two histories to misstate both realities and offend both communities.

In the first instance, the offense is more forceful in relation to blacks than to Jews. As Podhoretz sets up the terms of his analysis – integration, assimilation, and miscegenation, as the ascending elements in individual survival and group dissolution – one significant term is missing on the Jewish side of things: the word "conversion." Despite Podhoretz's implication to the contrary, assimilation is not miscegenation. Rather, assimilation, at least as it was and is popularly understood by Jews, is analogous for them to what integration represents for blacks.[64] In other words, when Podhoretz produces the word "assimilation" as what African Americans must achieve in the United States, above and beyond "integration," he is, in the first instance, advocating no more than what assimilation meant both to the Jews of Germany and to the Jews of America. For Jews, this meant gradually yielding certain aspects of their communal separatism (meaning, largely, elements of their religious life) without their becoming Christians. As Philip Roth once wrote concerning this strategy of nonconversion, "it is difficult for me to distinguish a Jewish style of life in our country that is significantly separate and distinct from the American style of life":

> What a Jew wants and how he goes after it, does not on the whole appear to differ radically from what his Gentile neighbor wants and how he goes after it. There does not seem to me a complex of values or aspirations or beliefs that continue to connect one Jew to another in our country, but rather an ancient and powerful disbelief . . . the rejection of the myth of Jesus as Christ. . . . The result is that we are bound together, I to my fellow Jews, in a relationship that is peculiarly enervating and unviable. Our rejection, our abhorrence finally, of the Christian fantasy leads us to proclaim to the world that we are

Jews still – alone, however, what have we to proclaim to one another?

What holds Jews together in contemporary America may be little more than their resistance to becoming *goyim*.[65]

When Podhoretz slides past the word "assimilation" right into "the brutal word" "miscegenation" – a term with no relevance at all to the contemporary American Jewish experience – he separates Jewish from African American history. Like Arendt before him, who also gets stuck on the idea of miscegenation, he transforms the name of the game. The analogue to miscegenation for blacks would be, for the Jews, conversion to Christianity. It would be actively to surrender their identity to the dominant culture. Conversion, in traditional discourse, is (as in Baldwin's image at the end of the *Fire Next Time*) very like a marriage. Therefore, to disappear into the dominant population as Jews would be – like blacks intermarrying with whites – for Jews to intermarry with or convert to (or at least raise their children as) Christians. Just as the numbers of whites versus blacks would reproduce a white world (despite the temporary dominance of melanin as a genetic factor; Faulkner quite clearly understands this at the end of *Absalom, Absalom!*), so, too, would interfaith marriage between Christians and Jews produce more Christians than Jews.

Podhoretz, I suggest, is not advocating the conversion of the Jews, even in America, although his view of European Jewry differs from his view of Jewish Americans in this regard. One must note, in this context, that although many (Jewish) readers took Podhoretz to be answering his question whether Jewish group survival was worth the death of a single Jewish child, Podhoretz does not actually attempt an answer to this question. Quite the contrary: he denies the question's answerability. In any case, he claims to understand exactly why the Jews of Europe felt compelled to survive as a people. This failure to see African American culture similarly as a culture worth preserving produces Podhoretz's major offense against the African American community, as several of his readers suggested. It causes him to misread Baldwin's "Letter" in the direction of advocating the "conversion" of the blacks out of their faith into the American dream. But Baldwin's lovers do not in the least become each other (convert each other to the other's position); rather, they are said to together create the consciousness *in others* of what Baldwin, throughout the essay, has been arguing for (although his readers may have missed this in him as in Ellison): the existence of a black cultural identity.

Such cultural identity, as I have already suggested, is, for Baldwin, already intrinsically part of American culture. White culture, however, including the Jews, has refused to see this. The mission of Baldwin's lovers, in other words, is not to let anything disappear. It is to retrieve and preserve a consciousness of black culture within both the black and the nonblack population.[66] For blacks as for Jews, conversion might seem an anathema, and multiethnic identity an impossibility, as when Nella Larsen has one of her characters say, quite against normative logic, that a classmate is "no longer a Negro or a Christian but had become a Jew."[67]

And yet, even as blacks and (European) Jews separate out in Podhoretz's essay, forcing an affront to blacks, the analogy he devises produces an equally problematical implication for contemporary American Jewry. Podhoretz understands why formerly Jews had not wanted to convert. He is not, however, at all convinced he sees any reason for them, any more than for blacks, to remain ethnically distinct in America. Podhoretz, I maintain, is still not advocating the active conversion of the Jews, which would be the counterpart to miscegenation for blacks, and which would thereby at least carry with it the same consequences (i.e., the disappearance of Jews as Jews). Therefore, he is evading as well the memory of the trauma of historical violation that conversion, like miscegenation, represented: forced conversion, in the case of Jews; rape, in the case of blacks. In an almost unthought-out way, however, Podhoretz is nonetheless ensuring the disappearance of the Jews as Jews – a fact evidenced by Podhoretz's own statement concerning himself: that he wrote as a white liberal, not as a Jew. Such disappearance might not occur through any actions Jews might or might not choose to take. Rather, it would happen because of their lack of attentiveness to who they are and what they imagine for their future as, or not as, Jews. This danger of assimilation, as unconscious, unpremeditated, and absolutely annihilating, is what may well have already taken its toll on the European Jewish community before the war. Cruse cannot see this about Jewish history. Nor can he see the complex relationship between assimilation, the resistance to assimilation, and Zionism, especially in the postwar years in the United States.

If the unexamined difference between integration and assimilation, exposed through the word "miscegenation" and its unspoken, rejected counterpart "conversion," produces a distortion in Podhoretz's position, a similar dynamic of inattentiveness concerning assimilation and Zionism characterizes Cruse's argument as well. Pressuring Cruse's text throughout is the fact that as much as Cruse wants

to release black intellectuals from Jewish domination, he is himself
so enamored of the Jewish example that he explicitly proposes it as
a model for black group solidarity, albeit as part of an anti-Jewish
strategy rather than as a feature of alliance. Since for Cruse the
name of this example is Zionism, this means advocating nothing less
than black nationalism. "Much more important than developing a
critique on Jews, is the challenge of learning the methods and techniques that the Zionists have developed in the art of survival against
all kinds of odds."[68]

Of course, one might immediately point out that this "survival
against all kinds of odds" did not prevent the annihilation of six
million Jews, which was the horrific condition without which it is by
no means certain that a Jewish state would ever have been estab-
lished. The success of Zionism is not only not synonymous with the
success of American Jewry but, in its own terms, it triumphed only
at enormous, devastating cost. But more pertinent to the issue of
domestic American politics, the political Zionism that Cruse would
advocate for blacks did not characterize the identity politics of the
majority of Jews preceding and following the war; Zionism does not
account for Jewish strength in America; nor is Zionism what Podhoretz is advocating in his essay, even though Podhoretz will indeed
later become a "Zionist" and an adamant defender of the State of
Israel. This makes Cruse's misreading of Podhoretz's essay and of
the 1960s Jewish community nothing less than prophetic – though
it is also possible to understand some measure of the Jewish turn
toward Zionism as a response to black intellectuals like Cruse, who
ejected Jews from the arena of domestic social struggle.

Like many Jewish intellectuals who proceed through black issues to
Jewish ones, so Cruse, in his effort to divorce blacks from Jews (his
countermove to both Baldwin's and Podhoretz's marrying them to
each other), makes Jewish history and culture a central component of
his thesis. But in order to make Jewish history applicable to African
American history, Cruse has to emphasize that feature that Podhoretz
has to blur. This is the Jews' unwillingness to convert. But in reversing
Podhoretz's emphases, Cruse proposes to his black audience a model
that does not exist and was not the major mechanism of American
Jewish identity. He also distorts the distinctions between internal
American politics (for both Jews and blacks, and in relation to their
own ethnic communities and to each other) and international affairs,
invoking a difficulty that will continue to divide American blacks and
Jews: the Palestinian issue. The "cultural nationalism" that Cruse
would advocate for blacks and which he believes to characterize Jews

is not, as he imagines, Zionism. Cultural nationalism, for Jews like Howe and Podhoretz, is assimilation; it is pluralism; and pluralism is exactly what failed the black community in the United States. "The path to more knowledge for the Negro intellectual," Cruse concludes one of the chapters in *The Crisis of the Negro Intellectual*, "is through cultural nationalism – an ideology that has made Jewish intellectuals into a social force to be reckoned with in America."[69]

Of major concern to Cruse in both his book and his essay is the same issue that galvanizes both Baldwin's and Ellison's concern: black cultural identity, making Cruse's hostility to Baldwin rather perverse and misdirected. Cruse's objection, for example, to "Jewish dominance in the Communist Party" from the 1930s on, is that it "bur[ied] the Negro radical potential deeper and deeper in the slough of white intellectual paternalism." Committed as it was (in Cruse's view) to "the preservation of Jewish cultural identity," the Jewish leadership, in Cruse's interpretation, did nothing less than deny the existence of such "cultural identity" to blacks:

> It evidently never occurred to Negro revolutionaries that there was no one in America who possessed the remotest potential for Americanizing Marxism but themselves. Certainly the Jews could not with their nationalistic aggressiveness, emerging out of Eastside ghettoes to demonstrate through Marxism their intellectual superiority over the Anglo-Saxon *goyim*. The Jews failed to make Marxism applicable to anything in America but their *own* national-group social ambitions or individual self-elevation. As a result, the great brainwashing of Negro radical intellectuals was not achieved by capitalism, or the capitalistic bourgeoisie, but by Jewish intellectuals in the American Communist Party.

For Cruse this denial of cultural identity to blacks could only have to do with international Zionism: "under Jewish Community prodding, the Communist Party took up the anti-Hitler crusade in the late 1930's."[70]

Thus, in order to defend his accusation against Podhoretz that, as already quoted, "what lay behind Podhoretz's avowals . . . was the fact that the Jewish community was in the process of reevaluating the position of Jews in American society," Cruse says the following:

> For example, on the evening of November 17, 1965, an influential rabbi – Arthur Hertzberg of Englewood, New Jersey – speaking at the Zionist Theodore Herzl Institute, stated that

American Jews were no longer among the "have-nots" but associated with the "haves." He stated that this required the Jewish community to reassess its entire relationship with American society, and also with the Negro civil rights movement. He declared that he was happy to be in the presence of such "positive Jews" as those associated with the Theodore Herzl Institute, who were unlike certain other kinds of Jews who go "crawling on their bellies to Rome." In other words, the rabbi was saying that today American Jews are a power in this land and should act accordingly. Behind this power, of course, is the State of Israel, which immeasurably enhances the new status of American Jewry as a "have" group.

Cruse's conclusions concerning what Hertzberg intended for Jews to do differently in the United States, now that they had power, are not at all substantiated by the materials he presents. That aside, the major problem with his statement is the easy equation between Jewish power in America and the force behind this power, which for Cruse is, "of course," the State of Israel. But let me quote a bit more before I more closely examine Cruse's error:

> . . . the American Negro must seriously reassess *his* relationships with American Jews. Such reassessment should have taken place immediately after the establishment of Israel in 1948. For the emergence of Israel as a world-power-in-minuscule meant that the Jewish question in America was no longer purely a domestic minority problem growing out of the old immigrant status tradition. A great proportion of American Jews began to function in America as an organic part of a distant nation-state. This power, in fact, was exerted beforehand, in the very formation of this state. During the 1948 presidential election, Senator McGrath, chairman of the Democratic National Committee, had to warn his party colleagues "that our failure to go along with the Zionists [on Palestine] might lose the states of New York, Pennsylvania and California. . . ." It was established that "the United States was primarily responsible for the creation of a Jewish State in the heart of the Arab world, but Soviet support made it possible." This fact attests to Zionist power in the United States. But the United Nations partition of Palestine did violence to the Charter's promise of "respect of the principle of equal rights and self-determination of peoples" and made the charter "look like unblushing hypocrisy." [Cruse is here quoting from the *UN Record* of 1955.][71]

There are several ungrounded moments of illogic in Cruse's text, not to mention the gratuitous introduction of a pro-Palestinian position. Primarily, however, the essay fails to take into account that Jewish and American support for the establishment of a Jewish state following the extermination of six million Jews did not (any more than the support of the many other nations who voted for the partition of Palestine in 1948) indicate that the great majority of American Jews were Zionists or that American Jewish identity was founded on Zionist principles. Cruse is right that "official Zionist policy has always been that of anti-assimilation, pro-Jewish group solidarity."[72] But the reverse, that "anti-assimilation, pro-Jewish group solidarity" has always been Zionist, is simply not the case. Quite the contrary, especially in relation to that major Jewish activity Cruse critiques in his book: Jewish social activism in the Communist Party and the Civil Rights movement. Indeed, many Jewish Marxists and Civil Rights workers were involved in redefining their Jewishness *as* their commitment to Marxism and social conscience. Jewishness, for many Jewish intellectuals from the 1930s and 1940s on, was, as it had been among European Jewish intellectuals before them, a card they played to lose, in order to win the hand and perhaps the game itself. The game in America was not Jewish identity but Americanization, assimilation.[73]

Irving Howe, in *A Margin of Hope,* poignantly describes this situation in relation to "socialism," which

> for many immigrant Jews, was not merely politics or an idea, it was an encompassing culture, a style of perceiving and judging through which to structure their lives. . . . Only radicalism seemed to offer the prospect of coherence, only radicalism could provide a unified view of the world. . . . Comparisons between radical politics and religious practice are likely to be glib. . . . yet in thinking back to these years I'm forced to recognize, not very comfortably, that there were *some* parallels between the two. Everything seemed to fall into place: ordered meaning, a world grasped through theory, a life shaped by purpose. Is that not the essence of conversion? . . . Unacknowledged motives were also at work, having less to do with Marxist strategy than our own confused and unexamined feelings about Jewish origins.[74]

Indeed, even after the 1967 war, which, even more than the creation of the state in 1948, turned American Jews toward Israel, an intellectual like Howe maintained a coolly non-Zionist stance toward Israel.

"Who could suppress a thrill of gratification," Howe confesses in an editorial in the July/August 1967 issue of *Dissent*, "that after centuries of helplessness Jews had defeated enemies with the weapons those enemies claimed as their own." But his "concern for the survival of Israel" comes accompanied by the following very explicit disclaimer: "we are not Zionists; or Jewish nationalists; or by any means uncritical of the state of Israel."[75] Most American Jews, even in the 1960s, were ideologically non-Zionistic, as were many prominent Jewish leaders before them, who, actively involved in the NAACP and other Civil Rights movements, had resisted Zionism. According to one account, this includes such figures as "Louis Marshall, Jacob Billikopf, . . . Boas, Melville Herskovits, and the Altmans, Lehmans, Rosenwalds, and Spingarns"; even the exceptions, like Judah Magnes and Felix Frankfurter, were "politically cautious and emotionally cool" on the issue of Israel.[76]

Many American Jewish intellectuals discovered, first through Marxism and socialism, later through the Civil Rights movement, ways of converting without converting – effecting just the inadvertent slide (like Podhoretz's in his essay) toward what is for most Jews, on the conscious level, unthinkable: their active conversion out of Judaism into Christianity. Indeed, as I have already suggested, it is Podhoretz's quite admirable desire to find a solution for blacks, whose identity Podhoretz can see only in terms of color, that forces him to imply acceptance of the similar disappearance of Jews, who are not, of course, for Podhoretz a racial group, at least not in the same way that blacks are. Similarly, confusing Jewish group solidarity and cultural nationalism (assimilation) with Zionism, Cruse, quite rightly admiring what Jews have succeeded in doing in America, produces a dangerously false model for blacks:

[D]eep within the social consciousnesses of these groups lie three nationalist ideologies – Anglo-Saxon nationalism, black nationalism and Jewish nationalism (Zionism). The first is both overt and covert, especially in the South; the second is openly avowed and vocal, but poorly organized and even more poorly directed; the third is the most highly organized of all – the most sophisticated, scholarly and intellectual, with the most highly refined propaganda techniques – and hence the most successful of the three. A study of Jewish Zionist organization and propaganda techniques reveals that influential Zionist thought sees Anglo-Saxon nationalism in the United States as its main potential political threat. Zionist thought also correctly sees the Negro civil rights drive for social equality and racial integration as a possible indirect threat to Jewish status, in the event that Negroes drive Anglo-Saxon nationalists into the radical rightist political camp. Hence, Jewish trends that are pro-Zionist and anti-Jewish-integration-assimilation, are forced to take a pro-Negro integration position and an anti-black nationalist position. *Thus, pro-Zionist influences within Negro civil rights organizations are strategically aiding and abetting Negro integration (assimilation) albeit Zionists, themselves, do not believe in integration (assimilation) for Jews.*[77] (italics in the original)

As I have already suggested, while Jewish Zionists do not necessarily believe in assimilation for Jews, most Jewish Americans, especially in the years when Cruse was writing, did. They could not see, however, that integration and assimilation did not mean, for them, the same things, and that although, from their perspective blacks might genuinely integrate into America because all that differentiated them from other Americans was their skin color, Jews, who, in their view, differed by virtue of religion, history, and culture, could not. Hence, black critics have recently observed, quite rightly, that Afrocentrism may be a white, rather than a black, construction of race, since it posits the existence of a homogenous, unified African continent, defined primarily by skin color. Nothing, of course, could be further from the sociopolitical reality of tribal Africa, in which difference is not defined by color but by national/tribal membership. To one black scholar, producing another of those black–Jewish convergences, it is not at all clear that this "pathetic" "quest of individuals for roots in Africa" is not, at bottom, the fault of "anthropological erudition, provided, very often, by Jewish anthropologists."[78] The names Boas and Herskovitz once again emerge as basic to the ongoing dialogues and disagreements between blacks and Jews; even as prominent a figure in the reformation of racial thinking as Boas seems to have shared certain of the racist assumptions of his time.[79]

This brings me back to Ralph Ellison and, in particular, James Baldwin, who from the 1950s on were claiming for black people cultural, rather than purely economic or political, identity, *in the United States,* which was, for both of them, the nation of the American black, not Africa. Where Cruse's argument goes most astray as it is actively confronting a Zionism it imagines as American Jewish identity, is in its refusal to hear that the issue between blacks and Jews, specifically between Baldwin and Podhoretz, has to do with culture, not nationalism, in America, and not in relation to some foreign place that one might imagine as an ancestral homeland.

Cruse's failure to take Baldwin seriously is especially perplexing because the Podhoretz essay to which Cruse so vociferously responds and on which he models his own "My Jewish Problem and Theirs" is itself a direct response to Baldwin's "Letter," which Cruse does not mention at all, though he does engage some of Baldwin's earlier statements concerning Jewish–black relations. Although these earlier statements, in Cruse's view, protect Baldwin from being labeled a "Jew-lover," they don't release him from the charge of being, like other black liberals, an "apologist for the Jews." Even though Cruse seems to be talking, especially in his contribution to *Black Anti-Semitism and Jewish Racism,* to Jews, his audience is his own community. And while he has some extremely harsh things to say concerning both Podhoretz and another notable American Jewish intellectual, Nathan Glazer, the real objects of his attack are what he refers to in *The Crisis of the Negro Intellectual* as "Jewish blacks" like Lorraine Hansberry, Leroi Jones, and James Baldwin who not only "reflect this white-Negro-Jewish ideological muddle," but who have been "uncritically pro-Jewish or critically tongue-tied" both in relation to "the international implications of Israel vis-à-vis black Africa or the domestic implication of Jews vis-à-vis the Negro movement."[80] And, Cruse continues,

> bending over backward to avoid criticism of Jews while pretending to be angry with whites, he overlooks the fact that if *American* Jews are "caught in the American crossfire" they are also very much in control of the situation and have their enemies well "cased" from all directions. Baldwin's unfortunate mismatch with Jewish intellectuals on *Commentary* magazine showed that Jews also have Baldwin well "cased" – only he does not know it. . . . When Baldwin discussed Negro problems with the Jewish intellectuals on *Commentary* magazine in the winter of 1964, he did not, and could not, ask a more pertinent question: where do you Jewish intellectuals of *Commentary* stand on the question of international Zionism?[81]

In fact, Baldwin produces a much more devastating challenge to his Jewish compeers during that *Commentary* roundtable that Cruse finds so distressing. For the American Jewish intellectuals in conversation with Baldwin in this symposium, the single overriding, foundational principle of government to which they subscribe and which defines their relationship to America – even if it threatens and perhaps even effects the disappearance of the Jews as Jews – is not Zionism but pluralism.[82] But as more than one African American intellectual will point out, liberal pluralism, which did enable Jews and other minorities to move into positions of power, did not afford African Americans that same success. It is what the black community must resist. If Cruse does not know this, James Baldwin certainly does.

Liberalism, Pluralism, and the American Family Fantasy
(Sidney Hook and James Baldwin)

What leads Cruse to his fiery condemnation of Podhoretz and the American Jewish community is what he perceives (largely correctly) as the community's double-standard vis-à-vis the issue of assimilation and integration. This double standard emerges powerfully in Podhoretz's dramatic, one might say even sensationalistic, use of the term "miscegenation." Cruse does not, however, register correctly the prior, internal, divisions within American Jewry, in particular pertaining to Jewish nationalism. Nor does he hear the ambivalence in Podhoretz's recurrence to recent Jewish history as he acknowledges that the once-legitimate desire for Jewish group survival may no longer have meaning in America. Nor does Cruse fathom the difference between Zionism and cultural nationalism, which is what Jewish American intellectuals meant by the term "assimilation." For this reason, Cruse imagines that the American Jewish faith in pluralism is a form of Zionist conviction, and this skews his relationship to and understanding of Baldwin.

What Cruse does hear, quite accurately, which Podhoretz and others do not, is a Jewish confidence in America, which is alien and inappropriate to the African American experience. Jews can talk about miscegenation because they themselves are in no need of converting. They have made it in America as Jews, and they have, many of them, in many respects disappeared, at least when viewed from the perspective of other forms of Jewish identity, such as religious or national (Zionist) identity. Because of this assimilation Howe and Podhoretz (and Lionel Trilling and others) could claim to speak not as Jews but as white liberal Americans.[83]

This feature of Jewish American identity emerges powerfully in the *Commentary* event that Cruse condemns, even though it lays squarely on its roundtable the essence of the philosophical divide between Jews and blacks in the 1960s. *Commentary*'s "Liberalism and the Negro," which appeared in May 1964, was, according to Cruse, "a disastrous failure" less because of its Jewish organizers than because of what its black participants failed to say:

> When Norman Podhoretz put the following question to Baldwin, the latter could not answer it, as he had neither the insight nor the knowledge to do so: "Mr. Baldwin, is it conceivable to you that the Negroes will within the next five or ten or twenty years take their rightful place as one of the *competing groups in the American pluralistic pattern* [italics added]?" . . . it was the most important question asked during the whole discussion, and Baldwin (along with Kenneth Clark) had to sidestep it. . . . Podhoretz, of course, was merely voicing *Commentary*'s contemporary understanding of an old question. For years American Jewry has been much concerned with the implications of cultural pluralism. Jewish intellectuals have written extensively about it, inasmuch as official Zionist policy has always been that of anti-assimilationist, pro-Jewish group solidarity.
>
> . . .
>
> If they were more like Jewish intellectuals and creative artists, they would not be as afraid of becoming propagandists for their own kind in politics and culture as they are about writing "Everybody's Protest Novel" – only to wind up writing bad protest plays. If Negro intellectuals could become more objective and less subjective about the Negro-Jewish "thing," they might be more perceptive about the prevalent Jewish intellectual and literary mystique that has developed in America.[84] [Bracketed notation "italics added" appears in the original.]

If it were not for Cruse's caution against Jewish–black relations, his advice to African American artists could be mistaken for Howe's advice to Ellison. But, of course, it is exactly that caution that violates the most essential ethical principle of Howe's (and Podhoretz's and Glazer's) thinking: the belief in American pluralism.

For Cruse, Jewish liberalism is nothing more than a cover for group identity, even exceptionalism. It expresses the opposite of the belief in competing groups taking their rightful places in a multiethnic America. In coming up with a similar accusation against Jewish liberals, Leslie Fiedler provides a useful definition of what Jews meant by such liberalism. He also explains some of the reasons that such a definition not only did not work for blacks, but created hostility between African and Jewish Americans:

What chiefly exacerbates relations between Negroes and Jews, as far as Jews are concerned, is the persistence among them of the mythology of Liberal Humanism . . . that all men desire freedom and full human status and deny that freedom and status to others only when it has been refused to them; that equality of opportunity leads to maximum self-fulfillment and social well-being; that the oppressed and the injured have been so ennobled by their oppression and injury that they are morally superior to their masters; that all men desire literacy and suffrage – and can exercise those privileges equally well when granted them. . . . Intertwined with this credo . . . is the Whig Myth of History which sees freedom slowly broadening. . . . How utterly unprepared they have been, therefore, to find a growing number of Negroes rejecting not only their credo but them in particular as its messengers. . . . "Hear our message and be saved," they cry only a little condescendingly, and are dismayed to hear in return: "All we want from you white mothers (or alternatively, Jew mothers) is to get off our backs and out of our road." Yet worse, much worse, is that fact that the Negroes . . . challenge by their very existence a basic article of the Liberal Faith: equality of opportunity will not grant very many of them, brutalized by long brainwashing and bred by a kind of unnatural selection, a decent life or the possibility of prosperity. What they demand . . . is *special privilege* rather than equality if they are to make it at all in the very world in which the Jews have so pre-eminently flourished. . . . Is "liberalism," then, only a camouflage for a special sort of privilege, a code by which the people who have long lived with the alphabet can triumph over all others?[85]

What Fiedler's summary, on the side of blacks against Jews, reveals about Cruse's criticism of Baldwin and Clark is the way in which it is directed at the Jews' so completely accepting the terms of liberal discourse, which Podhoretz's symposium assumes, that, in arguing both for and against the need of special privilege for blacks, they fail, in his view, to expose the camouflage of privilege that this so-called special privilege only replaces. And yet Baldwin, it seems to me, consistently does just what Cruse would have him do. Cruse, however, is so tied to his thesis of Jewish nationalism and so convinced that blacks like Baldwin cannot see past Jewish rhetoric to a philosophy of their own, that he cannot recognize this. Cruse is in good company here. The participants to the discussion are similarly deaf to what Baldwin is saying, exactly because it treads a line between nationalism (cultural or otherwise) and pluralism.

The participants of "Liberalism and the Negro" are Baldwin, Glazer, Sidney Hook, and Gunnar Myrdal, with the input of Kenneth Clark and several others, including Shlomo Katz, the editor of *Midstream* and the organizer of the special issue in which the above quoted statement by Fiedler appears. The question Podhoretz puts to them is this: Can one reconcile the principles of individualism with those of affirmative action? Quoting another contributor to *Commentary*, Podhoretz offers as way of clarification the following: "Over the past two or three years . . . a new school of liberal . . . thought has been developed which is based on the premise . . . that 'the rights and privileges of an individual rest upon the status attained by the group to which he belongs.'"[86] Affirmative action, of course, is one of those issues that sharply divided the Jewish and African American communities in the 1960s, and beyond.

Throughout their conversation with Baldwin, who naturally enough upholds affirmative action, Podhoretz, Hook, Glazer, and Myrdal consistently misunderstand Baldwin. Baldwin's essential point is that the very assumptions of liberalism, which produce the questioning of affirmative action in the first place, are illegitimate. The experience of African Americans, according to Baldwin, is in no way similar to that of white Americans, whatever their ethnic background (Hook and Glazer begin their statements by invoking the experience of German refugees and Nazism in Germany, as well as their own status as members of an immigrant society). Whereas "immigrant groups," Baldwin points out, "chose to come to America," "I was brought here. I did not want to come." For this reason, the very premises of the roundtable discussion – of "liberalism" and of what Hook repeatedly refers to as "ethics" – do not, in Baldwin's view, apply to the black situation. "If you are a Negro," he explains, "you have to operate outside the system and beat these people at their own game."[87] And yet, as he puts it most eloquently toward the end of what becomes a very fierce and angry discussion, this place Negroes occupy outside the system in no way changes the fact that African American history *is* American history, of whites as well as of blacks:

> The history which the Negro endured coming to this country and in this country was not only endured by *him*; it was endured on another level by all the white people who oppressed him. It is, Mr. Hook to the contrary, a collective history. I was

here, that did something to me. But you were here on top of me, and that did something to *you*. What happened to the Negro in this country is not simply a matter of *my* memory or *my* history; it's a matter of *American* history and *American* memory.[88]

Despite Baldwin's repeated insistence that the very notion of liberalism must be transformed to take into account the historical evolution of such liberalism within a shared American history of oppression, the rest of the members of the panel insist on retreating both to a conventional idea of liberalism and to the assumption that of course Baldwin's definitions and theirs are the same. Thus, when Baldwin counters Hook by saying that we have to talk about "the white people's problem" in America, and argues that "the presence of the Negro here is precisely what has allowed white people to say they were free; and it is what has allowed them to assume they were rich," Podhoretz reduces this to one small fragment of Baldwin's comment, that "in the beginning . . . Negroes were a source of cheap labor." Glazer is then able to remark, when Podhoretz asks for his response to this statement, "I'll get to that point eventually, I suppose, but I'd rather talk about liberalism first," as if the issue of black slavery in America is not already, as Baldwin makes clear, the issue of liberalism. And he is able to return to economic issues through the safer route of urban poverty, which sets the stage for Myrdal's more class-centered (Marxist) critique of the African American "dilemma" (as he calls it in his famous book): the black problem, in Myrdal's view, is part of the larger economic problems of contemporary America.[89]

Throughout the conversation, and underlying its various pretenses, dissimulations, and yet considerable goodwill and aspiration, is Hook's (and the others') commitment to what Hook repeatedly refers to as ethics. (The word emerges so frequently and so angers Baldwin that Podhoretz finally exclaims, in exasperation, that "it's unfortunate that the word ethics came into the discussion" – an odd statement to be sure, as Hook points out.) For Hook ethics underlie liberalism. They make it necessary to think in liberal terms, even when those terms are threatened or called into question by local political realities (like anti-Semitism or racism). "Our real problem – and this is how I interpret ethics," declares Hook, "is to work on all the specific projects by which we can bring our Negro fellow citizens into the 'kingdom of democratic ends.' "[90] Hook is extremely sensitive to what he takes to be Baldwin's message of hate. Baldwin pro-

duces in Hook a response very similar to Cruse's in relation to Podhoretz. And it leads him back (albeit obliquely) to Podhoretz's essay:
"If I read his most recent book properly," Hook says, "he actually
believes that all Negroes hate white people. . . . That's not true for
the Negroes I know, and it can't be true for Negroes who have
married whites. . . . I think we drug ourselves with rhetoric when we
advocate wholesale solutions like total intermarriage to make color
disappear. It seems to me this is an insult to the Negro population.
. . . The conception of democracy – which, as I keep repeating, is
fundamentally an ethical conception – is that we can live peacefully
together with our *differences.*"[91]

In relation to Podhoretz's essay, which Hook is indirectly criticiz-
ing, Hook, I think, is quite correct. He is also right to assert that the
objective of pluralistic democracy is to enable people to live together
with their differences. The problem, however, is that two hundred
years of American history, and two thousand years of European history, have suggested that, at least for blacks and Jews, it has not been
possible to live peacefully with their differences from their white and
Christian neighbors. This glaring contradiction might be expected
to produce the question that does not emerge for Hook (and
Glazer): Is pluralism the name of the game for blacks and Jews?

From Baldwin's point of view, Hook's faith has to be an affront to
blacks, as it might be as well to non-American Jews (in Israel, for
example), who just might feel themselves still to be living on un-
peaceable terms with the world. Without so much as a murmur,
Hook slides past Baldwin's reluctance to being admitted into a democracy that, systematically excluding him, can hardly be considered a democracy at all. Yet, as I say, to dismiss the ambitions of
pluralism as irrelevant or to discard ethics altogether does not seem
like much of a solution. How, then, might one understand pluralism
in terms that do not stubbornly refuse to confront the realities of an
illiberal world? Again, "miscegenation" emerges as a key term in
redefining black–Jewish relations.

White Negroes, Black Jews, and Invisible Men
(Norman Mailer, Leslie Fiedler, James Baldwin, and Ralph Ellison)[92]

One way out of the liberal dilemma, which was the route taken by
such writers as Leslie Fiedler and Norman Mailer, was to get rid of
the romantic metaphors of family that governed much thinking
about human relations, nowhere more than in the effort to dissolve
racial categories. The major objective of such studies as those of

Franz Boas and Melville Herskovits was to deny the importance of racial distinctions. Podhoretz and Arendt similarly wish to disregard race as a significant biological category of difference. These are certainly not aims to be trivialized or condemned, especially given the alternatives, which have once again reared their ugly head in a 1994 publication, *The Bell Curve: Intelligence and Class Structure in American Life.*

Still, as Leslie Fiedler so vividly points out, the myth of racial harmony and intermingling may be not only just that, a myth, but it may represent a dangerous fantasy as well. The family myth not only permits us to forget the history of race relations in America (as Baldwin cautions Hook), it enables the white population to imagine itself into a position of being forgiven (by blacks and Native Americans and thus by themselves as well) for its trespasses against its oppressed countrymen and women. The trope of the family of the human (reassuring as it is) yields an idea of pluralism (similarly reassuring), based on the shared category of the human. But pluralism has not yet proven itself capable of functioning as a family philosophy. And it is not clear that predicating human relations on romantic conceits of the human does not create more problems than it solves. The family metaphor puts race in the forefront of our consciousness in order to deny its significance. But the racial difference Baldwin is claiming for American blacks is cultural rather than or in addition to racial. This is what Baldwin means (and Podhoretz quotes him on this) by saying that race is a *political* category. Cultural difference (based on history, art, and tradition) is the kind of difference that American Jews would claim for themselves, but found it difficult (in these debates) to formulate in relation to blacks.

Thus advises one of the contributors to the *Midstream* symposium on "Negro-Jewish Relations," quite breaking ranks with his fellow Jews (as he does again in 1971 in a book entitled *Jews and Blacks*): "The basis for any healthy Negro-Jewish relation . . . is to understand and accept that we are dealing not with a family quarrel, but with the distinct and maybe even conflicting interests of separate groups."[93] Ben Halpern's statement recalls Kenneth Clark's observation, decades earlier, that Jews and blacks are not really willing to define the issues that separate them. And it coincides with the wisdom of several other Jewish intellectuals addressing the same issues in the *Midstream* symposium. "Is there a special Jewish stake in the Negro struggle?" asks another contributor. His answer is not intended to dissuade Jews from advocating civil rights for blacks. Rather, by responding "not really," he would force Jews to ground their commitment in something other than false assumptions of universal, or at least American, brotherhood.[94]

Sidney Hook, Nathan Glazer, Norman Podhoretz, and James Baldwin need some term other than pluralism, predicated on some historical and organic understanding other than family, to mediate the divide between them. And they need it urgently. The term, which is reinvented from within the American philosophical tradition by Ralph Ellison, Leslie Fiedler, and Norman Mailer, is that old Emersonian staple of American self-understanding: *self-reliance*. It is with this concept that I conclude this chapter on black–Jewish dialogue.

There is no white Jewish critic of the 1960s less enamored of liberalism than Norman Mailer, unless it is Leslie Fiedler, who writes specifically in relation to black–Jewish relations that "the liberal tradition in America – to which the Jewish intellectual has attached himself . . . insists on stumbling from one innocence to another with appropriate bouts of self-recrimination between."[95] I want to discuss both of these Jewish intellectuals as sharing a certain relation to each other and to Ellison and Baldwin through what turns out to be, for all four, a commitment to Emersonian self-reliance, especially as self-reliance pertains to the subject of American innocence – a popular refrain in the writings of all these authors. Ellison, we recall, had a fairly unpleasant comment to pass on Mailer's "White Negro" in his exchange with Howe. Nonetheless, Mailer's white Negro and Ellison's invisible man have a lot in common. This is the case in no area so much as in the Emersonian project they share.

The object of Mailer's essay is none other than that familiar Emersonian target "conformity." For this reason, he begins his project by explicitly invoking the context of Emerson's writings, both in the general tone of his essay and in its specific phrases, such as "questions about his own nature" or "a slow death by conformity" or "Know Thyself" and "Be Thyself."[96] Not too surprisingly, this Emersonian exploration of conformity and the self-reliant self takes him through the same route followed by Emerson in "Self-Reliance." It takes him through the issue of race. Ralph Waldo's other heir, Ellison, had already fathomed the same connection in *Invisible Man,* on which Mailer's essay, I believe, forms something of an extended, intellectual gloss.[97]

To get at what Emersonianism might give us here, it is useful to invoke the thinking of Americanist philosopher Stanley Cavell as he reinterprets Emerson, in particular in relation to the issue of slavery in the nineteenth century. Like a number of intellectuals, Cavell couples this subject with thinking about the Holocaust. For Cavell, this means interpreting Nietzsche's inheritance of Emerson and his passing on of Emerson to Heidegger.[98] For Cavell, Emersonianism is not a celebration of the solipsistic individual in rejection of society. Rather, it is a writing-mediated philosophy of social relatedness, in which the self-reliant individual turning away from society in resistance turns toward it again in acknowledgment and recommitment. As Cavell puts it,

> The relation of Emerson's writing (the expression of his self-reliance) to his society (the realm of what he calls conformity) is one, as "Self-Reliance" puts it, of mutual aversion: "Self-reliance is the aversion of conformity." Naturally Emerson's critics take this to mean roughly that he is disgusted with society and wants no more to do with it. But "Self-reliance is the aversion of conformity" figures each side in terms of the other, declares the issue between them as always joined, never settled. But then this is to say that Emerson's writing and his society are in an unending argument with one another – that is to say, he writes in such a way as to *place* his writing in his unending argument (such is his loyal opposition) – an unending turning away from one another. . . . hence endlessly a turning *toward* one another.[99]

Nonetheless, Emerson's philosophical assumptions, Cavell knows, present moral problems, especially in relation to the existence of slavery in the United States. Emerson wrote and spoke explicitly against slavery. Nonetheless, his major philosophical writings do not engage the issue of slavery as such, or, when they do engage it, they do so in extremely problematical ways. One such troubling moment occurs in the same essay in which Emerson offers his model of what Cavell describes as his "aversive thinking" – the essay entitled "Self-Reliance":

> On my saying, "What have I to do with the sacredness of traditions, if I live wholly from within?" my friend suggested, – "But these impulses may be from below, not from above." I replied, "They do not seem to me to be such; but if I am the Devil's child, I will live then from the Devil." No law can be sacred to me but that of my nature. Good and bad are but names very readily transferable to that or this; the only right is after my constitution; the only wrong what is against it. . . . If malice and vanity wear the coat of philanthropy, shall that pass? If an angry bigot assumes this bountiful case of Abolition, and

comes to me with his last news from Barbadoes [where slavery has just been abolished], why should I not say to him, "Go love thy infant; love thy wood-chopper; be good-natured and modest; have that grace; and never varnish your hard, uncharitable ambition with this incredible tenderness for black folk a thousand miles off. Thy love afar is spite at home."

According to Cavell, Emerson's objective here, despite the obliqueness of his language, is exactly not apolitical. Rather, invoking through the word "constitution" the knowing and willful violation of American values that slavery in the United States represents, Emerson, argues Cavell, produces a portrait of self-reliance as intimately tied to both public and private morality.[100] Emersonian self-reliance, in other words, is for Cavell the discarding of the self-protective armor of public conformity; it is, in the American context, to acknowledge the dissonance between the theoretical premises (and promises) of America's C/constitution, and its C/constitution in fact as a slave-holding society. Emerson's word "constitution" contains worlds of American history in its virtual silence on the particulars of that Constitution, and on the intolerable moral paradox at the center of American life.

Mailer begins "The White Negro" with the two large catastrophes of the Second World War: the atom bomb and the concentration camps. These have nothing directly to do with American race relations, though their introducing the essay once again forges the Jewish–black connection, as Mailer moves quickly to his subject: "the Negro [who] has been living on the margin between totalitarianism and democracy for two centuries."[101] For Mailer, as for Emerson before him, the Negro tests, and exposes, the limits of American self-perceptions.

In "The White Negro," Mailer outdoes Emerson in the play of language through which he revises the terms by which we understand and define America. "It is impossible to conceive a new philosophy," writes Mailer, "until one creates a new language, but a new popular language (while it must implicitly contain a new philosophy) does not necessarily present its philosophy overtly."[102] Mailer is Emerson's devil's advocate par excellence. In the extreme perversity of his logic, he aims at producing the radical transformation both of the individual reader and of the society to which the reader (like the writer) belongs. The hipster, writes Mailer, is a

philosophical psychopath, a man interested not only in the dangerous imperatives of his psychopathy but in codifying, at least for himself, the superstitions on which his inner universe is constructed. By this premise the hipster is a psychopath, and yet not a psychopath but the negation of the psychopath for he possesses the narcissistic detachment of the philosopher, that absorption in the recessive nuances of one's own motive which is so alien to the unreasoning drive of the psychopath.[103]

For Mailer, the psychopath's deep detachment from society, an *aversion* bordering on disgust, is a philosophical stance. And through this mode of philosophical reflection, Mailer's psychopath, like Emerson's somewhat less deviant individual, constructs a self-reliance that is also social revisionism. From Mailer's perspective, as from Emerson's, the moral issue of America most in need of such "aversive thinking" (to quote Cavell) is racism.

Thus, when Mailer produces the image of marriage and family that underlies as well the positions of Podhoretz and others, he does so unsentimentally. All of the violence (aversions) of American race relations remain fully intact. In "this wedding of the white and the black," Mailer insists, "it [is] the Negro who [brings] the cultural dowry" (a line of thinking Malamud follows in *The Tenants*). And:

> To take the desegregation of the schools in the South as an example, it is quite likely that the reactionary sees the reality more closely than the liberal when he argues that the deeper issue is not desegregation but miscegenation. . . . For the average liberal whose mind has been dulled by the committee-ish cant of the professional liberal, miscegenation is not an issue because he has been told that the Negro does not desire it. So, when it comes miscegenation will be a terror. . . . What the liberal cannot bear to admit is the hatred beneath the skin of a society so unjust that the amount of collective violence buried in the people is perhaps incapable of being contained, and therefore if one wants a better world one does well to hold one's breath, for a worse world is bound to come first, and the dilemma may well be this: given such hatred it must either vent itself nihilistically or become turned into the cold murderous liquidations of the totalitarian state.[104]

Mailer's is iconoclasm at its most extreme. But his essay cannot be brushed lightly aside, as Ellison, for one, would like to do. Mailer's antiliberalism, like Baldwin's, is deeply rooted in his critique of racism; and his miscegenation replicates no image so well as that of Baldwin's lovers. Whether or not Mailer's white Negro is identical to Ellison's invisible man, he is as much an Emersonian figure as Ellison's. He is, for that reason, his close kin, not by virtue of a fantasy of likeness but because of his self-reliant resistance to public and political conformity. Both Ellison's and Mailer's invisible and white Negro individuals are haters and nihilists, who follow Emerson's dictum in "Self-Reliance" to *examine* goodness to determine whether it indeed *be* goodness. They are vehicles of social regeneration.

Like Emerson and Thoreau before him, what Mailer would especially remove from white America's relationship to its African citizens is its (color) blinding innocence. For Mailer, as for Fiedler, this color blindness is figured as American immaturity, as contained in an unexamined notion of romantic love or family consanguinity. The solution to America's pathology is for Mailer miscegenation, not because, as in Podhoretz's use of the image, it makes race disappear. Quite the opposite: in Mailer's evolution of the concept, miscegenation pulls into focus the deeper juvenility underlying American race relations: its avoidance of the genuine issues between blacks and whites, which is like nothing so much as the avoidance, within tropes of romantic love, of that sexuality by which love is made concrete and humanly real. One might say of this turn in Mailer's essay that the specific object of his attack is a notion of Christian love similar to that which characterizes a novel like Harriet Beecher Stowe's *Uncle Tom's Cabin* – one of the texts Fiedler discusses. For Mailer hipsterism is still an expression of American immaturity, as, one could easily say, is Emersonian self-reliance ("if I am the devil's child . . ."). But it is an expression that in its radical sexuality produces a new and less innocent reality in the next generation.

Given this quality of almost prurient exposé and boldly adult sexuality, it is not surprising that Mailer's essay should appear as a central document in Leslie Fiedler's 1963 *Commentary* piece "Race – The Dream and the Nightmare." Nor is it surprising that Fiedler, like Mailer, should evolve an image of miscegenation in the most baldly sexual terms. Despite Fiedler's criticisms of Mailer, both in his "Race" essay and in "Antic Mailer – Portrait of a Middle-Aged Artist," Fiedler shares much with Mailer.[105] Both are impatient with American immaturity, especially in relation to issues of race and gender (Fiedler entitles two of his books *An End to Innocence* and, the one in which the *Commentary* essay is reprinted, *Waiting for the End* – both of these titles, I suspect, someplace behind the title of Harry Lesser's book in *The Tenants*). For Fiedler, as for Mailer, liberalism is innocence; innocence is self-deception and other-denying fantasy; and the fantasy must end.

Fiedler's essay "Race – The Dream and the Nightmare" picks up

important themes from his *Love and Death in the American Novel.* Like
that earlier work, it exposes a racist American fantasy of Adamic,
Edenic innocence, in which the white American male – this is a
sexist fantasy as well – imagines not only the Negro's and Indian's
forgiveness of him but the willingness of racially different others to
embrace and nurture the white oppressor. This myth, Fiedler argues, is almost at an end. But it is at this moment passing through
or is on the verge of another, almost as problematical, myth. This is
the myth of racial harmony, which, in his view, Mailer introduces in
"The White Negro":

> The dream which began with the Trapper Harry and flowered
> into the mid-19th-century cult of male friendship, seems to
> many contemporaries too sentimental, or wrongly sentimental,
> too blandly liberal, perhaps – at any rate, too *easy* to sustain us
> here and now. And in certain of our latest books, in the whole
> cluster of works, for instance, called "hip" or "beat," as in our
> recent life, we have seen the emergence of a new dream . . .
> [that]goes further, for it not only imagines joining with Indian
> or Negro in pseudomatrimony, or being adopted by some col-
> ored fosterfather – but being reborn as Indian or Negro, *becom-
> ing the other* . . . the White Negro.

Fiedler concludes with: "a new generation of Negroes are presently
learning in Greenwich Village, or at Harvard College, to be what the
hipster imagines them to be, imitating their would-be imitators. It is
the kindest joke our troubled white culture has played on them; and,
one hopes, the last."[106]

But what Fiedler proposes instead of the white Negro is exactly
what Mailer is also proposing: miscegenation. "Jewish writers," says
Fiedler, "from Mailer to Nat Hentoff, may try to escape the mytho-
logical hang-up by redefining themselves as imaginary or 'White Negroes' (the very term was of course, invented by a Jew) – just as their
more political brethren have tried to assimilate to a world which
mythologically rejects them by linking arms with Negroes in protests
and demonstrations. But though young Jews have an affinity not
only for protest but for folksongs, jazz and marijuana. . . . they have
trouble making it across the legendary line." Therefore, Fiedler puts
his faith instead in "the sight of young couples linked arm in arm":
"And I think our daughters ['pretty blonde daughters of Jews with
black boyfriends'] will save us, love (not big theoretical, but small
sexual love) will save us":

I remember a year or two ago riding a plane to Jerusalem and being told by the man seated beside me, who worked for a Jewish adoption agency, that the number of illegitimate Negro babies being produced by Jewish girls was mounting spectacularly. And were there also, I asked, legitimate ones, *even* legitimate ones? But I did not listen for the answer, knowing it was yes, and not quite sure why I needed confirmation. What sunders us may not be first of all but is last of all a sexual taboo; and that taboo is every day being broken, with or without benefit of clergy, Christian or Jewish; and its breaking is the beginning (though *only* the beginning) of the end.[107]

As Mailer and Fiedler evolve their images of miscegenation, what emerges (which is largely absent from Podhoretz's rather mechanical presentation of the concept) is the physicality and individuality of the act of sexual intercourse, the private choices and responsibilities it denotes within the private sphere (Arendt's point), out of which emerge the possibilities of abandoning mythologies and of entering history as such (this is only the beginning of the end, according to Fiedler). This history, as Baldwin so eloquently puts it in his rebuttal to Sidney Hook and Shlomo Katz in the *Commentary* roundtable, is "not simply a matter of *my* memory or *my* history; it's a matter of *American* history and *American* memory." Katz's question to Baldwin, and Baldwin's response, are crucial to the Emersonianism of Mailer and Fiedler. Asks Katz:

> Do you think it would ever be possible for . . . American Negroes to eradicate from their memory their specific, particular, unique history in the United States – a history which the rest of the population did not experience . . . if it is not possible, then won't there be new separations which in their own turn will engender differences leading again to discriminations?

To which Baldwin responds:

> What I would like to see happen in some day to come is a fusion between what I remember and what you remember. Then there will be no question about our separation. We are really one people and – this is part of our problem, in fact, we spend all of our time denying it.

Hook's response, missing Baldwin's point, seals the position of the old liberalism in its complete inapplicability to the American race issue. "Even if we succeeded in reconstructing American life," Hook replies, "there would still be Negroes with memories of their past. There would still be Jews with memories of their past. That's not the point. The important thing is whether the individual would be free to identify himself with a group or not. . . . We are fundamentally concerned here with the freedom of the human being to develop his personality and to make his own choices."[108]

Hook does not err in his assertion that the major concern both of the participants to the discussion and of the American people is the freedom of the human being. No one, least of all Baldwin, would deny that. Rather, a swerve in the argument takes place when Hook implicitly accepts Katz's possibility that memory can, and indeed must, be eradicated, as if human freedom existed outside of, even in defiance of, the place of human memory. For Hook and Katz, individuals come together (bridge their separateness) in a process of forgetting. This forgetting can occur because the memories of individuals or of individual groups are largely different memories, which, being witnessed by no one but the oppressed group, can thereby be forgotten. But our national nightmare, notes Fiedler, is produced by the fact that our history has been enacted in the presence of "*witnesses*."[109] Blacks and whites (as Jews and Christians in relation to anti-Semitism) can only remember themselves through their memories of each other.

Fiedler's view takes on Baldwin's assertion that the American memory of slavery and racial oppression is already collective. We could, of course, imagine wholesale American amnesia. But such amnesia would itself be unfair to blacks, since what blacks would be forgetting is oppression, whereas whites would only have to forget their oppressiveness, which they have in any case already willingly done. (As Philip Roth puts it in *The Counterlife*, in response to the idea of forgetting the Holocaust: they've already forgotten.) But barring such possibilities of both sides starting anew, what we remain with in Katz and Hook's idea of historical forgetting is the contemporary American status quo: white America's refusal to remember itself together with blacks in a shared interracial history, which is the only American history there is. If the American population hasn't already embraced miscegeny, its history has. America is biracial. It is the culmination of the process of the intercourse of the races, on all levels.

Hook and Katz's idea of the human being, which produces their liberalism, is romantic. Baldwin's idea of the people, on which he bases his affirmation of the group, is historical, political. For Baldwin the notion of "one people" and of "fusion" does not begin with the merging of bodies in love, but in the fact of shared memories, historically inscribed and politically enforced, which took cover under the myth of the nondifference of the American races and the absence of American racism – as Fiedler so perceptively describes it. Katz and Hook's "forgetting" would only reproduce this myth. So might Mailer's white Negro, were it not for his insistence that this hipster figure preserves unabridged, in his nihilism and radical sexuality, the memory of racism, which has so often tended either to segregate blacks or to whiten them. Mailer's white Negro, in other words, contains the knowledge of the degree to which the figure of the white Negro has, in its reverse minstrelsy, already figured within the American imagination as a denial of black identity.

For Fiedler and Mailer, as for Baldwin, the reconstruction of America as a nonracist society depends, as it did for Emerson before them, on the private rebellions that self-reliant individuals enact as they acknowledge one another within a shared social realm, and as, in that acknowledgment, they construct themselves in relation to each other. Such mutually aversive mutual constructions begin not in amicable sharings, but in genuine *aversions* and denials. Blacks and whites, whites and Jews, and blacks and Jews, Mailer and Fiedler insist, project onto each other not only their stereotypes of each other but their rejections of the stereotypes that have, in this process of mutual construction, been imposed on them. As Fiedler insists of Mailer's white Negro, "it scarcely matters whether the Negro whom the hipster becomes in his imagination ever really existed at all; for it is with the projection of our rejected self, which we have called 'Negro,' that we must be reconciled." Just as white America has invented black America, so, Fiedler insists, "the moment that he invents himself, the Negro begins to invent the white American, *his* white American, too; *must,* indeed, invent him out of the scraps he has left over, the human elements he has chosen – painfully or in apparent relief – to discard from his own image. And already there are white Americans who begin to see themselves as 'fay' or 'o-fay,' as everything the Negro thinks them when he names them so in contempt, just as all Negroes once, and many still, thought and think of themselves as Niggers."[110] The dire consequences of inventing oneself out of some other group's leftovers vividly inform Malamud's image of Lesser and Spearmint ransacking the garbage cans for each other's discarded manuscripts and destroying each other in the process.

Although Fiedler might seem to be effecting his own assimilation of the African American into his private psychic practice, he is, rather, involved, as is Mailer, with acknowledging the darker side of our mutual constructions. This is Baldwin's concern as well when he insists on "our" American history, which is the history not of black–white harmony in America but of America's racial condition as it is experienced jointly and differently by blacks and whites. And if such mutual construction projects outward the hostilities of one partner to the other in what emerges as a marriage less of Baldwin's lovers than of Cruse's enemies, it also internalizes that hatred and redirects it against the self, producing art: "So with minorities," writes Mailer, in direct response to Podhoretz's "Negro Problem"; "one must look for more than the insurance of their rights – one must search to liberate the art which is trapped in the thousand acts of perception which embody their self-hatred, for self-hatred ignored must corrode the roots of one's past and leave one marooned in an alien culture. The liberal premise – that Negroes and Jews are like everybody else once they are given the same rights – can only obscure the complexity, the intensity, and the psychotic brilliance of a minority's inner life."[111]

In this way Mailer sets the stage for the complex performances of African and Jewish American fiction (including his own), as, interacting with and entangled in each other, African and Jewish American writers give play to the psychotic brilliance of their inner lives. This produces the terms for a continuing African and Jewish American dialogue. It also creates a canon of literary texts that not only fully acknowledges America's racial history but assumes responsibility for it. To be sure, forces of competition, appropriation, and displacement persist. But this may be to say no more than that literary writing is as much an aggressive activity as it is a passionate one, and that the products of artistic conceptions, like the children of miscegenist unions, will be every bit as individualistic, independent, and embattled as their parents – and as brilliant. I now turn to some of those fictional performances of mutual African and Jewish American construction.

3

Race, Homeland, and the Construction of Jewish American Identity

A Diasporist . . . is a Jew for whom *authenticity* as a Jew means living in the Diaspora, for whom the Diaspora is the normal condition and Zionism is the abnormality – a Diasporist is a Jew who believes that the only Jews who matter are the Jews of the Diaspora, that the only Jews who survive are the Jews of the Diaspora, that the only Jews who *are* Jews are the Jews of the Diaspora.

Philip Roth, *Operation Shylock*[1]

When working-class Newarkian Neil Klugman in *Goodbye, Columbus* phones affluent Jewish American princess Brenda Patimkin and launches into his "you-don't-know-my-name-but-I-held-your-glasses-for-you-at-the-club" "speech," she answers him, quite naturally enough, by asking him what he looks like. "I'm . . . dark," he answers; "Are you a Negro?" she responds. "No," he replies. Pages later the conversation repeats, in painfully truncated form. Asked what his cousin looks like, he responds: "She's dark–" "Is she–" "No."[2]

How are we to understand the placement of this conversation in a novel essentially concerned not with blacks but with Jewish Americans? And what, further, are we to do with that "no," Neil's refusal of likeness between himself and the "Negro"? The answers to both questions might seem obvious enough, and wholly objectionable, on both Neil's part and on Roth's as well, were it not for an even more dominant and pervasive pattern through the novel. This is the book's affirmation of a genuine similarity, verging on consanguinity, between blacks and Jews, as much on Neil's part as on Roth's.

119

In this chapter I deal with works of fiction by Jewish American writers in which the writer constructs ethnic identity or otherwise deals with the subject through recourse to the cultural materials of black Americans.[3] By definition I am not interested in the vast majority of texts by Jewish authors, which do not deal with the black experience. Nor am I concerned with texts that refer to blacks but that are themselves not particularly invested in questions of ethnicity. Given the heterogeneity of the United States, it is absurd to imagine that the appearance of black characters and materials in Jewish texts is not, occasionally, just the consequence of America's multiethnic condition.

A number of texts are relevant to my subject, such as the ones noted by Leslie Fiedler in a 1966 essay entitled "Negro and Jew." Fiedler's notion of why Jewish American writers turn to the black experience is as pertinent to my subject as his list of texts. "This is a moment for questions," writes Fiedler,

> which is, perhaps, why fiction (a method of posing questions without troublesome question marks) seems the most promising method of attacking the problem of Negro-Jewish hostility. I am thinking of such books as Norman Mailer's *An American Dream* (1965), Nat Hentoff's *Call the Keeper* (1966), and Jay Neugeboren's *Big Man* (1966), as well as (hopefully) my own *The Last Jew in America* (1966). In a strange way it has now become incumbent on the Jewish writer to re-imagine the Negro in terms which will escape the old WASP clichés, sentimental and vicious, and the recent even more soupy and hysterical Spade ones.[4]

The novels that Fiedler mentions may be supplemented by a few other works, among them several that I do not discuss. These include Jo Sinclair's *The Wasteland* (1946) and *The Changelings* (1955); Isaac Rosenfeld's "King Solomon" (1956); Saul Bellow's *Henderson, the Rain King* (1958); Stanley Elkin's "Criers and Kibitzers, Kibitzers and Criers" (1961); Anne Roiphe's *Up the Sandbox* (1970); Cynthia Ozick's "A Mercenary" (1976); Bernard Malamud's *God's Grace* (1982); Lore Segal's *Her First American* (1985); and Francine Prose's *Primitive People* (1992). The works I have already taken note of or deal with in the chapter are several short stories by Lionel Trilling, H. J. Kaplan, Bernard Malamud, and Grace Paley; Issac Rosenfeld's *Passage from Home*; Philip Roth's *Goodbye, Columbus*; Saul Bellow's *Mr. Sammler's Planet*; and, of course, Malamud's *The Tenants*. I suggest that these fictions are not, as Fiedler claims, simply interested in reimagining the African American on more open, more human grounds (although it seems to me that they do this as well). Rather, they are equally, sometimes even more deeply, concerned to explore Jewish identity through the distance, difference, and safety afforded by the American black.

As much as fictions by Jewish writers about the black experience open into discussions with both blacks and other Americans, they are also components in an intra-Jewish conversation. This conversation is taken up by Jewish Americans in relation to other Jewish Americans, but it also, however, addresses non-American Jews, primarily the Jews of Israel. As I proceed in unraveling the multiple agendas of these texts of Jewish identity, I try to make explicit my own stake in a dialogue that, seemingly between blacks and Jews, comes increasingly to seem a conversation among Jews themselves, with extraterritorial as well as internal American messages. This is by no means to say that the Jewish writer's concern for blacks is not sincere. Rather, it is to identify in these texts another subtext, which, as in Malamud's *The Tenants*, is Jewish, rather than African American, identity. For this reason, what Fiedler says of the project of the Jewish writer reimagining the African American on more human grounds can be said with greater emphasis of this other, more Jewishly oriented project of the Jewish American writer: that this "task can prove in the end only one more possible source of misunderstanding and tension between the two groups"[5] – those groups being not only blacks and Jews but Israelis and Americans.

In many ways, both the African American–centered fiction of Jewish authors and the Jewishly oriented fiction of African American writers carry forward the dominant tendencies of the more academic conversations in which blacks and Jews have engaged over the last several decades. For the Jewish writers this means dissolving their specifically ethnic identity into a universalist mode, declaring such separateness, strangeness, and ethnicity as they wish to preserve through their identification with blacks. The African American becomes a nostalgic marker of what, as Jews, they feel themselves to have lost in their acceptance into the American mainstream. At the same time, the black character signifies the incorruptible and indestructible vessel of their own Jewish ethnicity. This ethnic component consists in the decision (as expressed in Cynthia Ozick's essay "Metaphor and Memory") to maintain the moral, ethical, pose of the stranger, despite their assimilation into the dominant culture.

For many Jewish American writers, in other words, the African American becomes a metaphor for their own eternal, internal strangeness. This strangeness is the vehicle of their ethical commitment. And it is lasting: the image of the American black further reassures Jews that their difference, albeit moral rather than physical, will no more rub off from them than color from black people. This recasts Jewishness as a variety of race. It guarantees the perpetuation both of the Jews as a people and of Jewishness as a moral position, with little conscious effort on the individual's part to preserve such difference (as adherence to something like a faith or a nationalism might seem to demand). American Jewish writers wish to become fully American. Simultaneously, for psychological and emotional reasons having to do with the Jews' long history of persecution and exclusion, they find themselves incapable of wholly denying their specifically Jewish identity. Therefore, Jews reconfigure themselves as a racial rather than as a religious or national group. In this way they are able to maintain an elusive difference that does and does not quite matter to them, in the same way that color may or may not matter to American blacks.

Jewish Americans cast themselves not as American Jews, as some terminologies would suggest, but as Jewish Americans. In other words, Jewish Americans are not one more community of Jews, the equivalent in the United States to what German Jews or Russian Jews or Israeli Jews are in their national settings. Rather, they are, as Werner Sollors among others would maintain, a community of Americans with some set of ethnic links abroad. The identification of Jewish Americans with African Americans helps to forge this American national identity, thus constituting the category "Jewish American" a phenomenon unto itself. In fact, the representation of the category "Jew" as race is coupled in many texts written by Jews with an idea of diaspora and homelessness. The Jew is defined by his or her lack of national homeland, except for that homeland shared with other Americans. These Jewish American agendas and strategies, as we shall see, cannot but lead them to positions concerning nationalism, Israel, and the Palestinian–Israeli conflict, which may not harmonize easily with Israeli positions (including my own) on these issues.

The Black Other and the Jewish Self: Transcendentalizing the Jewish Subject in Lionel Trilling's "Other Margaret" and H. J. Kaplan's "Mohammedans"

The double agenda of dissolving Jewish identity into universalist ethics and realizing the specificity of Jewishness in its displacement

onto the American black experience, comes into vivid focus in relation to two quite remarkable and neglected short stories by Lionel
Trilling and H. J. Kaplan. Kaplan's "The Mohammedans" appeared
in 1943, Trilling's "The Other Margaret" two years later. Both of
them, in Leslie Fiedler's opinion, are among the important precur-
sors of modern American Jewish fiction.[6] Both are stories about race
relations in America, not between blacks and Jews (as in most of the
novels written by Jews already cited and discussed below), but between blacks and white Anglo-Saxon Protestants. Yet each story produces a narrative that in oblique, almost subterranean, ways, insists
on going through the Jewish experience on its way to the black
experience. Therefore, each raises questions as to whether the Jewish author's interest is only or primarily in the question of race, or
whether Jewish ethnic identity is not (in part, at least) the concealed
object of the story's investigation.

It is relevant here that the publication date of both stories is the
1940s, when anti-Semitism in Europe was emerging in nothing less
than a Holocaust. Also relevant, both stories appear in *Partisan Review*, one of the journals associated with the New York Jewish intellectuals with whom both Kaplan and Trilling were affiliated. By the
mid-1940s, *Partisan Review* was printing numerous articles by
Hannah Arendt, many of them already concerning the German concentration camps. Sartre's "Portrait of the Anti-Semite" appeared in
1946 and Sidney Hook's "Reflections on the Jewish Question," in
1949. From 1948 Trilling served on the advisory board. As the
founding editor of *Commentary*, Elliot Cohen, put it, "the main difference between *Partisan Review* and *Commentary* is that we admit to
being a Jewish magazine and they don't."[7]

Trilling's story has primarily to do with an idea that circulates in
much of his literary criticism and fiction: the truth of personal responsibility. Whatever one's socioeconomic or political situation,
one had to assume responsibility for one's actions. For most of his
career Trilling engaged in a heated battle with American liberalism,
affirming many of its most salient beliefs but objecting strenuously
to the way in which it had become flaccid and unthinking. Such
concern with liberalism did not have to do, specifically, with Trilling's Jewish identity, although it does recall the Jewish universalism
that features so prominently in the Jewish intellectuals I have already
discussed (Irving Howe, for example). It is also not directly tied to
the issue of racism. Nonetheless, in "The Other Margaret" Trilling
takes up the battle with liberalism in relation to the subjects of anti-
Semitism and racism.

"Had he been truly the wise man he wanted to be," Trilling writes of the story's protagonist Stephen Elwin,

> he would have been able to explain, to Margaret and himself, the nature of the double truth. As much as Margaret, he believed that "society is responsible." He believed the other truth too. . . . It came suddenly, as no doubt was the way of moments of wisdom, and he perceived what stupidly he had not understood earlier, that it was not the other Margaret but herself that his Margaret was grieving for, that in her foolish and passionate argument . . . she was defending herself from her own impending responsibility. (p. 499)[8]

The story out of which this wisdom unfolds has to do with the Elwins' insolent and irresponsible black maid, Margaret, and the daughter of the family, also named Margaret. The daughter Margaret defends the maid on the grounds that "society didn't give her a chance. . . . She has to struggle so hard – against prejudice. It's so *hard* for her . . . it's not Margaret's fault" (pp. 498–99). Throughout the story, until the moment that Margaret the maid willfully destroys a clay sculpture the daughter has made for her mother's birthday, Margaret Elwin spouts the liberal clichés that she has learned from her socially minded schoolteacher. At the story's climax, however, when the child confronts the maid's responsibility for her actions, and (more to the point, perhaps) her own responsibility for judging those actions, we realize that "it was not because the other [maid] Margaret hated her that this Margaret wept, but because she had with her own eyes seen the actual possibility of what she herself might do, the insupportable fact of her own moral life" (p. 501).

Given the historical events transpiring in Europe during the writing of this story, it is not to be lightly dismissed that in "The Other Margaret" the figure of the Jew makes a dramatic appearance.[9] Trilling's major protagonists, the Elwins, are not Jews. "The Other Margaret," therefore, is not, like later works of American Jewish fiction, a Jewish, or even a Jewish American story. On the surface of it, at least, it is a purely American one. Therefore, when the issue of the Jew, nonetheless, and almost without any justification whatsoever, makes its entry into this story authored by a Jew, it is impossible not to wonder why Trilling (who was so assimilated a Jew that he was almost considered non-Jewish by the literary establishment) imports this "other" context into his fiction.

Trying to deflect her daughter's anger from her criticism of their maid, Lucy Elwin relates a disturbing incident on the bus. Her point, presumably, is that there is a lot of bad behavior around, especially among the poorer classes, who are now in charge of the city's major services. Oddly enough, this incident replicates her husband's experience of the same day, which also has to do with a bus conductor's misconduct in relation to one of his passengers. As in the major narrative concerning the Elwins, in neither bus story are the characters Jews. But, in Lucy's story the characters are expressly *not* Jewish, and this denial is what gives the reader pause. Lucy's narrative concerns "a young woman who had asked the conductor a question. It was a simple, ordinary question, Lucy said, about what street one transferred at. The conductor at first had not answered, and then, when he came around again and the question was asked again, he had looked at the young woman – 'looking her straight in the face,' Lucy said – and had replied in a loud voice, 'Vot deed you shay?' " Margaret's immediate assumption is that her mother, who has just been so severe concerning the black maid, is now making fun of the Jewishness of the conductor. This impression of her mother's racism is immediately countered by her father's intervention, only to yield to further misunderstandings, not only on the parts of the characters, but on the reader's part as well. The conversation proceeds as follows:

> "Mother!" Margaret grieved, "you mustn't do that." . . .
>
> "Why, do what, Margaret?" . . .
>
> "Make fun of – fun of –" . . .
>
> "Of Jews?" said Elwin . . . "Margaret, whatever makes you think that Lucy is making fun of Jews? She is simply repeating – "
>
> . . . "Oh," she said happily. "What the woman said to the conductor!"
>
> "No, Margaret. How absurd!" Lucy cried. "*Not* what the woman said to the conductor. What the conductor said to the woman."
>
> Margaret just sat there glowering with silence and anger.
>
> Elwin said to Margaret with a pedagogic clearness and patience, "The conductor was making fun of the woman for being Jewish."
>
> "Not at all," Lucy said . . . "she wasn't Jewish at all. He was insulting her by pretending that she was Jewish."
>
> Margaret had only one question to ask. "The *conductor?*" she cried with desperate emphasis. (pp. 492–93)

Ostensibly, from Lucy Elwin's own point of view, the story is rather straightforward. Without entering into the philosophical elements of her husband's thinking in the matter, it supports her husband's contention that individuals have to assume private, ethical responsibility, even, or especially, in the public sphere. What the scene, however, reveals, especially as the original incident gets caught up in the confusions of those telling and listening to the story concerning who is or is not a Jew and who is or is not expressing anti-Semitism, and how, is a flow of racist assumption beyond anyone's ability to control or define it. The next passage immediately follows the portion of text already quoted:

> And when Lucy said that it was indeed the conductor, Margaret said nothing, but shrugged her shoulders in an elaborate way and made with her hands a large grimace of despairing incomprehension. She was dismissing the grownups with this pantomime, appealing beyond all their sad nonsense to her own world of sure right reason. In that world one knew where one was, one knew that to say things about Jews was bad and that working men were good. And *therefore.*
>
> Elwin, whose awareness was all aroused, wondered in tender amusement what his daughter would have felt if she had known that her gesture, which she had drawn from the large available stock of the folk-culture of children, had originally been a satiric mimicry of a puzzled shrugging Jew. (p. 493)

What Trilling here adds to the sufficiently complex issue of identifying deliberate racism or anti-Semitism is the even more precarious task of locating, and judging, its inadvertent, reflexive expressions. The logic of the passages is something like this: Margaret is quite willing to believe her upper-class mother guilty of racism and anti-Semitism, or, for that matter, the woman passenger to whom she erroneously begins to attribute making fun of the Jew. She is quite unwilling, however, to imagine such anti-Semitism on the part of the "underpaid" conductor (p. 493). This mirrors her inability to imagine the black maid as harboring racist feelings toward her or her family. And she is completely unconscious of her own anti-Semitic caricature as in minstrel mimicry she enacts the mannerisms of the Jew.

The child Margaret's inability to get outside the racism she wishes to condemn represents both the inescapability of the flow of racist assumption within any cultural system and, just as important, the lack of consciousness, verging on a form of innocence, that characterizes most people's participation within cultural racism. This feature of institutionalized racism, set against the destruction of European Jewry that is going on even as the characters speak, produces the appropriate horror that innocence can momentarily conceal. The conductor's response, which is at this moment *not* directed at a Jew, we are given to understand by Margaret's own pantomime, has less to do with any direct experience of Jews than it does with taking on cultural mannerisms. And the conductor is applying to this language of anti-Semitism not in order to do damage to Jews (who are quite absent from the scene) but to assert his equality with or even his superiority to those very fabricators of the myth of the Jew: the white Protestant upper class. The conductor, in other words, uses the language of the dominant class in order to mimic and insult it, and simultaneously to join it. Margaret the maid behaves the same way when she assaults her employers by doing physical damage to their habits and possessions. Margaret the maid is not waging all-out revolution. Rather, she is subverting the culture from within.

Her final action of smashing the child Margaret's lamb reveals the underlying logic of her attack, and the conductor's. It also, however, exposes what Elwin himself – for all his intelligence, lucidity, and insight – cannot see. For Elwin, too, innocently and unconsciously participates in the same social pantomime he identifies in his daughter. If the gravity of the child's innocent expression of racism is brought into focus by the text's invocation, through the Jew, of the horrors of the Holocaust just then transpiring, it is also illuminated through the example of the archmoralist and -rationalist, Elwin himself.

In the opening scene of the story we are introduced to Elwin as he is buying a portrait of an African king holding a "flower" in his hand. Like so many Americans, as described by Leslie Fiedler, Elwin participates in a fantasy attraction to blacks, which complicates and calls into question his actual relationship to them. On the one hand, Elwin is genuinely sympathetic to black people. He lends money to his former maid. He recognizes her "need to think of herself as a person who pays her debts, as a responsible person" (p. 499). Elwin is not a racist in any typical or obvious sense. On the other hand, Elwin cannot relate directly to blacks. He must put between himself and them a romantic, artistic image of this other culture, an African king with a flower in his hand.

Trilling draws our attention specifically to the problem of American innocence in the final scene of the story. Casually, nonchalantly positioned at "the other corner of the sofa" where his daughter is sitting pouting, the maid just having angrily announced that she is "through here . . . I've had enough," is "the picture of the king with the flower in his hand." The child and the king balance each other on the sofa. Both face toward Margaret the maid as she enters the room. The child (and her parents) can only imagine Margaret hurling down the lamb in violent response to the child and to the family's (presumably) ill treatment of her. We, the readers, however, who share the maid's angle of vision, are invited to imagine another cause for the maid's reaction. Staring directly into this painting and clutching her napkin to her breast, all the "genteel contempt" gone from her face and looking only "frightened" (p. 500), the maid looks directly into the face of her own racial ancestry as that ancestry has been bought up and overlaid (romanticized and infantilized) by American culture.

What prompts the maid's violent display, then, is not just the socioeconomic dynamics of her relationship to her employers, whom she believes (erroneously, perhaps) to be exploiting her. Rather, it is their blind innocence toward the fact of their racist assumptions. This racism may be no more than an unexamined fascination with pictures of African kings or a casual shrug of the shoulder that has lost its explicit reference to the Jews whom such a shrug would mock. But it is there. It pervades the cultural realm. And it is so diffused into all areas of cultural formation (among whites, blacks, the lower classes, and the upper classes, men and women, children and adults) that it is barely perceptible, hardly susceptible of treatment. As intelligent as he is, Elwin cannot see in the conductor's or the maid's behavior the inevitable circulation of racist assumption through which the lower classes (sometimes wittingly, sometimes not) effect their most subtle, and damaging, revenge, their parodying and thus exposing the corruption of the dominant culture. More to the point, he cannot recognize the degree to which such cultural reflex marks himself, and how little innocent it is even when it emerges in something as benign as the purchasing of pictures or the shrugging of shoulders.

In this sufficiently complex calculus of cultural racism the figure of the Jew, in the first instance, serves merely to broaden the base of the story. As in many other works of American Jewish and African American fiction, the Jew doubles the black, and vice versa. The story does double duty, as it were, vis-à-vis two different groups of oppressed peoples. But the particular structure of Trilling's analogy between Jews and blacks, especially in a story that is calling into question our ability to perceive and identify the strands of racist assumption within ourselves, problematizes Trilling's story. Before I proceed, let me repeat what I have already said concerning the argument between Howe, Ellison, and others. I do not intend here to accuse anyone, least of all Trilling, of racism. "The Other Margaret" seems to me an extraordinary (and sorely underread) story. It is staunchly antiracist, and it brilliantly anticipates much of our contemporary thinking concerning the individual subject's lack of agency within the cultural constructions through which we evolve our sense of self and world. Yet Trilling constructs his argument concerning racism against blacks through the figure of the Jew. He constructs it, in other words, through a version of himself, because, however assimilated Trilling was, he was, like Howe, identifiably Jewish. At the same time, however, he does not identify himself or the consciousness of his story as specifically Jewish. By producing the image of a Jew not as a person but as a transcendental metaphor, above or beyond analysis, Trilling gets himself caught in just such a repetition of the cultural circulation that he is exposing in his protagonist and that he is endeavoring, through his story, to resist.

The dilemma of which the story is itself an example is produced by the asymmetry between its Jewish and its black referents. Throughout the story, the drama concerning the white Protestant Elwins and their black maid is detailed and specific. It presents a recognizable feature of contemporary American society, subject to all kinds of nuanced interpretation and reflection. At the center of this story, however, is the fact of anti-Semitism. It is as if the phenomenon of racism can be made fully comprehensible only by reference to this other, more traditional, form of discrimination, which, especially in these war years, upper-class white New Yorkers might be thought already to have confronted in more direct and self-conscious ways. Like other Jewish intellectuals, Trilling seems to assume that the case of anti-Semitism is more basic and familiar, also remediable. Therefore, reference to anti-Semitism (as to the Holocaust later) might be imagined as a way of clarifying, condemning, and ultimately redressing racism. For this reason, Trilling can represent such anti-Semitism in something of a cultural shorthand. It doesn't need any elaborate explanation. Trilling may be portraying something of this shorthand quality in the very construction of his dialogue: " 'Mother! . . . you mustn't do that.' . . . / 'Why, do what, Margaret?' . . . / 'Make fun of – fun of –' . . . / 'Of Jews?' "

Trilling's using the figure of the Jew at the center of a story about blacks and whites makes of the Jew a universal, transcendental signifier, outside the immediate cultural construction Trilling is describing. To compound the problem of this Jewish claim, Trilling as a Jew is distinguishing himself from the Christian Elwin and legiti-

mizing his moral right to speak as being different from and superior
to Elwin's. The Jew's right to speak of oppression is like that of the
blacks. But insofar as Trilling is a Jew not in either a religious or
even cultural sense but, rather, as an extrapolation out of Jewish
culture, he is himself transcendentalized and universalized. He is the
Jew as writer, intellectual, and moral voice of Western culture.

Trilling's purpose in the story, as I understand it, is to problematize the notion of the "other." Despite the similarities between the
two Margarets and the need of each to recognize herself in the
other, the situations of the two Margarets, the story shows us, are
utterly different. The fallacy Elwin labors under, which is first revealed in his purchase of the painting, and which later comes to
complicate all of his moral pronouncements, is that all human nature is analogizable to ourselves. He imagines that individually we
constitute models of ethical responsibility that enable us to emulate
and teach each other. In Elwin's view, black people are noble savages who confirm the possibility of ethical behavior as inherent
within us all. But the other Margaret (the maid), we are being asked
to see, is not another Margaret (the daughter). Rather, like the
African king, she is a fantasy projection onto the "other." She images
our desire for a universal rule of moral behavior governing all human beings, a rule that allows us to demand of the victim the same
code of ethics we demand of the victimizer. There is, the story reveals in its circulation of racist attitudes and assumptions, no position outside culture by which to judge culture. There are only the
stands we take within culture, by which we implicate ourselves alongside our culture.

The figure of the Jew disturbs this insight. It provides just such a
transcendental place outside culture as the complex logic of the
story actively works to disallow. As transcendental figure, the Jew is
not, like the black maid, subject to the story's critique of moral
responsibility. The figure of the Jew exists outside the complexities
of psychology, economics, and society. It is, as I suggested earlier,
cultural shorthand, the nation's language to itself, which only need
be referred to in order for the culture to understand what is being
said. It is the language of art and of authorship, which is to say, the
language of the writer. By including the figure of the Jew in the
story, the Jewish Trilling encodes in the story the fact of his own
Jewishness. At the same time, by introducing the Jew not as a person
but as a figure or phantom within the cultural constellation, he produces one position that remains outside the ungovernable flow of
cultural attitudes: his own position as (Jewish) author.

Similar problems inhere in H. J. Kaplan's use of the Jew as signifier of an extracultural, transcendental morality in his story "The Mohammedans." In this story, as in Trilling's, no literal Jews appear. Rather, the story, which may well have provided the seed for Malamud's *Tenants,* concerns an American writer in a decaying "ancestral mansion" (p. 211; it should have been "torn . . . down long ago" – p. 212), which is suddenly invaded by a sect of black Mohammedans. "Am I or am I not the lord of the manor?" asks the protagonist, when Wiley Bey (ancestor of Willie?) moves in (p. 214). But whereas Malamud's novel head-on tackles the problem of white and black America as the problem of blacks and Jews, for Kaplan the thinking together of blacks and Jews occurs by only the most circuitous route. This route adds a feature to Kaplan's thinking about blacks and Jews that involves as well, and far in advance of contemporary thinking on such matters, the relationship between Arabs and Israelis. It also exposes a concept of Jewish diasporism, almost imperceptible in much Jewish American writing and yet implicitly structuring it, which also complicates the black–Jewish relationship. In fact, this concept of Jewish diasporism informs Malamud's novel as well. Lesser's insistence on occupying the house, whether we understand that house to be literal real estate or a metaphor for American culture, puts him into direct conflict with both the immigrant Jew and the urban black. Both immigrant and black need Lesser to fulfill the traditional function of the Jew in contemporary society: to assume the position of homelessness that enables other people to get on with their lives.

Like the characters in Trilling's story, Kaplan's protagonist is *not* Jewish, although he is, we are told, sometimes taken for Jewish. In fact, the story is oddly punctuated with Charles Rodney Simon's denials of his Jewishness. These denials make the issue of the Jew as prominent a feature of Kaplan's story as of Trilling's, and equally oblique. "My background is Scotch-Norman," he tells Wiley (p. 213) at the beginning of the story; and in court he declares: "I am myself a Presbyterian, as was my grandfather, the first mayor of this town" (p. 283); and, at the end, to the police who have come to raid the building, he announces: "My family has been Presbyterian for six generations" (p. 291). As if Simon's credentials were not sound enough, he specifically denies he is Jewish: "The name sounds Jewish, but it's not" (p. 213). All of this makes Simon *sound* very much like a self-denying Jew or a non-Jew who suspects some Jewish ancestry (my family has been Presbyterian for six generations, he insists; and before? we might ask). The possibility that Simon is a crypto-

Jew, or at least descended of such Jews, is made especially vivid when he suddenly sees Wiley in Jewish terms not likely to occur to a non-Jew: "Solemn, ministerial, he suddenly reminded Simon of a Jew he had seen in Vienna, an old man who had emerged from the rear of his shop, clad in his colorful ritual garments, his eyes still lost in the misty distance of prayer" (p. 218).

Fundamentally Kaplan's story (like Trilling's) has to do with white racism, and the first tremors of black urban resistance. Charles Rodney Simon is the radicalized scion of American aristocracy who would recognize and try to correct the racial problem. He is already "thinking of Negroes" when the story begins (p. 210), and he knows already with a kind of protosocialist sensibility that *the house was not necessarily his* (p. 211). Still, unable to get past his own prejudices and self-interest, Simon not only fails in his efforts to argue the Negroes' case in court, but discovers himself at the end of his experience broken and abandoned in a ruined world, "just a crackpot," in the words of the police. The ending of Kaplan's story hauntingly evokes the conclusion to Melville's "Benito Cereno":

> *The house was his again.* The idea kept getting in the way of what he was trying to think. . . . What was it? But there's nothing, he said to himself bitterly, nothing you can make of it. Wiley Bey, for example, imagines he's proved some point or other. And suddenly Simon (who couldn't bear pain of any kind) began to bang his forehead hard against the wooden panelling between the two windows, saying aloud each time:
> "But he hasn't, he hasn't, he hasn't!" (pp. 291–92)

In Leslie Fiedler's terms, Kaplan's story (like Trilling's, and recalling Melville's short story as well) concerns white American fantasies of racial harmony. In these fantasies, white men realize their guilt and secure justice and equality for blacks, and blacks forgive them for all their previous deprivations:

> Consider for a moment what a chain of guilt must have produced a situation like this! The infinite multitude of mean and grandiose actions without which – without *all of which* – this world we cling to in desperation would not be ours. What Wiley Bey does not sufficiently realize – and who can blame him? – is that the Negroes in this country are only one link in the chain. They were dragged here by men who had sold their souls to the devil. They were set free as a matter of expediency, *and that was the only possible way*! . . . In this country . . . we're all Mohammedans. (pp. 285–87)

For this reason Simon fantasizes his and Wiley's "*first* [conversation] full of warmth and understanding. He would tell the Negro where he was wrong and where he was right. He would confess his own intimate sins" (p. 287).

As in Trilling's story, Kaplan's recurrence to the Jew expands the argument. Simon's being made to deny his Jewishness, with the concomitant suspicion it raises that Simon fears that someplace in his background there were Jews, helps locate what Simon, like most racists and anti-Semites, cannot get past: the anxiety of one's own genetic connection to the despised other, and the impossibility, therefore, of fully identifying with or sharing the other's experience. "I suppose you're a Mohammedan too," the police say to him, to which he responds, "with a nervous laugh, . . . Of course I'm not" (p. 291).

Like Trilling's "Other Margaret," Kaplan's "Mohammedans" also uses the figure of the Jew as more than a mere analogy to the situation of the black, or as a method of illuminating the racial situation. Both strategies are, as already suggested, problematical. But, like Trilling, Kaplan also surreptitiously encodes himself in the story. Both this encoding and the Trilling-like abstractualization of the Jew out of sociohistorical context produce a moral position beyond the local dynamics of the story. Insofar as Kaplan's black characters are also followers of Islam, this produces an odd extranational reference. This reference not only internationalizes the racial problem but places it within a Jewish debate concerning national and diasporic definitions of Jewish identity. Simon stands for the Jew as Christianized out of his Judaic identity, the Jew as universalist (like Malamud, for example). He is also the Jew who most realizes his Jewish identity in a form of diasporic consciousness centered on an idea of homelessness. All of this can be understood as responding to the internal Jewish debate, especially in the United States, as to whether Jews would do better to relocate in their national homeland or to continue to function in the other countries of their residence, in particular America.

If Trilling's "The Other Margaret" exposes how thinking through the ethnic position of the other through one's own unstated ethnicity might complicate and distort one's intentions vis-à-vis the other group, Kaplan's "Mohammedans" reveals how, reflexively, this process comes to alter the understanding of one's own group (and one's self) as well. Kaplan's story was published in 1943. The debate concerning the existence of a Jewish state, and the specific plan to relocate Jews in Palestine, were already issues on the American scene, especially as the world was becoming conscious of what was transpiring in Europe. Kaplan's story provides important insights into why American Jewish liberals rejected Zionism. It exposes how this rejection was also caught up in the relationship between blacks and Jews. For many Jews, including those who for political reasons supported, at least as a temporary measure, the establishment of a Jewish homeland, the Jewish function in the world was exactly not to establish a nation, either in Palestine or in America. Rather, the Jew was to contribute a transnational morality dedicated to the rights of the oppressed, including (as in the communist, socialist, and labor union movements) workers and blacks.

This did not mean, for Kaplan any more than for other intellectuals, necessarily giving up Jewish identity altogether. Rather, it meant imagining the possibility that Jewish identity might be realized through a universalism that nonetheless did not totally eradicate the Jew's distinctive markings. And this meant, in a sense, reimagining the Jew as black: Jewishness, not as culture but as a racial category, like color, that would precisely not disappear and would express itself, like black identity (as some imagined it), not in cultural or religious specificity but in physiognomy.

This is the central claim of Kaplan's fascinating and affecting essay entitled "A Minor Scandal in the Middle East," published in June 1949 in *Partisan Review,* just a year after the creation of the State of Israel.[10] Like "The Mohammedans," "A Minor Scandal" deals with Jewish issues only in their deflection onto other issues, in this case the Christian–Moslem conflict in the Lebanon. "I was due in Beirut," Kaplan tells us, "on a mission of peace and culture which had nothing, save very indirectly, to do with Palestine" (p. 607).

Kaplan does not, however, produce his commentary on the Jew only through implied analogy to the Moslem–Christian situation in the Lebanon. Woven throughout his contemplation of the Lebanon – itself a meditation on the story of Palestine and the Lebanon – is another, more powerful story. This is the story of himself and his father, which is to say, the story of the Jew in America. "It was the Lebanon itself, in the desperate intricacy of the Middle East, which constantly spoke to me of this distant stranger [my father], reminding me that he was a Jew (my author and creator!) fleshing those ancient problems which he and I had always, however obscurely, shared" (p. 605).

Of these ancient problems the two that emerge most powerfully are the question of what marks Jewish identity and whether, therefore, this identity in any way depends upon either ritual observance or a homeland. Kaplan's father's migration to Texas – which is for Kaplan, as he evolves it through references to the text of *Ulysses,* a figure for the movement toward, but never arriving in, the promised land – produces a text less about the Lebanon or about Israel, than about the American promised land. In this promised land, the high priest, descended of no lesser figures than Ulysses and Moses, is the Jewish Kaplan himself, to whom the mantle of priesthood has just been transferred by the death of his father.

The senior Kaplan, we are told, is "anti-religious" (p. 609) and a "heathen" (p. 606). He "could never understand, he once told me, why his son should return to his vomit": "while he went westward [to Texas] . . . I had gone back, first to his point of departure, the continent of Europe, and then even further east, to the land of his ancestors" (p. 604). What Kaplan there discovers (himself, he tells us, as much a heathen as his father) is not his lost connection to Judaism (which his mother tried but failed to repair). Rather, he locates in Cairo, in the Lebanon, in every place but Jerusalem, his link both to his father and to his Jewish past. This link has to do with the essential, biological, racial, nongeographical fact of his Jewishness.

This is Kaplan's definition of the Jew:

> Waiting in Cairo for my passport, I found myself thinking of the old man who gave me my name. He was anti-religious, on the style of the village-atheist, and he had no desire to see Jerusalem; yet he could have laughed at the suggestion that he, or his son, could choose to be anything else than a Jew. What makes a pigeon a pigeon, he would inquire, ironically? We observe this bird and we agree to call it a pigeon. (p. 609)

Kaplan is aware that "under new conditions" Jews may actually alter their genetic composition and stop looking like Jews. But, he goes on, "there was no time to work out this confusion" (p. 609). For the moment, Jews are Jews, as unalterably and irreducibly as pigeons are pigeons. And it is of utmost importance to Kaplan that we agree to call this bird known as the Jew by its proper name. For Kaplan this name is *Kaplan* or priest: "to bear such a name was like wearing a yellow star, or a beard with earlocks. . . . It exposed me and my children to massacre, simply because I hadn't the energy and courage of my apostasy. . . . [I]t invaded my life, which should have been entirely applied to the problem of being; and forced it to turn always about the problem of being-a-Jew" (p. 608).

In thus defining his Jewishness as biological or racial, Kaplan links into a long tradition of such definitions of the Jew, including the very recent racial theories of Nazi Germany. In voicing his own affirmation of Jewish racial difference, Kaplan, like contemporary African American celebrations of race, takes self-definition out of the control of the enemy. But Kaplan, even in this recovery of self-definition, is producing his portrait of the Jew as a consequence both of his experience of Arabs – who are also, many of them, racially distinct, and also in conflict over national as opposed to racial, cultural, or religious self-definition – and his experience of American blacks. Jews are as irreducibly Jews as pigeons are pigeons or blacks are blacks. In "The Mohammedans" the blacks are like the Jews. In "The Scandal" a reverse logic takes over. And both blacks and Jews are perceived in the light not only of racial conflicts, but of national controversies as well.

This playing out of Jew as black and black as Jew, and both as Arabs and Israelis caught in conflicts less over racial definition than over identification with the land, explains two important features of the plot of "The Mohammedans." Like *The Tenants,* which also seems to me indirectly to enter into the debate concerning Jewish nationalism, the story deals with territorial rights. It concerns not only black people generally, but a specific nationalist group of blacks, who have renounced their American citizenship and therefore refuse to serve in the American army. Although "The Mohammedans" is clearly a story denouncing race prejudice and its consequences, nonetheless it presents a highly critical view of its black Mohammedans as well as of its white Protestants. This view emerges as a consequence of what Kaplan sees, because of the circulation of these issues within Jewish culture, especially in the years of the Second World War (the war in which these black Mohammedans refuse to fight), as issues of nationalism rather than of race. Kaplan reads black Zionism through Jewish Zionism, and condemns such nationalism. *"The diaspora is not, except in the West, a Jewish phenomenon,"* he writes. *"It is the normal mode of communal existence in the Middle East"* (p. 615). Fifty years later, as the names of numerous books, journals, and articles suggest, it would become a major feature of thinking about non-Jewish communities in the West as well.

For Kaplan, as for Trilling and others, the Jews have a special mission to perform because of their homelessness. Of course Kaplan recognizes that without formal structures of identification Jews could, theoretically, disappear: "What becomes of those Jews who remain . . . in the Diaspora?" asks Kaplan, and he answers through Arthur Koestler's voice:

They can only disappear. . . . The Eastern European settle-
ments are already dead, with their distinctive language and
traditions. Their religion has long since transmitted its purely
spiritual values to the Christian Occident; for the rest, it has
survived merely as a mythology for the Return. But the Return
is now a fact. The perspective ("Next year in Jerusalem . . .")
once operated as a principle of cohesion. *The reality now imposes
a choice.* Let those who would be Jews make their way to the
Jewish homeland. (p. 609)

But what the example of the Lebanon and the Arab–Israeli conflict
teaches Kaplan is the equivalent dangers of statehood. Anticipating
Philip Roth's idea in *Operation Shylock,* Kaplan recognizes that gath-
ering the Jews together in Israel may simply provide a prelude to
exterminating them once and for all.

More important, however, Jewish difference is not inherently its
"ancestral attachment to a given land" (p. 613). It is rather something inscribed in their flesh. Therefore Jews, in Kaplan's view, are
not in danger of disappearing as Jews any more than black people
are in danger of disappearing as blacks. For this reason, the Jew
must act to protect the existence of "difference" (p. 620) in the
world. And this, again, defines the universalist mission of the Jew.
"What safety is there for any man, in a world which cannot assimilate . . . difference," Kaplan writes in direct response to the idea
(put forward by Sartre) that the Jews themselves assimilate and disappear. "And what pride? And what adventure?" Kaplan would insist on his difference as a Jew. This difference, however, is for Kaplan explicitly placeless and timeless. These are the concluding
words of the essay:

I close my eyes and dream a lovely letter. Is not the world
made richer, and more human, by those who take a passionate
interest in reasonableness and courage, if only because of their
names? I tell the old man that I am happy he's gone to Texas.
When I was a child, I saw him always with a hammer in his
hands, building houses. He has covered New Jersey with
houses. Never mind, there is plenty of land and much to learn,
in Texas. *I and my companions were old and tardy, says Ulysses,
when we came to that narrow pass, where Hercules assigned his land-
marks, to hinder man from venturing further. . . . "O brothers," I said,
"who through a hundred thousand perils have reached the West, deny
not to this, the brief remaining vigil of your senses, experience of the*

unpeopled world behind the sun."... And so they turned their poop toward morning, until *there appeared to us a Mountain, dim with distance; and to me it seemed the highest I had ever seen.* But a tempest arose from the new land and Ulysses was destroyed.

As pleased Another, he tactlessly says. (p. 620)

Like Moses viewing Canaan from Mount Pisgah, so Ulysses arrives at but does not enter the new land. For Kaplan, Ulysses – like that more direct descendant of Moses, his father – is a figure of diasporic consciousness. He is, also like his father, a wandering Jew or "roaming [Arab] tribesman" (p. 613), seeking home (even building houses) but never finding it. He is like the mountain itself, "an ambiguous sign" signifying "ambiguity" (p. 620). That Kaplan produces his figure of diasporic Jewish consciousness not through the figure of Moses but through the figure of Ulysses is itself testimony to this writer's commitment to his diasporic faith. Kaplan (like Trilling, Howe, and others) expresses his Jewishness in its displacement onto other issues and other traditions, as in his short story on "The Mohammedans."[11]

Kaplan knows that his strategy is from the Judaic point of view a "scandal," a word that, the dictionary tells us, has primarily a religious meaning. For Kaplan, however, scandal produces the only kind of religiosity that matters. Kaplan's is a conversion narrative, in which he finally assumes the imperatives of his name by becoming ("religious person" that he is) the priest of this scandalized new Jewishness, which, for him, returns Jewishness to its originary, mythic, universal, transcendental function. While the white Protestant narrator and black Mohammedans of Kaplan's short story fight to occupy the ancestral mansion, the Jew wanders, providing a model of moral consciousness for any and all to see. And insofar as this position of the wandering Jew is Kaplan's position as priest, the Jew emerges (vis-à-vis blacks and Arabs both) less as humble everyman than as a kind of divine, chosen presence that, insofar as it is also linked to the epic tradition, represents the voice both of Western civilization and of art. Like Trilling's, Kaplan's Jewish voice is the voice of the writer, and the voice of the writer is the voice of universal, Western morality. This position produces offense not only to populations who may come to seem inferior to the Jews, but to Jewish populations (such as the Israeli population or the religious community) who may believe that identity has to do with commitment rather than with race, with specificity rather than with general humanistic virtue.

"Ein Klug tsu Columbus": Jewishness and Race in Isaac Rosenfeld's
Passage from Home *and Philip Roth's* Goodbye, Columbus

The idea of Jew as transcendental signifier, and yet as genetically marked, conveying both a universal morality and a kind of ethnic authenticity, comes together in Isaac Rosenfeld's 1946 *Passage from Home* and Philip Roth's *Goodbye, Columbus.*[12] Before I suggest what such a definition of Jewishness leaves out, and why it might prove problematical for Israeli Jews or religious Jews, let me read Rosenfeld's and Roth's novels as providing further insights into the processes of Jewish redefinition going on in the United States in the 1940 and 1950s. Ironically, what gets lost in certain Jewish American self-definitions is exactly the move toward historical, cultural, even religious specificity that increasingly comes to characterize black writing during the same period. It may well be that Zionism, among certain segments of the Jewish American population, also owes a debt to black thinking, in unexpected ways.

The great informing theme of much Jewish American fiction from Anzia Yezierska's *Bread Givers* (1925), Abraham Cahan's *Rise of David Levinsky* (1917), Mary Antin's *The Promised Land* (1912), Mike Gold's *Jews Without Money* (1930), and Henry Roth's *Call It Sleep* (1934) to the present has been what Isaac Rosenfeld quite simply labels the passage from home. This passage from home does more than bring American Jewish immigrants and their American offspring into contact with native-born Americans. Rather, as in Henry Roth's epic representation of America's teeming cities at the beginning of the twentieth century, it proceeds through the experience of other ethnically different Americans, including those other native-born but painfully marginalized urban "refugees": the American blacks.

Certainly a part of the function of the black character in the Jewish novel of assimilation is to identify with this other victim of marginalization and oppression. Although there are no African American characters in Mike Gold's *Jews Without Money,* his naming of one of the major Jewish characters "Nigger" at least hints at a continuous feature of the tradition of Jewish American fiction. "The Jews had fled from the European pogroms," writes Gold, "with prayer, thanksgiving and solemn faith from a New Egypt into a new Promised Land. They found awaiting them the sweatshops, the bawdy houses and Tammany Hall."[13] They also, Gold indicates through the name of his character, found black people already resident in this new promised land, which might just turn out to be a new Egypt as well.

These black people form an analogy to Gold's Jews. They are also, however, savvy to the ways of the street, able, in Gold's view of things, to survive in ways most Jews as yet cannot. "Nigger" teaches the younger boys to steal and to flirt with prostitutes; he forms the vital communication between the ways of the old world and those of the new. For many Jewish authors, including Malamud and Rosenfeld, black experience provides striking parallels to Jewish experience, with an authenticity, specifically American, that does not quite characterize the Jews. As Rosenfeld puts it in one of his essays, "as a barometer of political calamity the Jews in this country are second only to the Negroes."[14] But as the name of Gold's character reminds us, however positive thinking together diverse ethnic experiences of racially or religiously different groups can seem, nonetheless it can, and often does, deliver us into problems of appropriation, displacement, and even inadvertent racism.

Like many Jewish American novels concerning the early immigrant and first-generation experiences, Isaac Rosenfeld's *Passage from Home* has less to do with the Jewish American community than with the growth into maturity of the artist. Typically, this portrait of the artist as a young man concerns a recognizably oedipal revolt against the parent, which is also, in the case of the Jewish child, a revolt against Judaism. Therefore, Bernard's rebellion consists mainly of his attempt to bring together two of the family's members, both of them largely alienated from the family and in particular from his father: his mother's sister, who was once extremely observant but who has broken with formal Judaism, and the non-Jewish husband of a now deceased cousin. "I remember the year in which I first felt respect for human intelligence," the narrator tells us. "I was fourteen, a precocious child, as sensitive as a burn. Human intelligence meant my own. Without growing more than an inch, I had suddenly shot up – that is, in my own estimation – and it seemed to me that I towered over life. Life meant the family" (p. 3).

Bernard's growth into maturity and artistic consciousness, in other words, has to do with realizing his outsiderness and alienation, for which his Jewishness becomes a primary metaphor. Elsewhere, Rosenfeld acknowledges that Jews lack the conventional criterion of the artist, "the security of a dignified neutrality." Nonetheless, as "marginal" individuals, "not completely integrated into society and yet not wholly foreign to it," they also enjoy considerable artistic advantage:

As a member of an internationally insecure group he [the Jew] has grown personally acquainted with some of the fundamental themes of insecurity that run through modern literature. He is a specialist in alienation (the one international banking system the Jews actually control). Alienation puts him in touch with his own past traditions, the history of the Diaspora; with the present predicament of almost all intellectuals and, for all one knows, with the future conditions of civilized humanity. Today nearly all sensibility – thought, creation, perception – is in exile, alienated from the society in which it barely managed to stay alive.

But alienation from society . . . may function as a condition of entrance into society. . . . No man suffers injustice without learning, vaguely but surely, what justice is. . . . Out of their recent sufferings one may expect Jewish writers to make certain inevitable moral discoveries.[15]

It is this metaphor of the artist as marginalized citizen that also prompts the text's application to the black experience.

"Why was he a Negro and I a Jew?" the protagonist asks himself. "Why not the other way around? Or both of us Negroes, or both Jews?"[16] And he continues:

The world was absolutely endless and complex: this was God, the imagination that kept on creating differences, face from face and life from life.

And yet, why was there so wide a gulf between person and person; differences so great that to breach them one would have to cross the world itself. Why, now on the street, should one man be a Negro, another having freckles on his nose, a third, a yellow moustache? . . . Why was I what I was? . . .

I was discovering it now, and yet I had always known it, always known the remoteness of reality, the distance that separated us from the truth. I had never been without the realization that an empty space, which one might never hope to fill, stretched between person and person, between ignorance and knowledge, between one hand and the other, condemning all to loneliness. And, without ever having been able clearly to estimate it, feeling the weight of it and haunted by its presence, I had always carried it with me as a token, both secret and obvious, of my own existence. For as a Jew, I was acquainted, as perhaps a Negro might be, with the alien and the divided aspect of life . . . I had come to know a certain homelessness in the world, and took it for granted as a part of nature: had seen in the family, and myself acquired, a sense of sadness from

which both assurance and violence had forever vanished. We
had accepted it unconsciously and without self-pity, as one
might accept a sentence that had been passed generations ago,
whose terms were still binding though its occasion had long
been forgotten. . . . "What am I?" (pp. 116–18)

The point of Rosenfeld's passage is to get to that question of identity
that every sensitive individual, and most especially the artist, must
ask: Who am I, and how am I different from others? For this reason,
Rosenfeld, ostensibly at least, applies to the example of the black as
well as of the Jew. But it is exactly at this point that the passage gets
itself, and the text, into trouble:

For as a Negro might ponder his outer body, asking himself
why it should differ from other men's when inwardly he felt his
common humanity, so I would consider my skin, my eyes, my
hair, and wonder why I should feel an inner difference when
outwardly I was the same as other men. (p. 118)

If I were black, Bernard imagines, I would be obsessed with my
blackness:

I should go about thinking, "I am black, I am black." . . . I
should constantly be thinking, "I am a Negro, I am black." And
yet, here we were, walking about in the street and no one gave
thought to it, no one inquired, no one imagined what the differences were between men.
    But I knew. I was discovering it now, and yet I had always
known it. (p. 117)

For Rosenfeld, as for other white (Jewish) liberals, black difference is purely physiological and hence superficial. It conceals similarity rather than proclaims distinctness. Jewish difference, however, is for Rosenfeld something else entirely. It is internal. It is
spiritual. And it opens into the philosophical knowledge of difference that is for Rosenfeld – as for writers like Malamud, Trilling,
and Kaplan – the secret moral knowledge of the Jew. Furthermore, this long-standing knowledge of the Jew of his spiritual difference becomes the basis for the transcendentalized Jew, the Jew-
as-artist, the Jew as the essential embodiment of moral knowledge
and behavior.
    Philip Roth's *Goodbye, Columbus* proceeds along similar lines and
gets itself into similar trouble. Although most readers probably do
not remember Roth's novella this way, *Goodbye, Columbus,* as I have

already begun to indicate, is virtually obsessed with the American black. "Over the next week and a half," Neil tells us concerning the major events of the book, "there seemed to be only two people in my life, Brenda and the little colored kid who liked Gauguin" (p. 42). Once one has noted the novel's deep investment in the African American experience, it becomes fairly easy to interpret the ostensible intention of the novel's references. Neil feels a deep "kinship" (p. 67) with the Patimkins' black maid Carlota, with whom he identifies as a fellow outsider, though he suspects, in a kind of reversal of racial/religious identification, that she feels more at home than he does with the Patimkins (p. 37). This kinship and identification between American Jews and African Americans is explored more fully in Neil's relationship to the "small colored boy" (p. 31) he meets in the Newark Public Library. What attracts Neil to the little boy, as to Carlota, is the position of outsidership and even inferiority that Neil feels himself to share with them. Furthermore, insofar as Roth locates Carlota as a poor black in an affluent white Jewish world, which is largely a domestic space, while placing the little boy against the public realm of white middle-class Christian culture, and then associating Neil with both of these positions, Roth suggests a further likeness between Jews and blacks. Their disenfranchisement is double. It is as much by class as by race/religion, and it occurs in relation to both the dominant culture and the minority culture (in this case Jewish culture) as well.

Roth, then, constructs the novella in such a way as to produce an image of the Jewish American as marginalized outsider, like the American black. In this sense the black and Jewish experiences parallel and illuminate each other. Roth's African American characters serve to indict the non-Jewish world in which American Jewry lives for anti-Semitism and racism both. Nonetheless, the focus of Roth's novel, which is highly satiric and critical of the Jewish community, is the Jew, not the black. In order to deepen his critique of American Jewry, Roth also registers the difference between African and Jewish Americans. And this difference, represented by Neil's "No" early on in the text, more than problematizes Roth's strategy.

One of the most insightful features of Roth's text, which affirms its antiracist intention, is its exposé of American racism, including a Jewish American racism largely indistinguishable from that of the white Christian majority. It is the yes-and-no quality of Neil's answer to Brenda, the ambivalent attraction to and desire for differentiation from the African American, which Roth, in the first instance, brings into view. "The next day," Neil tells us,

> I held Brenda's glasses for her once again, this time not as
> momentary servant but as afternoon guest; or perhaps as both,
> which still was an improvement. She wore a black tank suit and
> went barefooted, and among the other women, with their Cu-
> ban heels and boned-up breasts, their knuckle-sized rings, their
> straw hats, which resembled immense wicker pizza plates and
> had been purchased, as I heard one deeply tanned woman
> rasp, "from the cutest little *shvartze* when we docked at Barba-
> dos," Brenda among them was elegantly simple, like a sailor's
> dream of a Polynesian maiden, albeit one with prescription sun
> glasses and the last name of Patimkin. (p. 19)

Anticipating what has now become a common insight into black–
white relations, Roth represents the white world as simultaneously
partaking of black culture and forcefully distancing itself from it.
The passage, in other words, reveals how the Patimkins and their
world exploit the existence of peoples of color and supposedly
"primitive" cultures by imagining them as forces of sexual energy
and vitality to which they can apply and from which they can prosper
while simultaneously maintaining their cultural distance and superiority. In an essay entitled "Boxing on Paper," Ishmael Reed, quite
conveniently for our purposes, calls other forms of this process (for
example, the "widespread adoption of such Afro-American forms as
rock and roll") "cultural tanning."[17] Some pages after the passage
already quoted, the text again applies to this image when it describes
a group of young Jewish suburbanites "tanning" themselves at the
appropriately named *South Mountain Reservation* (p. 76). Black and
Carribean culture are not the only provinces of American exploitation. The "navaho"-faced Patimkin maid with a Spanish name recalls
this fact of a Native American and Mexican presence in America as
well, which the dominant white culture also exploits.

But no sooner has Roth laid out the dimensions of his cultural
critique than he gets himself involved in just the coil of identification and distancing that he seems to be trying to undo. The difference between blacks and Jews, Roth suggests, is only skin-deep. Thus
we hear Neil, who on several occasions makes fun of Brenda's nose
job, say of his tanning, peeling cousin (who is "dark" like him) that
"she is going to have her skin fixed" (p. 20). For Roth, Jews are not
blacks, and the difference between them is that Jews can far more
easily assimilate into WASP society than blacks. But, this is for Roth
also the blacks' advantage over the Jews: that they cannot assimilate.
What Jews, therefore, can discover from the black experience is, as

in a wonderful Grace Paley story entitled "The Long-Distance Runner," a kind of authenticity no longer available within the Jewish world.[18] This authenticity that Roth would retrieve from blacks is problematic. First of all, as it emerges in Roth's own text, it is a white person's construction of racial authenticity. Second, and more important, it participates in already existing patterns of institutional racism in the United States, which has already availed itself of the fantasy of black authenticity in order to keep African Americans in a subordinate place within the culture. In this, it leads back to the major feature of Trilling's, Kaplan's, and Rosenfeld's texts: that Jewish difference is more spiritual, cultural, and transcendental, and it must be maintained.

The first "offense" delivered (inadvertently, perhaps inescapably) by Roth's novella is the white (and Jewish) construction of race. The image of race to which Roth's little colored boy is drawn, and which then functions in the book itself as an image of racial purity, is a white artist's representation of race, in which (as in Trilling's story) race primarily stands for a romantic conception of the natural and the primitive. This narrative device offends through its implication that people of color need white artistic representations of race in order to achieve cultural coherence. By having a child of African descent identify with a portrait of Tahitian racial difference the book enters into the fallacy (or is it just inattentiveness?) that all people of color are of the same color. This fantasy functions within much racial thinking about Africa itself: that all Africans share an undifferentiable racial identity and that the racial marker is a primary source for Africans of transnational unity. Tahiti, the Carribean, Polynesia, and Africa all blend together in Roth's novella as the site of black racial difference, in which such difference stands for a natural authenticity to which all of us (black and white) can apply.

More crucially, however, despite its knowledge of the white exploitation of racial difference, the novel tends not so much to correct what it figures forth as a major deformity in white American culture as to slip into some manner of (sensitive and creative) repetition of this exploitation. Even in the critique of the New Jersey suburban matrons, Brenda emerges as a "Polynesian maiden." More extensively, as Roth sets up the story, the African American child in the library, in love with the pictures of Gauguin, represents, not only to Neil but within the structure of the novel itself, a vitality and sexuality absent from white America, and most especially Jewish America. The child serves Neil (and us) as a counterforce to the sterile world of the Patimkins, with their superficial, ignorant, and highly commercial notions of Jewish identity: a smattering of Yiddish words and a few leftover Jewish holidays and traditions.

Not accidentally, the vitality, power, and naturalness the young boy incorporates is expressly sexual. Roth is not the first American Jewish writer to connect Jewish authenticity with sexuality. Bernard's passage from home, especially as it involves him in the love affair of his aunt and uncle, also marks the young Jew's passage into sexuality and the procreative future. Rosenfeld makes his point more explicitly in "Adam and Eve on Delancey Street," an essay that drew forth the wrath of the Jewish community as only the fiction of Philip Roth would later do: "It is sad evidence of the sexual displacement in Jewish living that the sexual forms in the popular Jewish conception should derive not from the Song of Songs or any indigenous source within the presumably rich and close-textured contact with life Judaism maintains, but from a forbidden exogamy, symbolized in food taboos." Such taboos, Rosenfeld reveals later in the essay, amount to a "sexual taboo not only of exogamy, but of the sexuality of the tribe itself. It is the taboo of sex as such."[19] If, on the one hand, Rosenfeld, like Trilling and Kaplan, wants to prioritize the importance of the spiritual over the physical, on the other, he, like Ludwig Lewisohn before him, wants to maintain the physical both as marker of difference and as vehicle of authenticity and procreative power.

It is the sexualization of the black that enables Roth to slip easily from Neil's appreciation of the child to his infatuation with Brenda. Without a doubt, Roth is satirizing his narrator when Brenda metamorphoses for Neil into a "Polynesian maiden." Only the most pathetic leap of the imagination could reconceive Short Hills, New Jersey, as "rose-colored, like a Gauguin stream" (p. 35). But how differently does the "wide-eyed" "lion tamer" of Newark, who is finding his way back to cultural origins through the painter Gauguin, function for Roth in his portrayal of the exhaustion and sterility of American Jewish culture? In keeping with this idea of cultural authenticity as a form of primitive sexuality, the major issue between Neil and Brenda, which brings the story to its unhappy climax, is his desire (and her resistance to that desire) that she buy a diaphragm for, in his words, "the sake of pleasure" (p. 64), "my pleasure," as he later adds. Neil would "wed" Brenda to himself through some form that would reverse and undo the unnecessary complications and obfuscation of culture. Neil would have them restored to a state of nature such as is represented in Gauguin's paintings.

The recovery of the idea of sexuality both as positive and as evidencing cultural authenticity proceeds for Neil as it does for white culture generally through the image of native black culture. White racism in this formula is voyeuristic sexual repression, as when Neil's (non-Jewish) co-worker in the library expresses the suspicion, which he will not even name directly, that the black child who seeks out Gauguin's sensuous representations of native women is in the library masturbating. "You know what those boys *do* in there . . . there is touching . . . and there is touching," he says, after which he makes the additional important point, linking the racist stereotype concerning sexuality with political bigotry and fear: "You know the way they treat the housing projects we give them . . . They're taking over the city" (p. 33). Roth sexualizes McKee's racism in order to condemn, in the rejection of that racism, the troubled attitude toward sexuality that such racism also expresses.

For McKee is not mistaken about the sexual aspects of the boy's attraction to Gauguin. His error lies in his devaluation of sexuality itself. Therefore, when the little boy exclaims "that's the fuckin life . . . ain't that the fuckin *life*" (a remark, the text notes, for which he could have earned "eternal banishment from the Newark Public Library and its branches" – pp. 34–35), he is not, in the view of the book, expressing some pornographic sexual urge, as if he were flipping through pages of *Playboy* or even *National Geographic*. Rather, coming as he does from the slums of the inner city, the little boy (Roth's text makes clear) appreciates the uninhibitedness and purity of Gauguin's women, their authenticity. In the context of the book's other references, this authenticity must be taken as also representing the cultural autonomy and purity of colored peoples not overtaken and enslaved by asexual white (and American Jewish) culture.

Sexuality, in this text, is a figure (for Roth as much as for Neil) of wholesomeness and wholeness both, by which it is possible to measure not only McKee's racism but his personal degeneration and sterility. Sexuality is exactly what defines the natural and the normal against the decadent and the corrupt. One need hardly note, in this context, the representation of Jews in classic anti-Semitic literature as swarthy and lascivious, or the post-Freudian countermove that this produced in writers like Lewisohn and Rosenfeld, in which Jewish sexual potency was linked directly to the preservation of genuine Jewish identity. Brenda's appeal for Neil is what he imagines (incorrectly) as her authentic, unspoiled, and uncompromising sexuality. This sexuality makes her not only a native like him (dark, a *shvartze*). It also transforms her into the most purely and innocently "Jewish" of the book's characters. But because Roth's idea of Jewish sexuality and authenticity proceeds through the image of the American black, it cannot but carry forward the same cultural equation he is condemning among the residents of Short Hills, New Jersey. In this way, the book replicates the dynamics of race appropriation and discrimination it brings into focus.

For all its sliding into the problem of the inevitable repetition implicit in his application to the African American experience, Roth's *Goodbye, Columbus* nonetheless reveals what inevitably also emerges from these mutually constructed black–Jewish fictions: the evidencing of the mutual construction itself, which enables the reader to see through the artifice of cultural claims to the artifice itself. The final image of Roth's book, with Neil staring at his reflection in the glass of Harvard's Lamont Library, could be read as reproducing Roth's conceit (as opposed to the object of his critique) of the fantasy of the self-creating self. In the views of a whole line of American writers, from Cooper and Hawthorne through Fitzgerald and Updike, this fantasy characterizes one form of American personality. But, searching for an image of self, what Neil is forced to see instead, looking through the dark glass, is a wall of books. Neil comes to confront the fundamental textuality of all self-constructions, including his own, and including the African American and Jewish materials that he (like others) has applied to this self-construction:

> From the light of the lamp on the path behind me I could see my reflection in the glass front of the building. Inside, it was dark and there were no students to be seen, no librarians. Suddenly, I wanted to set down my suitcase and pick up a rock and heave it right through the glass, but of course I didn't. I simply looked at myself in the mirror the light made of the window. I was only that substance, I thought, those limbs, that face that I saw in front of me. I looked, but the outside of me gave up little information about the inside of me. I wished I could scoot around to the other side of the window, faster than light or sound or Herb Clark on Homecoming Day, to get behind that image and catch whatever it was that looked through those eyes. . . . I looked hard at the image of me, at that darkening of the glass, and then my gaze pushed through it, over the cool floor, to a broken wall of books, imperfectly shelved.
>
> I did not look very much longer, but took a train that got me into Newark just as the sun was rising on the first day of the Jewish New Year. I was back in plenty of time for work. (pp. 103–04)

From Roth's perspective, there is no essential Neil Klugman any more than there is any essential Jew or black. But this means as well that there is no Neil Klugman who is not configured by such identities as Jew and black, which exist outside of his private self-conceptions.

In using African American materials to get at a fundamental falsehood within Jewish American self-conceptions, Roth involves himself in a repetition of his own insights into American and Jewish American culture. At the same time, however, in resisting cultural essentialism in both its black and its Jewish versions, Roth produces a study of American individualism as always a cultural construction. Neil, in the final scene, returns to work on the Jewish New Year, continuing to mark time Jewishly, but realizing that his place is in the workaday world of a distinctly non-Jewish, biracial, culture. It is not so much that Neil denies his Jewishness as that he refuses to remain any longer "disguised as an Orthodox Jew" (p. 95). This may well prompt more traditional Jews to say, in relation to their assimilated children: *ein klug tsu Columbus* – a curse on Columbus, for having given the Jews this opportunity to assimilate. But from Roth's point of view, America is the reality in which the American Jew lives, and American Jewish identity is all the identity they have. As we will see, Alice Walker and Toni Morrison come to fairly similar conclusions in several of their novels.

The Black, the Israeli, and the American Jew in Saul Bellow's Mr. Sammler's Planet

By the time Saul Bellow came to write *Mr. Sammler's Planet* in 1969, black–Jewish relations had exploded. As in Malamud's *Tenants* (which may well be indebted to Bellow's novel) one does not find in the Jew's passage through black culture either Jewish–black affinities or still viable bases for a Jewish self-reconfiguring based on the black experience. At the same time, another complicating factor has entered the American Jewish self-definition: the existence of the State of Israel. As we have seen, Israel was already a factor in American Jewish self-construction. Even before the creation of the nation, American Jews had pondered the implications for them of a Jewish national homeland. But in 1967, just as American race relations (including relations between blacks and Jews) were swinging out of control, the Jewish people were once again threatened with annihilation. Israel won a stunning, if extremely problematical, victory over its Arab neighbors.

For many American Jews, including Bellow, the Six-Day War would reawaken a sense of responsibility and guilt vis-à-vis the Jewish people. It would also imbue them with a new Jewish pride. And it would bring into painful focus the difference between American Jewish loyalties to their new promised land and Jewish national aspirations, both ancient and modern. In thinking about Zionism, especially in relation to Israel's Arab citizens and the Palestinian population put in its control by the 1967 war, Bellow, as American Jewish writer, would take an old familiar path on his way to resolving his conflicts as an American. He would think through his own situation as an American Jew by thinking through the situation of American blacks. He would do this, however, in order, finally, to differentiate himself not only from blacks but from Israelis as well. For many Americans the black power movement and the subsequent success of black studies programs throughout the United States signaled the renewal of ethnic pride for all American minorities, Jews included. Bellow, I suggest, resists this American move toward identity politics and multiculturalism. As in the major trajectory of his fiction, Bellow's *Sammler* is an empassioned plea for rationality and humane balance. It is a highly moral text, treading between political excesses in order to define an ethical norm. In so doing, however, it may create problems for both its black and its Israeli readers. For Bellow's African American character serves as a code and a warning in relation to two related phenomena. He represents American ethnicity as power gone wild. And he stands for that other national identity that proved for many Jews (the writer of this study included) irresistible and that might also be seen in the light of power and violence unleashed: the State of Israel. Not accidentally, Bellow incorporates many of the ideas implicit in *Mr. Sammler's Planet* in his autobiographical *To Jerusalem and Back,* which he as much addresses to Israeli Jewry as to his own fellow Americans.

No reader of *Sammler* is likely to forget its most compelling, troubling, and potentially offensive scene when a black pickpocket corners Mr. Sammler in his apartment house and exhibits his penis to him:

> He was never to hear the black man's voice. He no more spoke than a puma would. What he did was to force Sammler into a corner.... There the man held Sammler against the wall with his forearm.... The pickpocket unbuttoned himself.... He was directed, silently, to look downward. The black had opened his fly and taken out his penis. It was displayed to Sammler

with great oval testicles, a large tan-and-purple uncircumcised thing – a tube, a snake; . . . Over the forearm and fist that held him Sammler was required to gaze at this organ. No compulsion would have been necessary. He would have in any case looked.[20]

As is clear from most readings of Bellow's novel, the scene is meant to contribute to the book's general depiction of the degeneration of the human race, especially in the aftermath of the Second World War and its various catastrophes, including (but not exclusively) the extermination of European Jewry:

> New York was getting worse than Naples or Salonika. It was like an Asian, an African town, from this standpoint. The opulent sections of the city were not immune. You opened a jewelled door into degradation, from hypercivilized Byzantine luxury straight into the state of nature, the barbarous world of colour erupting from beneath. It might well be barbarous on either side of the jewelled door. Sexually, for example. The thing evidently, as Mr Sammler was beginning to grasp, consisted in obtaining the privileges, and the free ways of barbarism, under the protection of civilized order, property rights, refined technological organization, and so on. Yes, that must be it. (p. 8)[21]

And later:

> From the black side, strong currents were sweeping over everyone. Child, black, redskin – the unspoiled Seminole against the horrible Whiteman. Millions of civilized people wanted oceanic, boundless, primitive, neckfree nobility, experienced a strange release of galloping impulses, and acquired the peculiar aim of sexual niggerhood for everyone. (p. 130)

The black man who assaults Sammler is rendered by Bellow as being not only a crook but also a sexual degenerate. He figures both criminality and hedonism as the twinned conditions of corruption in the modern world, a world that stretches back to include prewar Germany.

But by using a black character to represent moral and sexual degeneracy, especially when its major concern is Jewish history, the book cannot escape troubling racist implications. This potential racism is rendered more central, and more offensive, by the passages comparing New York City to Africa, with the currents of corruption coming from the "black" side. It is not helped much by the fact that the black pickpocket is also rendered in Bellow's novel a figure of power and energy. He is, clearly, a deeply felt, deeply internalized alter ego and fantasy image of Sammler himself. He is potent in a way that the similarly aristocratic Sammler never quite was and certainly, in his old age and halfblindness, never can be again. As in all such projections, in which we both identify with the other but feel, to some degree, both our superiority to and inadequacy in relation to the other, Sammler yields to a bitterness and disgust as intense as his admiration.[22] Surely Bellow is sensitive enough a writer, especially in the aftermath of both the Civil Rights and black power movements, to have been conscious of the overtones of his imagery. It is even more difficult to believe that Bellow either intended, or even inadvertently launched, a racist attack against blacks, whatever the objects of his social satire in the book (including black radicalism). Remarkably, very few critics have done more than note this extremely disturbing aspect of Bellow's novel.[23]

One must immediately point out, of course, as a kind of first line of defense, that in the book's characterization of modern man/woman as more brute than human, the black pickpocket is hardly an isolated figure. Bellow's cast of Jewish characters, most of them Holocaust survivors at one remove or another from the events in Europe, are as morally and sexually compromised as the pickpocket.[24] Sammler's own daughter, Shula, is very much "like the Negro pickpocket" (130) when she suddenly steals an entire manuscript. His perpetually masturbating cousin Bruch, who obsesses over women's arms, and Angela and her ex-boyfriend, with their sexual orgies and fixations, are only two more instances in this panoply of American Jewish perversion. Even Sammler's nephew Elya, the best of the lot, has dealings with the Mafia, performs illegal abortions, and has money hidden in his suburban home.

What may be happening here is, simply, that, like many other American Jewish intellectuals after the Second World War, for whom anti-Semitism is the European event, racism its American version, Bellow is drawing together these two phenomena in terms of what might be understood as the consequences of slavery/racism and genocide for the victims of such persecution. All of the characters in Bellow's book, black and Jewish, bear scars. In this case, the racism of Bellow's text is not, therefore, as one critic has argued, Bellow's "cultured, traditional revulsion against the scatological metaphysics of [books such as] Mailer's *An American Dream*" (the passage concerning sexual niggerhood would seem to recall Mailer's "White Negro" as well). Rather, it stands for what Bellow is holding up for criticism. As Susan Glickman points out, "Sammler is shown up from the start as a posturing and self-righteous figure." At most he is a caricature of Bellow; and his voice is not that of his author.[25]

Even though *Sammler* is not a first-person narrative, for the most part the events and meditations of the story are presented through Sammler's consciousness. It is Sammler, therefore, not Bellow, who may be understood to be likening New York to Africa and its youth to monkeys. It is Sammler who does not want his daughter marrying a dark-skinned Indian and who obsesses over the black pickpocket. Sammler, who doesn't have much use for "Protestant America" either (p. 85), is, simply put, a racist. Nor is he the only Jewish racist in the book – and this, even though most of these Jewish characters (including at moments Sammler himself – p. 34) ostensibly sympathize with blacks. Angela, for example, is actively involved in Civil Rights activities (p. 11), while what interests Margotte about Sammler's black pickpocket is "his origins, his class or racial attitudes, his psychological views, his true emotions, his aesthetic, his political ideas . . . Was he a revolutionary? Would he be for black guerilla warfare?" (p. 14). Nonetheless Bruch is sexually obsessed with people of color: "they had to be youngish, plump women. Dark as a rule. Often they were Puerto Ricans . . . At F. A. O. Schwarz or in antique shops he bought wind-up monkeys who combed their hair in a mirror, who banged cymbals and danced jigs. . . . Nigger minstrels had fallen in price" (pp. 48–51). In the same vein, the Indian Dr. Lal, with whom both Shula and Sammler's niece Margotte (who is also sexually overactive) fall in love, is described by Sammler as a "bushy black little fellow" (p. 211). "What a woman wants," says the other niece, Angela, is "a Jew brain, a black cock, a Nordic beauty" (p. 55). Her statement can be read as thinking together the adoration and devaluation of blacks that everywhere in the book characterizes its Jewish characters.

This ambivalent love–hate (Roth's "yes–no") feeling of Jews for blacks is nowhere in the book rendered more completely than in relation to Sammler. Sammler, despite his comment on Lal, entertains the idea of his own cultural otherness as Asian: "himself, a Jew, no matter how Britannicized or Americanized, was also an Asian. The last time he was in Israel, and that was very recent, he had wondered how European, after all, Jews were. The crisis he witnessed there had brought out a certain deeper Orientalism" (p. 94). For him the German he shoots to death during the war is "white" (p. 112), and he identifies with Native Americans as well (p. 111).

Thus, in Sammler's view, the black pickpocket, though a "beast," is "handsome" and "striking," a "prince" (p. 14) – indeed, a "Solomon" (p. 57).

Therefore, the question to ask about *Mr. Sammler's Planet* is not why Bellow gives voice to a racist stereotype of blacks. He doesn't, at least not in his own voice. Rather, the question is why, in a book about the Holocaust and its Jewish American survivors, Bellow creates a cast of (for better and for worse) black-obsessed Jews and a protagonist/focalizer with clear racist tendencies. Bellow's book, more than almost any other novel in American literature and atypical of Bellow's other fiction, goes out of its way to acknowledge the occurrence of the Holocaust, and to penetrate to its absolute, unmitigatable, unspeakable horror. Why should Bellow want to compromise that depiction of the Holocaust by redirecting his focus away from the Holocaust and toward the American race issue, producing a racistly inclined protagonist in the process? As I have already suggested, Bellow's cast of characters speaks to the terrible psychological, ethical distortions produced by anti-Semitism and racism. Sammler's racism may be one of the consequences of his experience, as, we might extrapolate, anti-Semitism or antiwhite racism among blacks may be the consequence of theirs.

For the black pickpocket has another antagonist and double in Bellow's text, who is also an antagonist and double for Mr. Sammler himself. This is Sammler's Israeli son-in-law, Eisen. Like the pickpocket, Eisen stands for a virility lacking in the American Jewish refugee. He provides an image of Jewish power akin to the black power embodied in the pickpocket. *Mr. Sammler's Planet,* I suggest, is as much, perhaps even more, about the relationship between American Jews and Israelis as it is about American Jews and blacks. And the central black character functions for Bellow not only (or at least not directly) as a way of constructing American Jewish identity, but of portraying the Israeli identity that American Jews must also resist.

Of central importance to Bellow in this novel is the dark and unsettling question: Does surviving persecution or discrimination in any way produce morally superior human beings? Does the experience of racism or anti-Semitism, in other words, yield moral clarity and a greater capacity for human sympathy across barriers of cultural, religious, and racial difference? And what, then, about that nation of survivors, Israel, whose very claim to legitimacy and whose defense of its political and military policies (especially post-1967) depends on its survivor status? Sammler's "*experiences* were respected," we are told, because of "the war. Holocaust. Suffering"; "he, personally, was a symbol. His friends and family had made him a judge and a priest. And of what was he a symbol? . . . Was it because he had survived? . . . He had lasted" (pp. 63, 75). But survival does not transform Sammler into a nonracist. Quite the opposite.

It is not that surviving – lasting, in Bellow's view – does not matter. As Earl Rovit has pointed out, an important feature of Bellow's text is Sammler's status as "survivor" rather than as conventional hero. In so identifying the Jew, *Sammler* as a Holocaust novel participates in a more general tradition of what many critics have identified as a Jewish as opposed to a Christian mode of thinking about suffering and death – a tradition that took on special significance after the Holocaust. Western civilization, argues Terrence Des Pres in his study of the death camps, has tended to celebrate the experiences of suffering and finally of death as the quintessential path to spiritual purity and redemption. Moral knowledge, in this tradition, evolves through the experience of pain. Grace, whether in secular or religious terms, is the consequence of a death nobly engaged. Heroes are the individuals who rebel against the condition of their lives, and martyr themselves for a higher cause. Such views, which in Des Pres's understanding are specifically Christian, distort and compromise the position of the Holocaust survivor. In the context of the Holocaust, the sheer fact of survival, with some human dignity and ethical integrity left intact, must be granted its status. Such a valuation of survival has always, Des Pres insists, characterized Jewish thinking.[26]

As survivor, especially set against such flashy rebels as the pickpocket (who functions in this book as both rebel and survivor) and the Columbia University students (not to mention some of his own relatives), Sammler is the figure and voice of morality in an immoral universe. He preserves tenuous ethical distinctions. Sammler persists in the mild and moderate human attempt just to exist as a decent human being. This view of Sammler accords with a major element of Bellow's text: its emphasis on assuming responsibility for the historical past. As Judie Newman has pointed out, *Sammler,* with its focus on H. G. Wells and on the moon landing, has everything to do with fantasies of escape, with specifically American imaginings of starting history all over again from some Edenic moment before the beginning of human time: "New worlds? Fresh beginnings?" muses Sammler, and he objects: "Not such a simple matter" (p. 110).

This fantasy of the new is also a part of the black pickpocket/ primitive Africa/innate sexuality/culture of youth complex of images: America would back itself up out of history, and with its new-found innocence it would begin history anew.[27] Not only Sammler but Bellow oppose this ahistorical imagination, which seems to characterize one large impulse of the American mind. There are, for Bellow and Sammler both, no apocalypses to rebirth the world. There are only catastrophes that annihilate human beings. Bellow is here rejecting a whole trajectory of Enlightenment thought, with its emphasis on individualism and on reason as the instrument of individual morality. Even reason, in the view of this book, is too much to hope for. All there is, is the simple, pragmatic, human and humane, capacity for survival – no mean feat, set as it is against a force as powerful and consummately evil as the Holocaust.[28]

And yet, even as Bellow's *Sammler* revalues the survivor experience against its various alternatives, it also calls that experience into question. It discovers the link between the passivity of a survivor like Sammler and the militancy of a survivor like Eisen or like the pickpocket. All of them project onto others fantasies of power. They transform themselves from victims into victimizers. *Sammler,* in other words, wonders whether survivorship is not its own kind of myth, a celebration alternatively of passivity (as with Sammler) or of militancy (the black pickpocket and Eisen). Behind Bellow's thought here is the example of Nazi Germany itself. In the 1930s, Germany, like Israel or the American black community in the 1950s, was a nation of survivors. The black pickpocket, with his "masterful" expression and his "certitude" and "Lordliness" and his "authority"-affirming "penis" (pp. 42 and 46), becomes a figure of the master race.

No wonder, then, that in the final scene of the novel both Sammler and Eisen go at the black with a vengeance more befitting an attack on an SS trooper than a pickpocket. "Old Sammler with his screwy visions" responds to 1960s America as if it were 1930s Germany:

> He saw the increasing triumph of Enlightenment – Liberty, Fraternity, Equality, Adultery! Enlightenment, universal education, universal suffrage, the rights of the majority acknowledged by all governments, the rights of women, the rights of children, the rights of criminals, the unity of the different races affirmed . . . the privileges of aristocracy (without any duties) spread wide, democratized, especially the libidinous privileges, the right to be uninhibited, spontaneous, urinating, defecating, belching, couples in all positions, tripling, quadrupling . . . now all the racism . . . had broken up but the mental masses,

inheriting everything in a debased state, had formed an idea of the corrupting disease of being white and of the healing power of black. . . . Like many people who had seen the world collapse once, Mr Sammler entertained the possibility it might collapse twice. (pp. 28–29)

But the black pickpocket is no murderer, and New York City, where his crimes take place, is hardly the Germany of the Holocaust. Hurling excremental epithets and indulging in sexual promiscuity do not make the students of Columbia University fascists. Illegally performed abortions are not infanticide. And no one in New York City is rounding up, deporting, and murdering anyone, least of all the Jews. Bellow's reduction of the scene of moral turpitude suggests the inappropriateness of Sammler's Holocaust analogizing, as of Arendt's in her 1959 essay on segregation in the South. It suggests the dangerous directions that misapplied philosophical inversions can take. If the moon is not, nor ever likely to be, Mr. Sammler's planet, neither, in the 1960s, is the past world of fascist Europe. If this is the case for American Jews, it is even more true for those Jews living in Israel. In his commitment to violent action, the romantic, artistic Israeli survivor Eisen reincarnates nothing so much as the myth of Faustian rebellion and heroic self-sufficiency, which survivorship initially seems to replace.

The existence of the State of Israel, especially in its relation to the Holocaust, hovers as insistently over Bellow's novel as the Holocaust itself. "No Zionist, Mr. Sammler, and for many years little interested in Jewish affairs. Yet, from the start of the crisis [in 1967], he could not sit in New York reading the world press. If only because for the second time in twenty-five years the same people were threatened by extermination: the so-called powers letting things drift towards disaster; men armed for a massacre. And he refused to stay in Manhattan watching television" (p. 115).

Sammler's first visit to Israel, ten years earlier, to rescue his Catholic/Jewish daughter from a bad marriage, is completely different. It has nothing at all to do with feelings of Jewishness. In fact, his experience of Israel at that time is distinctly non-Jewish: Nazareth, Capernaum, the Mount of the Beatitudes, all the places associated with Jesus and the New Testament. But Jewish endangerment, paralleling the ascent of black power, forces in Sammler a significant shift of position. It is of this shift on the local landscape that Bellow is taking stern, critical notice.

As Kurt Ditmar has pointed out, Sammler and Eisen are "tragic equivalents" of each other: "Eisen sticks to the inflexible opposition of either killing or being killed, of 'in' versus 'out,' whereas Sammler's disinterestedness represents a paramount, a kind of existential 'out' meant to transcend all possible conflicts."[29] Clearly Eisen, after the 1967 war, stands for an Israeli as opposed to an American Jewish response to Jewish history and to what are perceived of as continuing threats to Jewish existence. This is a response that is deadly in the extreme, and not only to the enemies of the Jews, of which the black pickpocket forms an appropriately racialized representation. Eisen's violent stance is as much an assault against Sammler, and, by extension, against the Jewish community that Sammler represents (including, I would suggest, Bellow himself) as it is against the ostensible enemy (either the black pickpocket or the Arab nations). Sammler as American Jewish refugee is an "old" man, a "*past* person": he "lacked physical force. He knew what to do, but had no power to execute it. He had to turn to someone else – to an Eisen!" (p. 232). "Eisen" who is "mad" and "belonged in the mental hospital" is a "homocidal maniac" (p. 236).

Presented with the reality that his self-defense rests in the hands of this wife-beating, savage, mad Israeli, Sammler returns his loyalty to the American black: "How much Sammler sympathized with him – how much he would have done to prevent such atrocious blows!" (p. 236). If there is going to be violence, the text seems to suggest, better it should be directed against, rather than by, Jews. No Zionist himself, Bellow had the following to say about the establishment of the Jewish state in *To Jerusalem and Back:*

> Was it necessary for them to establish a new state in one of the world's danger zones? Nationalism, [Elie Kadoury] implied, was an evil the Jews did not need to add to their too painful history. He was saying, I think, that he regretted this, not that he blamed anyone. In going beyond his statement, the responsibility is my own. But it is difficult to apply reasonable propositions to the survivors of the Holocaust. To them it might have seemed that they had escaped from a deeper and madder spirit than the rest of us can know, a fury remote from the minds of learned historical explainers or from the "causes" that students of psychology and society normally deal in – a more wicked wickedness than most of us take into account in our hypotheses. Perhaps many of those who had gone through the horror of the death camps wanted to be together afterward. Their desire was to live together as Jews. Anyway, it is idle to

speak of alternatives. The founding of a state was inevitable. It was a desperate, naked need that sent Jewish survivors to the Middle East. They were not working out historical problems in the abstract. They had to face extinction.[30]

In the final analysis, Bellow uses the black pickpocket to make a statement to American Jews about Israeli Jews. Neither "Eisen with his art" nor "the Negro with his penis" (p. 223) provides a path for American Jewry to follow. As Sammler swings back from his allegiance to and dependence on Eisen to a renewed admiration for the princely pickpocket, we see how desperate Sammler, and by implication Bellow, are to find some way in which to act that will not require of them lavish actions of self-defense. Nonetheless, even though on the domestic scene the black pickpocket represents a danger and a threat to be opposed, he still mounts less of a threat against American Jewry than the Israeli. It is the Israeli, finally, who might well seduce his American brethren not only into danger but into a violent response to such endangerment.

For Bellow, as for many American Jews, a basic text in such criticisms of Israel is Arendt's *Eichmann in Jerusalem*. *Eichmann* serves in *Mr. Sammler's Planet* as much as a caution to the Jews as to anyone else. Bellow agrees with other intellectuals of the period that Arendt's thesis concerning the banality of evil is an insult and an affront. But he will use this critique of Arendt as much against the Jews (especially Israeli Jews) as Arendt did her original thesis:

> Murder . . . is a very old human knowledge. The best and purest human beings, from the beginning of time, have understood that life is sacred. To defy that old understanding is not banality. There was a conspiracy against the sacredness of life. . . . This woman professor's enemy is modern civilization itself. She is only using the Germans to attack the twentieth century – to denounce it in terms invented by Germans. Making use of a tragic history to promote the foolish ideas of Weimar intellectuals. (pp. 17–18)

Of this denunciation of the twentieth century, which makes use of a tragic history to promote foolish ideas (including, as Sammler makes clear, Freudianism and Marxism), Bellow accuses, equally and alongside Arendt, American youth, the black power movement, American Jewish intellectuals, and Israelis. Bellow rejects Arendt's argument concerning the banality of evil. He accepts the other part of her claim, which the majority of American Jews largely ignored: that the

State of Israel violated basic principles of justice in kidnapping Eichmann and bringing him to trial.

In Sammler's view, and Bellow's, no evil is banal. This is true in
relation to the black pickpocket, who sees the world through his
experience of racial prejudice. It is true in relation to the State of
Israel, which sees the world through the vision of the Holocaust.
Bellow stages the scene of violent confrontation between black and
Israeli in order to make this point to his American Jewish audience,
which sympathized, alternately, with the one distorted view of reality
or the other – although for the most part, whatever its sympathies,
it remained, like Sammler, finally passive on both the issues of Civil
Rights and the State of Israel, rarely acting on either of its sympathies or on any of its convictions.

It is this passivity that Bellow's novel presents as an ideal of Jewish
behavior, placing Bellow directly in the line of Jewish universalists
for whom Jewish ethics had to do with the dissolution of specifically
Jewish identity. In his own reading of *Mr. Sammler*, Andrew Furman
defends Bellow as treading a delicate balance between defense and
critique of the Jewish state.[31] But might it not seem to an Israeli Jew,
as to an African American, that such passivity as Sammler represents,
with its abandonment of religious, ethnic, cultural, and racial identity, was itself responsible, in the long history of these peoples, for
their continuing persecution; that assimilation and integration, by
granting the terms of the dominant culture's belief, promoted
rather than defied racism and anti-Semitism? Certainly, viewed from
the distance of Israel, and through the lens of black cultural critique, Bellow's Sammler, sympathetic a character as he is, seems just
that kind of Uncle Tom who has reassured the dominant culture
that it was right all along. To what degree the emergency of survival
in an embattled nation (as the emergency of Civil Rights for African
American readers of this and other texts) determines my response
to Bellow's depiction of the American Jew is not easy to decide, nor
is the question of whether group survival (to return again to Norman Podhoretz's piece on the subject) is ever worth the life of even
a single child. But the issue is no less an issue than that, and if
Bellow's novel gets recast by the implied target of its critique, is this
revision of the book not occasioned by the text's own politics of
revision?

4

Cultural Autonomy, Supersessionism, and the Jew in African American Fiction

Jews, as such, until I got to high school, were all incarcerated in the Old Testament, and their names were Abraham, Moses, Daniel, Ezekiel, and Job, and Shadrach, Meshach, and Abednego. It was bewildering to find them so many miles and centuries out of Egypt, and so far from the fiery furnace.

James Baldwin, *The Fire Next Time*[1]

In 1987, Toni Morrison published a book that quickly became a classic of contemporary American literature. Like much African American literature, especially by women, *Beloved* focuses on the African American experience independent and autonomous of the white world. White society does not by any means disappear from the text. It is not, however, a subject in its own right. Instead, as if reversing the dominant assumptions of much fiction written by whites, it hovers over the story as both context and pressure, an informing principle to be understood only through reference to black life itself.

Beloved, in other words, deals only obliquely with white people. It deals not at all with Jews or Jewish history. Yet Morrison prefaces her text with two statements that might seem to turn the book toward just this subject of the Jews. One such piece of text is her dedication to "Sixty million and more." In the American context, this dedication cannot, especially to a Jewish readership, but recall the "six million" of the Holocaust. The other textual fragment is the epigraph taken from Saint Paul's Epistle to the Romans, from which

161

Morrison harvests the title of her novel: "I will call them my people,/ which were not my people;/and her beloved,/which was not beloved."[2] This is one of the major statements in the New Testament, justifying the displacement of the Jews by Christianity. It is also a statement frequently cited in anti-Semitic contexts.

The number "sixty million and more," moreover, does not stand outside the thematics and imagery of the text. The centrality of the number is recalled and reenforced through the designation of one of book's most heroic characters as Sixo. Similarly, the citation from Paul is underscored in the book by the fact that all of the male characters in this novel except Sixo and Halle are named Paul. That the Paul who becomes Sethe's lover and, figuratively at least, Beloved's father is Paul D, may signal an even further scriptural relationship. Paul may be marked as within the messianic line of David, which eventuates, of course, in the birth of Christ and the history of Jewish–Christian relations attendant upon that event. The text from the Old Testament, which Morrison's title and major figure in *Beloved* evoke, is also recalled (at least for some Western readers) by the title and major conceit of *Song of Solomon. Beloved,* it is clear to most readers, concerns an African American exodus from slavery, paralleling the major event of the Old Testament. It also portrays the crucifixion and resurrection of a beloved savior, in parallel with the New Testament.

Given the acts of historical recovery that motivate Morrison's fiction, Morrison's dedication to "sixty million and more" and her biblical allusions, both in *Beloved* and *Song of Solomon,* serve obvious important functions. According to Morrison's own account, this "figure is the best educated guess at the number of black Africans who . . . died either as captives in Africa or on slave ships."[3] *Beloved* would remember not only slavery and its aftermath, but the horrific slaughter and death that preceded it, which American culture (both black and white) has, in the imagery of *Song of Solomon,* as we shall see, overwritten, or which, according to the concluding chapter of *Beloved,* has been willfully and violently "disremembered." Mae Henderson has explained Morrison's use of materials in *Beloved* as follows:

> Dedicating her novel *Beloved* to the "Sixty Million and more" who failed to survive the Middle Passage, Morrison sets out to give voice to the "disremembered and unaccounted for" – the women and children who left no written records. The epigraph from Romans 9:25 prefigures the writer's purpose to reclaim

this "lost tribe": . . . In her citation of a New Testament passage that repeats with little difference a passage from the Old Testament, the author not only problematizes the nature of the relationship between the past and the present, but also thematizes the importance of historical Reclamation and Repossession. As Jehovah reclaimed the Israelites after their apostasy . . . so Morrison seeks to repossess the African and slave ancestors after their historical violation. Further, Morrison reinscribes the tension between Old Testament Law and New Testament spirit. Significantly, it is the epistles of Paul . . . which announce that the doctrine of justification by deeds under the Old Dispensation of the Law is revised through justification by grace under the New Dispensation of the Spirit. Engaging the Scriptures as a kind of intertext, Morrison enacts in her novel an opposition between the Law and the Spirit, redeeming her characters from the "curse of the law" as figured in the master's discourse. In her rewriting of Scripture, Morrison ushers in an ironic new dispensation figured not by the Law of the (white) Father, but the Spirit of the (black and female) child, Beloved. Thus Morrison challenges the hegemonic status of the (primarily male) slave narratives as well as the "canonical" history embodied in the master('s) narratives in a project which seeks to make both more accountable to the "disremembered and unaccounted for."[4]

In Henderson's reading, Morrison's novel would subvert white male hegemonic power. The objective of its acts of displacement is Christian history itself. But whether Morrison's biblical texts would substitute African American for Christian rather than for Jewish history does not lessen the consequence for Jewish history, which sits at the bottom of this heap of textual displacements.

This displacement of the Jews might not be terribly troublesome were it not for the history of Jewish–Christian relations, which has attended the substitution of the new law for the old. This is the history that culminated in the very recent past, in Europe, in the Nazi Holocaust, the event that is invoked, perhaps to be overwritten, in Morrison's dedication. It is an event that, as we shall see, comes to play an explicit role in *Song of Solomon* as well.

In the context of a wide-ranging recasting of black history, Paul Gilroy, in *The Black Atlantic: Modernity and Double Consciousness,* has forcefully defended Morrison's Holocaust reference in *Beloved.* The main purpose of Gilroy's book is to resist simplistic versions of Afro-

centricism, which would posit an unbroken continuity between African culture(s) and contemporary black life. Such Afrocentricism,
according to Gilroy, denies the decisive intervention of modernism.
For Gilroy, modernism includes the slave experience and the impact
of that experience not only on black people but on Western culture
generally. His book, like several of the fictional texts he discusses,

> accepts that the modern world represents a break with the past,
> not in the sense that premodern, "traditional" Africanisms
> don't survive its institution, but because the significance and
> meaning of these survivals get irrevocably sundered from their
> origins. The history of slavery and the history of its imaginative
> recovery through expressive, vernacular cultures challenge us
> to delve into the specific dynamics of this severance.
>
> The conclusion of this book is that this ought to be done
> not in order to recover hermetically sealed and culturally ab-
> solute racial traditions that would be content forever to invoke
> the premodern as the anti-modern. It is proposed here above
> all as a means to figure the inescapability and legitimate value
> of mutation, hybridity, and intermixture en route to better the-
> ories of racism and of black political culture than those so far
> offered by cultural absolutists of various phenotypical hues.[5]

Gilroy's position is everywhere informed by a rare sensitivity to the
pains and possibilities of transnational, transcultural, and transracial
interactions. It takes into account, and powerfully (I think) recasts,
the Jewish experience alongside that of Atlantic blacks:

> In the preparation of this book I have been repeatedly drawn
> to the work of Jewish thinkers in order to find both inspiration
> and resources with which to map the ambivalent experience of
> blacks inside and outside modernity. I want to acknowledge
> these debts openly in the hope that in some small way the link
> they reveal might contribute to a better political relationship
> between Jews and blacks at some distant future point. (pp.
> 205–6)

Gilroy continues: "It is important to emphasize that any correspon-
dences that can be identified between the histories of blacks and
Jews take on a radically different significance after the Holocaust"
(p. 213).

Nonetheless, Gilroy insists, the histories of blacks and of Jews derive mutual benefit from each one's taking into account the experience of the other, and, of course, from acknowledging the entangle-

ment of the two histories that is part and parcel of their simultaneous presence on the scene of modernism. To this end, Gilroy recovers Elkins's "misguided but extremely influential attempts to import the Holocaust" into thinking about slavery, which, Gilroy points out, have been "comprehensively forgotten" (pp. 213–14).

In order to make the above statements, Gilroy takes on Stanley Crouch's criticism of Morrison's *Beloved* – that it is a Holocaust novel in blackface. According to Gilroy, Crouch places Morrison's novel

> in the shadow of [a] theory of art which is for him merely a theory of black martyrdom in which the downtrodden were canonized before their misery could be sifted for its special, moral magic. He attacks the novel as a list of atrocities rather than an explanation of "the mystery of human motive and behavior." His final, cruel charge against Morrison is that "Beloved, above all else, is a blackface holocaust novel." It is, he continues, a book that "seems to have been written in order to enter American slavery in the big-time martyr ratings contest."

Crouch, Gilroy concludes, does not consider

> the possibility that there might be something useful to be gained from setting these histories closer to each other not so as to compare them, but as precious resources from which we might learn something valuable about the way that modernity operates, about the scope and status of rational human conduct, about the claims of science, and perhaps most importantly about the ideologies of humanism with which these brutal histories can be shown to have been complicit. (p. 217)[6]

Insofar as they project an ideal of interracial, black–Jewish thinking, Gilroy's arguments are extremely appealing and persuasive. Morrison's intentions, I suspect, are, as Gilroy represents them, to move away from ideas of autonomy and continuity toward a realization of hybridity and the mutualities of cultural construction. Nonetheless, Gilroy may not be fully taking into account either the actual language of Morrison's novel or the cultural context in which this fiction is being written – especially for her Jewish readership. The line between acknowledgment or allusion, on the one hand, and, on the other, displacement or supersessionism, may not be all that sturdy.

Before I temporarily leave Morrison's novels to examine other works of African American fiction that also make recourse to Jews and Jewish history in their pursuit of a different ethnic agenda, let me just note the existence of similar problems of black–Jewish, and specifically Holocaust, reference, in two other texts. One is Alice Walker's *Temple of My Familiar*, which contains the following epigraph to one of the chapters: "Remembrance is the key to redemption. – *Inscription on a memorial to Jews who died in World War II concentration camps, Land's End, San Francisco.*" The other is Leslie Marmon Silko's *Almanac of the Dead*, which notes, "Sixty million Native Americans died between 1500 and 1600. The defiance and resistance of things European continue unabated. The Indian Wars have never ended in the Americas. Native Americans acknowledge no border; they seek nothing less than the return of all tribal lands." What is problematical about both these references is not their alluding to the Holocaust, which might of course (as in Gilroy's terms) be a constructive move toward intertextual acknowledgment. Rather, it is the coupling of these statements with other statements in the novels, which move in quite the opposite direction. Thus, a bit earlier in Walker's novel she has one of her characters remark that "when my . . . parents . . . first came to Africa they taught the gospel inherited from the Jews, who were the earliest Christians" (a highly charged statement from the Jewish perspective). She then goes on a few paragraphs later, having made the point that "all evil, like racism or sexism, is a result of sickness," to say that "the child will always, as an adult, do to someone else whatever was done to him when he was a child. It is how we, as human beings, are made. I shudder to think what Hitler's childhood was like . . . but anyone can see that the Palestinians and their children are reliving it under the Israelis today." Similarly, Silko, early in her book, records a newspaper headline having to do with the "Middle East. There is killing everywhere. Jews and Arabs."[7]

While one might not want to go as far as Stanley Crouch in calling Morrison's *Beloved* or any other work of recent African American or Native American fiction a black or Native American "holocaust novel," nonetheless one might still feel compelled to account for the impulse in these texts to rival Jewish Holocaust rhetoric. Another way of framing this is to ask the question, What does it mean that a writer, with a particular ethnic agenda, writes to a community (both national and international) of readers who have their own conflicting, even mutually exclusive, ethnic concerns? What is a writer's responsibility for the sociopolitical realm in which a text is produced? What does one do with one's anger (legitimate and illegitimate) vis-à-vis other communities? Reversing direction, what is the reader's (my own, for example) responsibility to the text, which, in pursuing its own ends, brushes against one's own? And what degree of self-skepticism does one have to bring to bear upon such comments as my own? It is by no means clear to what degree I myself tilt these texts in order to see an offense not intended or even not there.

I return to Morrison's *Song of Solomon* and *Beloved* at the end of this chapter. I discuss them again at the beginning of the next chapter, where I invoke some of the recent context of black–Jewish debate, specifically concerning the Holocaust, and I dip into another area of sensitivity for Jewish readers like myself: the American intellectual (Jewish and non-Jewish) relation to the State of Israel. I will also put the Morrison novels into conversation with several other texts, including William Styron's *Sophie's Choice* and three works by Jewish authors, namely, Philip Roth's *Ghost Writer*, Cynthia Ozick's *Shawl*, and Grace Paley's "Zagrowsky Tells." At that time, I will also deal more explicitly with my own stake in this conversation between American blacks and Jews, as I carve out the oppositional position of the expatriate American Jew, resisting and reflecting both black and Jewish constructions of identity. First, however, I want to present the internal logic of the African American response to the American Jew, as the Jew figures as both a social entity and a representative of the Judeo-Christian scriptural tradition, an Israelite rather than either a Jew or an Israeli.

"Not the words of Rosie nor the words of Marx, but the words of Jesus Christ": Chester Himes's Lonely Crusade *to an African American Faith*[8]

Because of the radically different agendas of black and Jewish writers in the United States, there are fewer texts by African American authors that deal with Jewish materials than vice versa. As I have already suggested, the dominant trajectory of Jewish American writing, from its earliest texts through the contemporary period, has been toward assimilation into American culture. It has been the intention of the writers, almost in imitation of the founding Puritans, to discover in the United States all the promised land there is, for themselves and others. There may even be some measure of glee in the discovery by Jews that the American national myth is so "Jewish," as when Mary Antin titles her autobiography *The Promised Land*. Nonetheless, Jewish writing has tended less toward usurping the American myth, or Judaizing it, than finding its place in it.

Although African American writing is also linked to this biblical trope of the promised land, nonetheless from Zora Neale Hurston and Richard Wright (most notably in a text like *Uncle Tom's Children*) the effort of the tradition has been to project and claim a cultural uniqueness, which simultaneously underscores the indebtedness of the larger culture to its folk origins in the black experience of enslavement and exodus. In other words, if blacks and Jews are agreed with each other and with a dominant tradition within American writing generally that the United States is an Israel of sorts, for Jews this Israel is universalist and pluralistic, whereas for black writers (at least from Du Bois onward) it either originates in or is fundamentally formed by the black experience of enslavement. Black writers (especially black women writers) would have white America remember, and acknowledge, that however America has served (as in Emma Lazarus's poetry) as a promised land for those who reached it from other shores, within America itself the drama of emancipation was enacted not by its immigrant populations but by its black citizens. For the black writer, therefore, representing the plurality of the United States, and constructing black identity through an identification with that plurality, is directly contrary to the cultural work that black fiction must perform.

As with Jewish American fiction, so with African American writing there are texts that fall outside my primary concerns, even though they are interesting to consider in relation to issues of interethnic cultural construction. I am not, for example, going to discuss Zora Neale Hurston's *Moses Man of the Mountain* (1939). *Moses* seems to me less a head-on collision with contemporary Jewish culture than a fairly traditional "midrash" or commentary (albeit an African American and Christian one) on a Jewish text. Sometimes Jews are not Jews but Israelites, a no longer "extant" people, as Alice Walker so succinctly puts it in *Meridian* (1976), a text that actually will concern me because of how it combines both theological and sociological concerns.[9] Although Hurston may have been turned toward her narrative by her extensive contact with Jewish anthropologists like Franz Boas and Melville Herskovits, nonetheless *Moses Man of the Mountain* has little to do, directly at least, with American Jews or Jewish history.

Nor am I concerned with the Jewish lawyer in Richard Wright's *Native Son* (1940), the Jewish female activist in Ralph Ellison's *Invisible Man* (1950), the interfaith couple in Lorraine Hansberry's *The Sign in Sidney Brustein's Window* (1964), or the numerous African and Jewish American interactions in Ishmael Reed's *Reckless Eyeballing* (1986). In these texts the Jewish characters function as vivid evidences of Jewish–black political and social engagement. Therefore, they also constitute vehicles for the exploration of self-identity. But the Wright, Ellison, Hansberry, and Reed narratives do not lift Jewish–black relations off the social axis into the realm of myth and psychohistory.

Chester Himes's *Lonely Crusade* (1947) evolves in another direction. It continues the task, begun in the writings of Du Bois, toward the writing of a black scripture. This black scripture has as its ostensible function the displacement of the texts of white Christianity, which have disadvantaged and disenfranchised black people, religiously and culturally as well as politically. In the process of producing a new African American faith, complete with its own testament and savior, it cannot escape confrontation with Jewish scripture as well. In fact, in order to prevent the rewriting of scripture from seeming like a return to an older faith, the Judaic text may have to be made specifically to give way, as once it had been made to yield by Christianity, to the new law. This is the same textual logic we have begun to glimpse in Toni Morrison's two novels, and which informs Alice Walker's *Meridian* as well.

Like Jo Sinclair's *The Changelings* and Lore Segal's *Her First American*, Himes's *Lonely Crusade* directly confronts black anti-Semitism and Jewish racism. It does so within the specific context of Communist and labor unionizing in the 1940s, making the book a direct descendant of Wright's *Native Son*. Like Wright, Himes is concerned with black violence as it is provoked by the formal institutions of racism. More important, Himes (again like Wright) is interested in racism's more casual, less easily specified manifestations, even among white liberals, Communists, and labor activists. But more like Ellison than Wright, Himes is primarily interested in exploring black identity, both cultural and personal. He aims to recoup an African Americanism that white racism has deformed but not destroyed, and that can emerge triumphant not only in relation to African Americans but in relation to America itself.

In many ways, *Lonely Crusade* is a very modern book dealing with issues not only of race but of gender. Even more than Ellison, Himes understands the necessity for highlighting African American cultural and political uniqueness, and the need this produces, at least temporarily, to sever the relationship between black and white culture in the United States. Central to Himes's depiction of black identity is the figure of the Jew. The Jew does not, however, figure, as in Wright's or Ellison's novels, either as one more representative of white culture or, as in his own earlier *If He Hollers Let Him Go* (1945), as another of its many victims. In *Lonely Crusade* a very powerful, humane, and inspiring Jewish character plays a major role in the development of Himes's protagonist and thus in the novel's construction of black cultural identity. In the final analysis, this Jew will have to be pushed aside for the novel to achieve its specifically African American purposes. But the hero will have to proceed through the Jew, as through women, on his way to realizing both his humanity and his manhood.

Toward the middle of *Lonely Crusade,* Lee Gordon penetrates to the question that, in Himes's view, must be asked and answered in order for his protagonist to achieve both personal identity and human integrity: "what did he, Lee Gordon, want of Lee Gordon?" The question is very American, having to do with the self as the center of social integration and societal commitment. And, in an equally American fashion, the asking of the question proceeds through a gallery of other racially, religiously, and sexually dissimilar individuals, all of whom contribute (some negatively, some positively) to the asking of the question and to the consolidation of self that the asking produces.

At the center of the passage, as at the center of the novel, is the figure of the Jew:

> What did he, Lee Gordon, have that so many people wanted? he asked himself. And why did they all deny him the one small thing he needed? What was happening in this world that he did not seem to know?
>
> What was the union's angle? Did they really need him to organize the plant? or was his job just another form of Negro charity?
>
> And why would Foster go to the trouble of making a job for him? Surely Foster did not think that by so doing he could hurt the union. But what else could one lone, dark Negro boy, haunted by fears and weakened by uncertainties, mean to a man as Foster?
>
> Rosie? What did Rosie want of him? – giving him that long lecture on the psychology of the Jew. What did Rosie expect him to do about the Jew's oppression?
>
> And Jackie [his white Communist mistress]? It tortured him to think of her. . . . For a moment he hoped wistfully that she really liked him more than just sexually – liked him as a person. No one but his wife had ever truly liked him, and she didn't like him anymore.

And so at last his thoughts came back to where they always
ended and began – his wife. (pp. 197–98; cf. p. 84)

In this passage Himes presents a veritable panoply of American
types and options, all of which test the protagonist, and none of
which represents a final repository of value and meaning. The Jew
may be one of the most central components of Lee Gordon's recon-
figuration, but he is hardly the only factor. And like all of the other
characters and institutions, he represents both positive and negative
aspects. Both the Communist Party and the union, for example, are
exploitative and, in varying degrees, racist and anti-Semitic. Nonetheless, both are aimed at important goals, the significance of which
(as Lee discovers at the end) cannot be denied. Similarly, Foster,
the white capitalist and the most unequivocally evil of the characters,
is a scoundrel, a tyrant, and a bigot. But he does, in odd and inadvertent ways having to do with the very commitment to Americanism
that makes him anti-union and anticommunist, reach out to blacks
and even contribute to black progress.

Furthermore, Foster is clearly balanced, on the black labor side
of things, by the activist Luther McGregor. Luther clearly promotes
the interests of the union. But he is as self-serving and dishonest as
Foster and, finally, he is a murderer as well. Similarly, Lee's white
mistress, Jackie, is neither simply hero or victim. Jackie initially se-
duces Lee in order to control him for the party. Eventually, however,
she comes to love him, only to betray him out of her own despera-
tion and fear and an inherent racism she simply cannot shake. Nor
is Lee Gordon himself, or his wife, Ruth, a simple emblem of black
nobility. Both are highly compromised and compromising characters who, try as they might, cannot function effectively either in the
world at large or in their relationship to each other.

As this cast of characters suggests, a major thrust of Himes's novel
is toward exposing the ways in which the conditions of racism pro-
hibit both its victims and its perpetrators from escaping the ugly,
manipulative web of racial hatred (a feature of the text reminiscent
of Trilling's "The Other Margaret"). No character in the book can
function outside the racist condition, which for some of the book's
characters is an active position, but for most is nothing more than a
reflex. There is "no malice in the voice" that refers to "niggertown,"
"only forgetfulness of a Negro's presence" (p. 21). Similarly, it is
accorded "a natural mistake" by the "city administration" when a
black man is "mistaken for a burglar by policemen and shot to
death" (pp. 34–35). No one in the world of Himes's text is free to

act except as the conditions of racism dictate, unless at the risk of
death.

Death is exactly the risk Lee Gordon takes in the final moment of
the text, when he grabs the union banner and, "holding it high
above his head, began marching down the street" with the white
police officer's gun "leveling down on him" (p. 398). Whether that
gun goes off, the text does not say. What we do know, however, is
that, wanted for murder, Lee has put himself in the hands of the
authorities, who, on more than one count, want to see him dead.

The consequence of his action is that, at the cost of his life, Lee
achieves his freedom. He achieves as well considerable purpose for
the union and for his people. This makes Lee something of a martyr,
indeed a Christ. The union banner is his cross, and the "human
race" (blacks, whites, Jews, and Mexicans, all of whom represent the
oppressed of Himes's novel) is the object of his "crusade" (p. 386).
"Without warning, song broke from his lips, that great inspirational
battle hymn of the Christians . . . 'Oh when the saints . . . go marching onnnnn . . . Lord I want to beeeee in that numbahhhhh.' . . .
[W]hat kept ringing in Lee Gordon's mind like some forgotten liberty bell was not the words of Rosie nor the words of Marx, but the
words of Jesus Christ: 'Blessed are the meek, for they shall inherit
the earth' " (pp. 384, 394).

Lonely Crusade, in other words, is a book of religious conversion.
It asserts black cultural identity as nothing less than religious, salvational. It is capable of redeeming not only the nation (both black
and white) but Christianity itself. Indeed, like other books in the
African American canon (including such different texts as James
Baldwin's *Fire Next Time,* David Bradley's *Chaneysville Incident,* and
Toni Morrison's *Beloved*), *Lonely Crusade* can be read as a last final
book of scripture, superseding the religious tradition that precedes
it. "These were the words that Moses heard," Lee realizes as his
fellow blacks oppose his union activism. But Lee will not be dis-
suaded from leading his people into a new promised land (p. 366).
In this structure of supersessionism, and the construction of the
African American as a new Christ, with the picket sign his cross, the
American Jewish Communist, in the figure of the extremely sympathetic Rosie – Abe Rosenberg, the patriarchal Abraham – has a very
particular role to play. Just as Lee must come through communism
on his way to laborism and a commitment to the union, so he must
go through the Jew on his way to becoming an African American
Christian Moses and a messiah. And just as Lee must also leave com-

munism behind, so he must also exceed the Jew and what he represents.

To some degree, Himes's employment of Jews and Jewish materials in *Lonely Crusade* is fairly conventional. As in *If He Hollers,* many of the references do no more than attest to the uneasy multiethnic texture of America. In *If He Hollers,* Jews or references to Jews make a few isolated appearances, mostly as indices of the pervasiveness and multivariousness of American racism. They constitute the punchline of a racist joke, the object of the protagonist's own anti-Semitism, a potential figure of identification for blacks.[10] In *Lonely Crusade* these references achieve a density verging on an obsession. References to Jews are part of a virtual mantra, as the protagonist attempts to break through the suffocating atmosphere of American racism by giving voice both to its victims and to its perpetrators: "Nigger, white man, gentile, Jew . . . Niggers alongside nigger-haters. Jews bucking rivets for Jew-baiters. Native daughters lunching with Orientals" (pp. 130–31; cf. p. 96).

As in Sinclair's *Changelings* or Baldwin's essays, in *Lonely Crusade* the interest in blacks and Jews is dictated in part by the fact that these two groups share social and economic areas, where they compete for space, as in the WPA (p. 40) or in the white neighborhood where Lee and Ruth find accommodations early in their marriage: "cheap Jewish markets nearby" and the warning from gentile neighbors that "the Jewish people down below were trying to get the white people to drive them from the neighborhood" (pp. 124–125). In this context, Lee's anti-Semitism (pp. 157–58), while hardly condoned by the text, is nonetheless made comprehensible. Blacks expect more of Jews, Lee tells Rosie, anticipating Baldwin's similar comments; therefore, they are all the more bitter when they feel they are receiving less than they would from the gentile majority (pp. 156–57).

Rosie's rejoinders to Lee constitute an extremely powerful, nuanced defense of Jewish behavior and of black misperceptions and expectations. Importantly, they secure Himes's text from any charges of complicity in the protagonist's anti-Semitic views. *Lonely Crusade,* however, is an African American, not a Jewish or even a multiethnic, novel. Therefore, Himes is also very clear that his primary concern is with Jewish misperceptions of the black experience and not the other way around. "You're lucky you're not a Jew," says one of the Jewish characters in *If He Hollers* to the defeated and abused black protagonist (p. 160). In *Lonely Crusade,* Himes picks up

this thread of Jewish self-pity and misunderstanding with a vengeance, and answers it. "You, of all people, should know," Rosie says
to Lee, what "freedom" is and isn't in the United States (p. 88);
"Another Jew joined the conversation. 'Russia must be saved!'/'For
who? You Jews?' Lee asked harshly./'You a Negro and you say that?'
'I say that because I am a Negro. Russia is no haven for me. Not
even an ideological defense.'/'How is it any more an ideological
defense to the Jew than to you? You are human too, aren't you?'
'Not in this country. And this is where I have to live and die. I don't
see any collection being taken up to fight the Negro problem.' "
"There's a great deal of anti-Semitism going on right now too," says
another of the Jewish characters, to which Lee responds, "Well – yes.
How many Jews were there lynched in America last year?" (pp. 89–
90). The answer, they all agree, is none.

In the pattern of black–Jewish relations that the book constructs,
the Jew functions as both counterpart to black victimization and, far
more important for Himes's purposes, a survivor of such oppression,
who may either help blacks or contribute (either willingly or inadvertently) to their further victimization. Nonetheless, Jewish suffering is elsewhere. It is *not* American and therefore does not hold a
central position within the *American* cultural equation. And for this
reason, while Jews may imagine themselves helpful to blacks, and
some of them may actually be helpful to blacks, nonetheless their
power and position within the American Communist Party has to be,
from the black perspective, suspect.

We are barely into the story when we meet "Benny Stone . . . a
short, curly-haired Jew with sharp, dark eyes, who was acting financial secretary of the local. Benny's effusive greeting brought a recurrence of the old troubling question: On what side did the Jew actually play?" (p. 19). This question concerning Jews in positions of
power (specifically, financial power) takes on even more powerful
dimensions in relation to "Jewish Communists" (pp. 47, 121), such
as the self-hating, racist (mannish and one-armed) Maud Himmelstein. Himmelstein is supremely jealous of the WASP Jackie (pp.
244–46), and like the far more sympathetic, wholly human and affecting, and yet also (from the black protagonist's point of view)
"grotesque" Rosie (p. 383), she is humanly distorted.

It is important to Rosie's function as the text's most powerful
proponent of Marxism, and as a foil to Lee, that he speaks before
he is actually introduced into the narrative. Despite his powerful
humaneness, Rosie is more the embodiment of an ideology than a
fully fleshed human being. Lee has something intellectual, aca-

demic, to learn from Rosie, even though the black protagonist will eventually have to get beyond this knowledge to a more spiritual plane that will return him to a personal, private Christian and American faith. What Rosie has to teach him, both "as a Communist . . . and also as a Jew" (p. 155), has to do with the hard truth of historical necessity: the political and economic old law that Himes's African Americanism will transform at the end of the novel. This truth of historical necessity is, as Lee himself knows, in part theoretical Marxism. "Freedom," Lee quotes Marx early in the text, is the "appreciation of necessity" (p. 88). It is also, he comes to understand later, a part of Jewish experience as well, the training that Jews, unlike other Americans, receive in what Rosie calls "reality" (p. 379).

Rosie is the novel's consummate Marxist, so much above political intrigue, beyond both parties and individuals, that even when he is expelled from the party at the end of the novel he continues to articulate Marxist theory. "Marx," he knows, "did not establish the truth of materialism, no more than did we . . . He merely employed the dialectical conception of it to demonstrate the cycle of capitalism" (p. 86). Rosie's objective is to separate the truth of Marxism (which is dialectical materialism) from Marx himself, in other words, from the Communist Party and from religion as well, including the religion of Marxism. "The peasants in Russia," Lee argues, "have just swapped the Greek Orthodox faith for the Communist faith," with which Rosie agrees: "To be sure . . . That only illustrates the truth of dialectical materialism" (p. 87).

The essence of the Jewish experience, as Rosie explains it to Lee, and the reason for the Jews' success in America, is their similarly embracing the law of necessity, whether within the political context of communism or in their simple assimilation into American society. The Jew, as Rosie represents him (or her) is less a person than an idea, a set of attitudes, a moral configuration. But it is in the move from religious faith and personal identity into dialectical materialism that, from Himes's point of view, the Jews get themselves doubly into trouble. "Jews think in terms of self-preservation," Rosie tells Lee, by way of defending them against Lee's anti-Semitism:

> Most of their manifestations of both prejudice and progressiveness are directed toward that end. The Jew has been oppressed, not only today, but for nineteen hundred years; he has been oppressed in practically every nation where he has wandered, in every historical era through which he has passed. The fact that he has survived is not an accident. The Jew has survived by

developing habits of survival. He bears the stamp of his oppression – just as the Negro bears the stamp of his oppression. If
this is what you dislike in the Jew, you must also dislike it in
yourself.

To which Lee replies, "I do" (p. 160).

From Rosie's perspective, Jewish oppression and self-interest, like
black oppression and self-interest, will eventually serve the needs of
revolution. While this excuses neither Jewish nor black behavior, it
does render that behavior functional in terms of larger aims outside
the control of any single human being. But this view of historical
necessity, devaluing human agency, produces a mechanistic rather
than a spiritual or divine view of human beings:

> For out of the people's oppression has come every new way of
> life. . . . "It is not the consciousness of men that determines
> their being, but, on the contrary, their social being that deter-
> mines their consciousness." This is the source of most of our
> Western culture, civilization, religion, ethics; the source of
> American democracy, Russian socialism. The Mosaic laws came
> out of a people who had been enslaved; Christianity was the
> haven for the Jewish forgotten man when he was being perse-
> cuted by the Rabbis and the Caesars; democracy grew from
> colonial subjugation; Marxism out of industrial exploitation – .

"Therefore out of Negro oppression – " Lee interrupts. "Might come
Communism to America," Rosie answers (p. 160).

But Himes's aims are not Rosie's, and like Christianity's superseding Judaism through the new law of love over the law of justice, so
Lee will, through the experience of black oppression, deliver to
America not a mechanical, antihumanistic and antitheological communism, but a divinely humane black Christianity. In this process
Rosie, the Jewish communist, will be his "savior," a "minister," working "to save [his] immortal soul" (pp. 376, 383). This will mean for
Lee discovering himself as a "man" and a "Negro." "You think being
a Negro is important?" Lee asks Rosie, to which Rosie replies: "To
me? I do not mean to me. I mean to you, because you are a Negro
just as I am a Jew, and being what you are is as important to you as
being what I am is important to me" (p. 376). If for Rosie being a
Jew means essentially dissolving his religious or ethnic identity into
his political cause, for Lee being an African American means realizing himself, through his lonely crusade for his people, as an individ-

ual black man, solely responsible for his own fate and in this way for the destiny of his race:

> And now at last this brought him face to face with himself in the loneliness of the night. And he knew beyond all doubt that he could not excuse his predicament on grounds of race. This time he alone was to blame – Lee Gordon, a human being, one of the cheap, weak people of the world.
>
> Being a Negro was a cause – yes. . . . But it was never a justification – never! . . . Because being a Negro was, first of all, a fact. A Negro is a Negro, as a pine tree is a pine tree and a bulldog is a bulldog – A Negro is a Negro as he is an American – because he was born a Negro. He had no cause for apology or shame. (p. 361)

Lee's essentialism recoups and reverses the essentialism expressed earlier in the novel. In this essentialism blacks emerge as inferior, as in the following assessment of blacks, oddly invoking another Jewish intellectual, who had an extensive relationship with Richard Wright: "As Gertrude Stein might say a nigger is a nigger is a nigger was a nigger and can see nothing in life to indicate that he will not always be a nigger" (pp. 55–56).

Like many American writers, Himes is a self-reliant (p. 365) Emersonian, resisting conformity to any social movement, including unionism and the Communist Party. Therefore, throughout the novel Lee's struggle is represented as having to do primarily not with his commitment to social causes, but with his manhood, where "manhood" is not just a careless lack of attentiveness on Himes's part to the gender specificity of the term. In his pursuit of self, Lee proceeds not so much through violence against white people (although he does, like his predecessor in *If He Hollers,* flare up now and again) but through the abuse, first of his wife Ruth and then of his white mistress, Jackie. In tandem with insights of Zora Neale Hurston and anticipating the direction of much contemporary African American women's fiction, *Lonely Crusade* focuses a powerfully critical lens on the black male and his relationship to the black woman. The novel understands all too well that "a man had to stand on somebody, because this was the way it was" (p. 143). The nearest person on which the black man might stand was his own wife.

This relationship between male and female is brought into clearer focus by two other characters in the book. If Rosie is one foil by which we come to know and evaluate Lee, Lester McKinley and

Luther McGregor are two black characters who serve similar purposes. Both embody deep hatred and bitterness; both simmer on
the point of explosion; and both have white wives, who manifest the
displacement onto sexuality of the desire to destroy white people
and achieve masculine identity. For Lester, we are told,

> race had come to be within him not a designation of a people,
> but a real and live emotion, stronger than love or hate or fear,
> containing the compulsion for self-identity so urgent at times
> he felt that nothing less than murder would create the accep-
> tance of his humanity in this living world. . . . [T]o overcome
> the fixation of racial inferiority, McKinley must possess a white
> woman. He must marry her and have children by her – this to
> overcome the psychosis of race. Within the society where he
> lived, he might never overcome class. So he must marry a white
> peasant girl because he was of peasant stock himself. . . . Mc-
> Kinley had married Sylvia, a second-generation Russian Jew
> from New York's lower East Side. (p. 70)

McKinley, plotting the murder of Mr. Foster, is "insane." McGregor,
who actually succeeds in killing a white policeman, is similarly crazy.
He is a murderer who is himself killed in the process of trying to
escape. Lee, who incorporates aspects of both of these characters,
releases himself from their cycle of violence by severing his relationship to the white woman, and then rendering himself the object
rather than the perpetrator of racial violence. "You are a Negro of
revolutionary potential," Rosie tells Lee, to which Lee responds,
"frankly," "as one individual Negro afraid of being framed for a
murder rap," "my potential points more toward execution than revolution" (pp. 381–83).

The instruments of his recovery from the Lester/Luther position
are therefore both his black wife, Ruth, and his Jewish friend, Rosie,
who thus double each other even as they double and reflect aspects
of Lee himself. Indeed, Himes's Jewish Communist is not called
"Rosie" for nothing: like Ruth, Rosie, who nurses Lee back to health
and who, throughout, tries to protect him, is feminized alter ego, a
part of himself that Lee must learn to accept if he is to produce a
masculinity founded not on violence (against either white people or
women) but on love. Lee realizes about himself that

> he was a man in flesh and blood and bone, in brain and heart
> and senses, but in the indefinable essence of manhood there

was something missing. Something in the hope that has kept man struggling through all history for a better world; in the faith of man on which were built all civilizations; in the charity by which man sought an understanding; in the love from which man has drawn man's humanity to man; in the self-reliance, honesty, integrity, and honor that have always kept man above the beast; in the convictions that are the measure of a man; and – most of all – in the courage by which men die for these convictions. (p. 365)

Lee, in other words, takes on the Christian doctrine of love, which can be thought to characterize Christ's feminine aspect. When, next morning, Lee awakens in a room "filled with sunrise" (p. 384), not only the "battle hymn of the Christians" breaks forth from the lips of this new Moses but "ringing in his mind" are the words of Christ: "Blessed are the meek, for they shall inherit the earth" (p. 366).

Both Ruth and Rosie nurture and empower Lee. However, like Emerson shunning father and mother and wife and brother, Lee must leave both of them behind when his genius calls. In the final scene, Himes positions Rosie and Ruth in the crowd observing the union strikers, begging Lee not to risk his life. But Lee will have to do just this in order to realize not the large purposes either of the union or of his people, but his own independent selfhood, on which the success both of the union and of blacks in America ultimately depends. Rosie enables Lee to accept his death. But that death, in which Lee, taking his life into his own hands, transforms execution into crucifixion, is a place Lee knows he must travel to alone. Lee is Emersonian crusader, securing an American Jerusalem for black Christendom.

In Medius Dies: *Alice Walker's* Meridian *as African American Scripture*

"Indian and black"; "the black and the poor, the Indian, and now all those illegal immigrants from the West Indies"; "the poor and the black" (pp. 185, 189, 201) – this litany of victims produces the refrain of Alice Walker's *Meridian,* as the novel constructs its vision of nothing less than a new human world. Like all of Walker's fiction, and in keeping with the dominant mode of most contemporary African American fiction by women, *Meridian* is essentially about black people. In particular it is about black women, who are, in Walker's

world, the double bearers of the cross of racism and sexism. Nonetheless the two major characters aside from Meridian are a black
man and a Jewish woman, Truman Held and Lynne Rabinowitz.

Both characters are (in different ways) in love with Meridian. But,
they are the ones who marry, become estranged from each other,
and have a child who becomes the victim of interracial violence in
New York City. In some ways, *Meridian* is nothing less than an allegory of the Civil Rights movement and the subsequent turn toward
violent protest. Clearing away both white Northern (and Jewish) ideals, as embodied in Lynne, and black male activism represented by
Truman, and sacrificing the product of their union, the novel produces in Meridian a black female Christ. Meridian is capable both
of leading her own people to salvation and of providing a model of
Christianity to the white world as well – including the world of white
Jews, as we shall see.

To understand the role of the Jewish Lynne Rabinowitz in Walker's novel, one needs first to isolate the features of its revision of
Christian faith. The novel's climactic moment occurs when Meridian
returns to the church. At first the church, and the faith it represents,
seem to Meridian "unchanged" (p. 193). But Meridian is quickly
disabused of this illusion, when "a large photograph of a slain martyr
in the Civil Rights struggle" is brought from behind the altar. Both
the words and the melody of the church, Meridian suddenly understands, have undergone a profound transformation:

> The minister . . . spoke in a voice so dramatically like that of
> Martin Luther King's that at first Meridian thought his inten-
> tion was to dupe or to mock. . . . [S]he began . . . to listen. Da-
> vid and Goliath were briefly mentioned, to illustrate a point.
> Then the preacher launched into an attack on President Nixon
> . . . He looked down on the young men in the audience and
> forbade them to participate in the Vietnam war. . . . God was
> not mentioned, except as a reference. (pp. 195–96)

At the center of this new African Americanist Christianity is not
the divine savior but the "martyred son" of one of the congregants.
This son, "Strong, beloved, knowing through his father's eyes his
own great value, he had set out to change the ways of the world his
father feared. And they had murdered him" (pp. 196–97). Like
Christ, "beloved" and a "jewel" (p. 197), the young man has his
transfigured iconographic counterpart in the "stained-glass" representation, not "of the traditional pale Christ with stray lamb" but,
rather, of "a tall, broad-shouldered black man," entitled "B. B., With

Sword" (pp. 198–99). " 'Let the martial songs be written,' [Meridian finds] herself quoting Margaret Walker . . . 'let the dirges disappear!' " (p. 195). The church militant has replaced the traditional meekness of the lamb. And this transformed church finally produces in Meridian a commitment to what she has heretofore resisted: militancy, even violence. "How, she wondered, could she show her love for someone who was already dead?"

> The people in the church were saying to the red-eyed man that his son had not died for nothing, and that if his son should come again they would protect his life with their own. . . .
>
> In comprehending this, there was in Meridian's chest a breaking as if a tight string binding her lungs had given way, allowing her to breathe freely. For she understood, finally, that the respect she owed her life was to continue, against whatever obstacles, to live it, and not to give up any particle of it without a fight to the death, preferably *not* her own. . . . Under a large tree beside the road . . . she made a promise to the red-eyed man herself: that yes, indeed she *would* kill, before she allowed anyone to murder his son again. (pp. 199–200)

Through her love for the already dead son, who just might come again, Meridian, in a conventional conversion pattern, takes on the imperatives of the church. In the transfigured black church this means as well assuming the role of Christian soldier or crusader, who will kill before the redeemer is himself again murdered.

But this is not the final position at which Meridian arrives. Not accidentally, Meridian's revelation comes to her by a large tree on the roadside. The direction of Meridian's rebirth is toward life, not death. Therefore, Meridian is not simply black Christ but black female Christ, much like Toni Morrison's Pilate in *Song of Solomon,* as we shall see. In her progress toward a militant Christlikeness, Meridian has to move through and beyond the passivity of the church, which is represented largely by her own mother. She also has to outgrow the desire for self-abusive martyrdom that she, in resisting her mother's position, initially embodies. But then she must recoup these female positions in order for a truly female Christian form, which transcends violence, to emerge.

"Her mother's life," we are told, "was a sacrifice. A blind, enduring, stumbling . . . through life. She did not appear to understand much beyond what happened in her own family, in the neighborhood and in her church" (p. 77). Pouring all of her disappointment and frustration into religious observance, Mrs. Hill produces in her

daughter not faith but "guilt" (pp. 49–51) and a "longing for forgiveness" (97). These manifest themselves in Meridian's desire (reminiscent of her mother) for self-destruction:

> Meridian found, when she was not preoccupied with the
> Movement, that her thoughts turned with regularity and inten-
> sity to her mother, on whose account she endured wave after
> wave of an almost primeval guilt. . . .
>
> Meridian felt as if her body, growing frailer every day under
> the stress of her daily life, stood in the way of a reconciliation
> between her mother and that part of her own soul her mother
> could, perhaps, love. She valued her body less, attended to it
> less, because she hated its obstruction.
>
> Only during a crisis could she forget. While other students
> dreaded confrontation with police she welcomed it, and was
> capable of an inner gaiety, a sense of freedom, as she saw the
> clubs slashing down on her from above. Only once was she
> beaten into unconsciousness, and it was not the damage done
> to her body that she remembered when she woke up, but her
> feeling of yearning, of heartsick longing for forgiveness, as she
> saw the bright lights explode behind the red blood that cur-
> tained her face, and her feeling of hope as the harsh light of
> consciousness began to fade. (pp. 96–97)

Walker's depiction of Meridian's masochism and suicidal longings, specifically in the attenuation of her body (she suffers both
from paralysis and an inability to eat), strongly evokes archetypical
portraits of the Christian martyr, especially, as Caroline Walker
Bynum points out, the female martyr. This is the martyr who would
replicate in the barely living flesh the emaciated body of Christ.[11]
"Why not go all out . . . and put rocks in your shoes?" Truman aptly
asks her (p. 192). In this context, Meridian's abandonment of her
child also functions as a recognizable moment in the progress of the
saint, when (as Emerson paraphrased Christ) one leaves family behind in order to follow one's genius.

But if the object of traditional Christian suffering is Christ, as for
Christ it is God the Father, for Meridian (in the transposed gender
terms of the story) it is her mother. For Meridian, as female Christ-
child, the parent for whom one must make oneself available as sacrificial victim is the mother, not the father. Indeed, in biographical
terms, Meridian's father represents no obstacle to her career as redeemer. Like Christ's mother, so Meridian's father, with his attachment to the land and his relationship to the Native Americans, is the

body through which the savior moves on her way toward the fulfillment of her mission. In further keeping with the gender transloca-
tion of the female paradigm that Walker is producing, the course
the female savior must chart is away from crucifixion and toward a
regeneration more like procreation than like death – although Meridian (divine rather than merely mortal figure that she is) will not
herself go on to assume a reproductive role. It is not incidental to
Walker's purposes that the chapter recording Meridian's conversion
back to Christianity is named after Lynne and Truman's murdered,
martyred daughter, Camara.

In keeping with this different religious emphasis, the symbol of
the new African Americanism the novel is evolving is not the dead
wooden cross but the living Sojourner tree. The Sojourner is "the
largest magnolia tree in the country." Its profound flourishing is
attributable, according to the story, to what is buried at its roots: the
tongue of a slave woman hideously rendered silent by her master for
repeating the (literally) deadly folk legends of her native Africa. This
tree provides the center for the women at Saxon College for the
expression of their joys and griefs and spiritual awakenings. Early in
the novel the women of Saxon cut down the tree in a fit of female
self-punishment much like Meridian's (p. 48), even though, in the
specific instance of the tree, Meridian begs that it not be sacrificed.
By the end of the story, however, the tree, in almost magical sympathy with Meridian, begins to blossom again (p. 217).

Not accidentally for the supersessionist revision that Walker's text
performs, Meridian's mother's Christianity is still tightly tied to the
Old Testament and to the Israelites. Meridian's mother, we are told,
"did not learn very much beyond a rudimentary knowledge of the
birth and crucifixion of Christ . . . , and of the miracle of Ezekiel's
wheel . . . , and of the Exodus, under the command of Moses, of the
children of Israel (a race, unfortunately, no longer extant)" (p. 78).
And this brings into view the role of the Jewish female activist in the
text's religious economy.

It is clear what function the black male Civil Rights activist plays
in Walker's text. Truman Held is no abuser of women, like some of
Walker's male characters. Nonetheless he is dismissive, even con-
temptuous, of women. And like other of Walker's male protagonists
he has something to learn, not only about women but about humanity itself. He can only learn this through a woman. It is less
clear what Lynne is doing in this text. Yet her role is as critical as
Truman's.

In incorporating the white Jewish activist, Walker is to some extent being merely historically accurate, like Wright, Ellison, and Himes in relation to their depictions of Jewish involvement in the American Communist Party and their special investment in black rights. As the text itself recalls in its reference to the three Civil Rights workers, two Jewish and one black (Cheney, Goodman, and Schwerner), who were murdered in Neshoba County, Mississippi (p. 130), Jews were heavily involved in the Civil Rights movement in the 1950s and early 1960s. Lynne, whose Jewishness, in the first instance, is indicated only by her name (p. 101), enters the story as one of several white female exchange students. In this grouping, Lynne functions less as a Jew than as a conveyer of Northern politics and philosophy. She is also the vehicle for exploring black male desire for white women (pp. 106–10). Truman, with whom Meridian herself is in love, sleeps with all of the white exchange students, not only with Lynne. And finally Lynne is raped by one of Truman's friends, not because she is a Jew but because she is "guilty of whiteness" (p. 133).

But if Lynne's Jewishness is a part of her whiteness, it nonetheless also functions separate from that whiteness. Again, Walker's purposes may be primarily historical: to expose Jewish alongside general white bigotry. Lynne's family disowns her and pronounces her dead when she takes up with Truman. She is treated with angry contempt by the Jewish owners of the Southern deli where she and Truman shop. Just as there were Jewish Civil Rights activists, Walker would have us understand, so there were Jewish racists, whether such racism represented something innate to Judaism (as seems to be the case with Lynne's family) or whether (as with the deli owners) it reflected a peculiar and finally self-destructive desire to assimilate into white American culture:

> [T]hey were transplanted, as they had always been, to a place where they fit like extra toes on a foot. Where they were trusted by no one, exploited, when possible, by anyone with political ambitions. Where they lived in a delicatessen, making money hand over fist because they could think of nothing more exciting to do with their lives. Making money to buy houses – garish, large, separate – outside the city. Making money to send their Elaines and Davids to law and medical school, without a word of official Hebrew, except when they visited in synagogues in the North where they also felt like strangers.

The (nameless) Jewish deli owners finally close it after the local synagogue is bombed: "They were shocked, the papers said. Aghast at the bombing! She laughed at their naïveté. Laughed at their precarious 'safety.'

Laughed with such bitter contempt that she could not speak to a Southern Jew without wanting to hit him or her" (p. 180).

But the specific details incorporated in Walker's portrayals of Jewish racism, and their intensity, deflect from a purely realistic reading of Walker's intent here. They lead directly into her larger purposes in writing what is a redemptive text, an African American scripture. A major feature of American Jewish culture, in Walker's representation of it, is its deadness, the fact that it contains at best only moribund traces of a once "extant" people. Until her awakening to the black cause, there are not only no "black faces" decorating the walls of Lynne's room, there are also no "Jewish faces" (p. 154). There is no Jewishness at all except the *"nu"* or *"Oy vey"* that lingers in her father's and her own speech (pp. 152, 148), and her mother's panic at the thought of her daughter sleeping with a black man:

> When her mother tracked her to Truman's house they heard her screaming from three blocks away, because it was then that her mother noticed that she had tracked her only daughter – who had slipped out of the house as furtively as a rabbi from a pogrom – to a black neighborhood. . . . [The] harsh buzz [of the bell] followed by the continuation of her mother's, by then, howl, rested in the back of Lynne's brain like a spinning record on which the sound was turned down. It was never to leave her, even when she was most happy. Like the birth cry to a lucid mother it existed simultaneously with the growth of herself away from and apart from her mother. When she died she knew it would still be spinning soundlessly there. (p. 155)

If Meridian's rebirth as prophet and savior involves her in a reconciliation with her mother, Lynne's merely mortal rebirth as a decent human being is wholly directed away from hers. Like the image of the Jews in the New Testament, Walker's representation of contemporary American Jewry provides the justification for the emergence of a new law, which will replace them, if a Jew like Lynne is not to become (as the deli owners would have her become) an "Unliving creature. Maker of money. Slicer of salami. Baker of Challah!" Indeed, even at the height of her Civil Rights activism Lynne cannot get beyond a pallid aesthetic relationship to African Americans. "To Lynne," we are told, "the Black people of the south were Art" (p. 130), a position not so different from that of the photographer Truman – a similarity between them conveyed in the name of their daughter, Camara.

By assimilating into white America, Jews, according to Walker's representation of them, have lost not only their special tradition and any claims they might once have had to victimization or to chosen-ness, they have lost their culture as well. In response to Lynne's saying that "black folks aren't so special," Meridian counters, "Maybe . . . the time for being special has passed. Jews are fighting for Israel with one hand stuck in a crack in the Wailing Wall. Look at it this way, black folks and Jews held out as long as they could" (p. 181).[12] *Meridian* is, therefore, in some sense a threnody for Jewishness (as for an older form of Christianity and African Americanism). Like "whiteness" this Judaism hangs like a pall on American Jews. It is a whiteness "beyond" whiteness, which engulfs the Jewish family "like a shroud" (p. 179).

Already in her first direct reference to Lynne as a Jew, Walker puts her cards on the table. "I wants to feed y'all real good," says Mrs. Turner, one of the black women Meridian and Lynne are trying to register for the vote, " 'cause I don't believe in votin'. The good Lord He take care of most of my problems. You know he heal the sick and race the dead. Comfort the uncomfortable and blesses the meek." In a manner very typical of rebellious young college students, the argumentative, combative Lynne cannot help but respond con-temptuously to Mrs. Turner's simple religiosity: "So God fixes the road in front of your house, does he? . . . Jesus Christ must be pleased to let you live in a house like this. The good Lord must get his jollies every time you have to hop outside to that toilet in the rain. The Holy Ghost must rejoice when your children catch pneu-monia every winter." Walker, through Meridian, at first attributes Lynne's response to her "Northern logic." But Mrs. Turner knows better: "You sounds just like a blasphemer to me. . . . You sound like maybe you *is* kin to Judas Iscariot" (p. 102).

Truman and Lynne – the black man and the white Jewish woman – become Meridian's disciples in her new African American faith. It is they who will have to take on the mission Meridian has be-queathed them. By the end of the novel Lynne and Truman are reconciled to each other, not as husband and wife but as brother and sister (p. 213; cf. p. 199). They are pilgrims in Christ. At the beginning of the novel, sexuality had been a major factor complicat-ing the relationships among all the characters – especially among Lynne, Truman, and Meridian. Sexuality, linked with reproduction, had also produced for Meridian, as for her mother, the condition of her enslavement within the patriarchal construction of black as of white American society. As black female Christ Meridian transcends sexuality. She enables her disciples to transcend it as well. Her feel-

ing for Truman is no longer "sexual. It was love totally free of pos-
sessiveness or contempt. It was love that purged all thought of blame
from her too accurate memory. It was forgiveness" (p. 173). "My
love for you changed," she tells him; "I set you free . . . You are free
to be whichever way you like, to be with whoever, or whatever color
or sex you like – and what you risk in being truly yourself, the way
you want to be, is not the loss of me" (p. 216). Having become
Lynne's "brother," Truman also assumes a "maternal" feeling in relation to Meridian, and in the final scene he takes on the filial position: crawling into her sleeping bag, putting her cap on his head,
Truman wonders "if Meridian knew that the sentence of bearing the
conflict in her own soul which she had imposed on herself – and
lived through – must now be borne in terror by all the rest of them"
(p. 220).

Taking on the Christ role, Meridian also passes it on, in a process
of continuous rebirthing outside the biological laws of reproduction
and transcending both race and gender and, we might add: religion.
For in the pattern of religious supersessionism that the novel constructs, not only will black feminist Christianity overtake both militant and pacificist black Christianity of the male variety, it will overtake both white Christianity and white Judaism as well. And more: it
will convert white Christians and Jews alongside traditional black
society in the formation of a new church as broad as America itself;
and as nontranscendent, as imminent and human, as Meridian.

The symbol of this female black Christ is not the crucifix, with its
dead wooden slats, but the living Sojourner, her language (of
tongues?) a specifically female language not of a resurrected son
preaching truth to the benighted, but (as her name suggests) of a
sun risen at high noon, producing light and warmth for the living.
"[A]ll the people who are as alone as I am will one day gather at the
river," Meridian tells Truman. "We will watch the evening sun go
down. And in the darkness maybe we will know the truth" (p. 220;
the Sojourner tree recalls Sojourner Truth as well, of course). In the
meantime, Meridian (as again suggested by her name) will embody
the nontranscendental truths of human temporality: the pinnacle or
apex of power and health and splendor realized in nothing more
deific than high noon.

Another meaning of meridian, we are told at the beginning of
the novel, is a line bisecting not another line, as in a cross, but a
circle. This meaning of meridian corresponds as well to the image
in the book's epigraph of the "broken and scattered" "hoop" without
"center." It resonates with the final view of the Sojourner: the pho-

tograph of the "gigantic tree stump" as "an enormous bull's eye."
"The sacred tree is dead," pronounces Black Elk. By the end of
Meridian, the sacred tree is once again alive: a "tiny branch, no larger
than his finger, . . . growing out of one side" (p. 217). And the once
silenced Black Elk, as the once silenced black woman speaks again;
and when she speaks, she speaks in no less than the voice of a black
female God.

Toni Morrison's Songs of the Beloved: Jewish History and the African American Experience in Song of Solomon *and* Beloved

Unlike Himes's *Lonely Crusade* and Walker's *Meridian,* Toni Morrison's *Song of Solomon* has nothing to do with black–Jewish interaction, political or otherwise. Like many twentieth-century African
American fictions, it is primarily an odyssey of self- and cultural discovery. In the tradition of Zora Neale Hurston, it takes place within
the largely autonomous domain of the black community in America.[13] The book records the story of the (male) protagonist's return
to the place where his ancestors first arrived in America, the place
to which they brought their African traditions and where those
traditions still flourish, albeit decisively transformed. As the protagonist puts together the puzzle of the past (which is the puzzle of his
own identity), he discovers two important facts. He learns that a
coherent and uniquely black culture exists. He also, however, comes
to understand that this culture (alongside Indian culture, to which
the text, like Walker's *Meridian* and *Temple of My Familiar,* also sensi-
tively responds) has been violently overlaid and displaced by white
culture. He comes to see how the culture has maintained itself by
complying (apparently at least) with the white desire that it remain
silent and invisible.

As he is traveling back from Virginia to Michigan, Milkman experiences a revelation of the meanings that "lay beneath the names" of
American places, names as common as "Ohio, Indiana, Michigan."
These names are now "dressed up like Indian warriors from whom
their names came." "How many dead lives and fading memories
were buried in and beneath the names of the places in this country.
. . . Pilate had taken a rock from every state she had lived in – because she *had* lived there. And having lived there, it was hers – and
his, and his father's, his grandfather's, his grandmother's. Not Doc-
tor Street, Solomon's Leap, Ryna's Gulch, Shalimar, Virginia. . . .
Their names. Names they got from yearnings, gestures, flaws, events,
mistakes, weaknesses. Names that bore witness."[14]

The important historical work that Morrison's novel performs is the recovery (most definitively set forth in the writings of Walter Benjamin, and signaled in Morrison's own *Playing in the Dark*) of the minority history that the majority culture has consciously or unconsciously, violently or merely passively, repressed. It is, therefore, with a shock of sudden recognition that the reader of this novel realizes that the song of Solomon (which Milkman has known all his life and which the reader similarly has known since the opening pages of the novel, indeed, from the title) may not be an allusion to white Judeo-Christian culture. Rather, it may constitute an act of historical recovery, where the object of that recovery is black, not white, culture. Insofar as the novel has to shock us into this recognition against the grain of our cultural bias, the book also constitutes an accusation against white culture, which cannot imagine a song of Solomon that is not its own.[15] This shock of recognition is a part of the brilliance of the novel.

But the text, we soon begin to realize, may be doing more than reclaiming black cultural integrity and its place within the constellation of ethnic cultures by which America has constructed itself. It may also be claiming autonomy, even priority. In other words, in isolating an uninterrupted non-white non-American tradition reaching from Africa to the United States, it may also be attempting to set that tradition in the place of Judeo-Christian culture as the originating culture of the Western world. In this possible motion from claims of coherence and integrity to assertions of autonomy and anteriority, the problem of the book – in particular vis-à-vis Jewish culture – emerges. Like the place names of American geography, or like the bones that Pilate carries around with her (which she thinks to be those of a white man, but which turn out to be those of her own father), the origins of white Judeo-Christian and American culture, this book hints, may be black, not white.

In the first instance, the novel invokes the biblical Song of Solomon in order to turn it aside and deny it as allusion. But an allusion, once launched, can never wholly be disavowed. This puts us in mind of something about the biblical text, which the white reader (Jewish or Christian) might only barely recall and which the biblical text may or may not intentionally be concealing. This something is the text's own possible relationship to African culture. "I *am* black, but [and?] comely, O ye daughters of Jerusalem. . . . Look not upon me, because I *am* black, because the sun hath looked upon me: my mother's children were angry with me; they made me the keeper of the vineyards; *but* mine own vineyard have I not kept . . . My beloved *is* mine, and I *am* his" (I. 5–6).[16] Morrison's text raises the possibility that not only may black culture in America have enjoyed a separate, autonomous evolution, but that if black and white culture are indeed linked in some way, that linkage may expose the black (not to mention female) origins of white Judeo-Christian and American traditions, and not the other way around.

According to the novel, the word "Solomon" in the African American song of Solomon is a corruption of the original African "Shalimar"/ "Shaleemone." This Americanization of the African language causes the confusion between the two songs of Solomon. And this in turn enables the average American listener or reader to mistake the African American song for a version of or an allusion to the Judeo-Christian text. Of course, the word "Solomon" is also a corruption of the Hebrew *Sh'lomo.* Furthermore, *Sh'lomo* is itself a variant of an earlier biblical form, hauntingly close to Morrison's African *Shaleemone: Salmon,* which could well be pronounced *Shalmon* (Hebrew spelling: *sin, lamed, mem, vav, nun* – *shin* and *sin* are identical letters, voiced differently). This earlier variant on the Hebrew *Sh'lomo* is part of the genealogy that appears at the end of the Book of Ruth (need I recall here that Milkman's mother is named Ruth?). According to a recent commentator on the text, this genealogy was likely tacked on after the story was complete. It leads from Peretz through the house of David (with S[h]almon an ancestor of Boaz, the father of Ruth's son), to Solomon and directly on to Christ, on his father's side, if Christ had had a human, biological father.[17]

In the context of the unusual lineage of Christ, proceeding through a series of illegitimate unions – including Judah and Tamar, Ruth and Boaz, and David and Bathsheba – several baffling features of Morrison's *Song of Solomon,* not to mention her later novel *Beloved,* begin to take on special cultural and religious significance. I refer to the highly unusual circumstances of the births, first of Pilate, then of Milkman, whose birth comes about through Pilate's intervention. Pilate, we are told quite emphatically, and more than once, is born after her mother's death. "I don't remember my mother because she died before I was born," Pilate explains to Milkman's mother, Ruth; "she died and the next minute I was born. But she was dead by the time I drew air" (p. 141; cf. pp. 27–28).

It is for this reason, perhaps, that Pilate has no navel. This lack of a navel at first signifies a simple gender difference. Upon first seeing a navel on another woman, Pilate recognizes that "it was just like the thing her brother had on his stomach. He had one. She did not. He peed standing up. She squatting down. He had a penis like a horse did. She had a vagina like the mare. . . . She thought it was one more way in which males and females were different" (pp. 143–44). But as the woman who shows Pilate her own navel informs her, the lack of a navel is not so easily explained. A navel, she tells Pilate, is "for people who were born natural" (p. 144). This attribution to Pilate of a supernatural birth is matched by the somewhat less fantastic but still extraordinary conditions of Milkman's birth. Pilate doubly facilitates this birth. First, she feeds Milkman's father the herbs that arouse his dormant sexual passion for his wife. Later, she protects Milkman against his father's desire to abort the pregnancy.

In this context of the *Song of Solomon*'s Christological agenda, several dimensions of Morrison's *Beloved* also come into focus. In at least one strong reading of the text Beloved is not a human being but a ghost. She is, specifically, a reincarnation or resurrection of the "Beloved" murdered child. Like Pilate, in other words (and like Walker's *Meridian*), she is a figure for a black female Christ, the word "Beloved" being another name for Christ. At the same time, the name links her to the same Song of Solomon and its relationship to the Davidic, messianic line that is so strongly evoked in *Song of Solomon*.

Nor do the intimations of Beloved's miraculous birth, and its Christian meaning, end here. As Beloved's appearance on the scene of the novel is staged, she both is and is not the product of a natural conception:

> [F]or some reason she could not immediately account for, the moment she got close enough to see the face [of Beloved], Sethe's bladder filled to capacity. . . . Not since she was a baby girl, being cared for by the eight-year-old girl who pointed out her mother to her, had she had an emergency that unmanageable. She never made it to the outhouse. Right in front of its door she had to lift her skirts, and the water she voided was endless. . . . like flooding the boat when Denver was born. . . . there was no stopping water breaking from a breaking womb and there was no stopping now. (p. 63)

Ostensibly, naturally, the father of Sethe's "child" is Paul D, who has just appeared on the scene and entered into a sexual relationship with Sethe. He is also closely associated with her deceased husband, Halle, who is the literal father both of Denver and of the original child who reappears as Beloved (the Sweet Home boys, we are told, were largely interchangeable with each other).[18]

But insofar as Beloved is not a natural child, she has no father, except perhaps a divine one. In this sense her conception is not sexual but immaculate. This feature of Beloved's divine status as immaculately conceived is reenforced by Beloved's becoming pregnant herself. Although Paul D is again the ostensible father (raising knotty and not irrelevant intimations of incest), nonetheless it is difficult to imagine the terms by which a ghost can become pregnant through purely mortal means. Immaculately conceived and immaculately conceiving, Beloved might just recall the Virgin Mother, who is similarly the product of and the producer of an immaculate conception. She combines Ann and Mary, and Mary and Christ, as they are, I think, also connected in Pilate, who is also a supernatural child and, insofar as she assists in Milkman's conception and birth, supernatural mother as well.

Threaded throughout this already complicated procreative situation (all of it suggestive rather than definitive, as if the text is less reading and revising a tradition than intuitively responding to it) is a further element, also present in Song of Solomon. This is some degree of sexual illicitness, even incest, in the various unions that produce the major offspring – a feature rendered most prominently in Beloved through Paul D's sexual relationship with his "daughter," and in Song of Solomon through the implications of possible or potential incest between Ruth and her father, between Milkman and Hagar, and between Macon and Pilate, as Pilate intervenes to produce (conjure?) her brother's wife's pregnancy. All of this remains quite tentative in the text, just a hint in the direction of something not to be articulated directly. It is one of those "unspeakable things unspoken," to pick up one of Morrison's own terms in a context that only seems not to have anything to do with this figuration in the novels. Part of what Morrison (like other African American writers) unearths both in her fiction and in her criticism is the unwillingness of American culture to recognize what amounts to cultural miscegenation, that is, the degree of the culture's involvement with African culture. "I'm a soft-fried egg," Milkman tells Guitar, to which Guitar replies: "Negro's been a lotta things, but he ain't never been no egg. . . . Can't be no egg. . . . Something about his genes. . . . Eggs is difficult, complicated. Fragile too. And white." "They got brown eggs," says Milkman. "Miscegenation," says Guitar (p. 115).

At the same time, however, that she is making a point about American racial heterogeneity, Morrison is teasing out through her African Americanist revision of scripture the odd feature of the lineage of Christ – that, as I have already noted, it proceeds through a series of illicit unions, which the divine birth, in a move that finally differentiates Old Testament from New, cancels out by denying the lineage that the text itself has claimed. The immaculate conception, in other words, both duplicates the extraordinariness of the line of conception outside the realm of purely human terms and redeems it by bypassing human sexuality altogether. This strange supernatural genealogy actually begins almost at the beginning of the Old Testament, with the birth of the first patriarchal progeny, Isaac. Born after his mother's reproductive capacity is already terminated, Isaac's entry into the world is something of a matter of divine miracle (Pilate's own birth after her mother's death and her intervention in Milkman's birth and Beloved's entry into the world as ghost recall this). Christ's birth revives the idea of the miraculous birth (which appears elsewhere in the Old Testament as well, as in the birth of Samson). It also literalizes it. In canceling the Davidic line of adulterous unions, Christianity produces a savior completely freed of the taint of (adulterous) human intercourse.

Pilate's supernatural birth and her magical skills in relation to Milkman's equally miraculous entry into the world reinforce the novel's major claim concerning African American culture, which is brought forward by the song of Solomon itself: that it enjoys autonomous origins outside the United States, in Africa, and these origins may even be (as in Christianity and other religions) deific or supernatural. But also as in the example of the song of Solomon, it is quite possible that what is being claimed here is more than autonomy or separateness. As Pilate's name, chosen randomly from the New Testament, reminds us, African *American* culture is also a product of American, which is to say, Christian, influence. As Guitar says to Milkman, and as Milkman comes to learn in the course of the novel, everything that African Americans have acquired in the United States, including their names, is a part of their heritage.

Pilate is more than a figure for an autonomous black female savior, in disrelation to any Christian paradigm, as if African American culture did not happen in Christian America. "Christ-killing" (p. 19) Pilate becomes the goddess of this text through an act of deicide. The move has both racial/religious and gender implications. The absence of Pilate's navel may not be only a mark of gender difference, but it is that as well. Like Walker, Morrison is producing a specifically female African Americanism that stands in contrast both to male African Americanism and to American Christianity. "Already without family, she was further isolated [by her lack of a navel] from her people, for, except for the relative bliss on the island, every other resource was denied her: partnership in marriage, confessional friendship, and communal religion." She develops instead a "deep concern for and about human relationships" (pp. 149–50).

This form of black female religion stands opposed to Christian scripture. It also resists the ancient text of African Americanism, the African song of Solomon, which, as Milkman discovers, has fundamentally to do with an idea of escape, in particular escape from family. Pilate's final words, as she is sacrificed by the black activist Guitar on a rock that recalls the place of the *akeda* (the binding of Isaac), not only recall the Christian doctrine of love that she embodies but set Pilate's idea of love against the Seven Days' idea of masculine revenge. "You can't marry," Milkman says to Guitar; "Have children. . . . What kind of life is that? . . . There's no love in it," to which Guitar responds: "No love? No love? Didn't you hear me? What I'm doing ain't about hating white people. It's about loving us. About loving you. My whole life is love" (p. 160). This idea of love, associated as it is with the divine creator through entitling the group the "Seven Days," is not Pilate's idea of love at all. Nor, for that matter, does it reflect Morrison's, which is far more family- and community-centered. "I wish I'd a knowed more people. I would of loved 'em all. If I'd a knowed more, I would a loved more" (p. 340), Pilate tells us.

It is important to the novel's construction of Pilate as a black female Christ that it is Milkman who opposes Guitar's radical, militant doctrine and that it is Milkman who witnesses the scene of Pilate's death. As I have already hinted, in some sense Milkman, the only son of Pilate's only brother, who comes into the world through Pilate's intervention, is as much Pilate's son as Ruth's ("He ought to have a son. Otherwise this be the end of *us*" – p. 125, italics added). For this reason, perhaps, Pilate introduces Milkman to her granddaughter Hagar as her brother (pp. 43–44), a fact the text does not simply note in passing but dwells on for several sentences. Indeed, insofar as the family of Pilate, Reba, and Hagar seems to exist almost without benefit of males, and insofar as Pilate stages Milkman's conception and birth, this attribution to Milkman and Hagar of a sibling relationship hardly seems an inconsequential detail. Pilate is matriarch/virgin mother/God not only to her almost immaculately conceived daughters (who embody a fairly recognizable feminist fantasy of all-female reproduction) but to her almost immaculately conceived son as well. It is this son who stands poised in the final lines of the novel to either kill or be killed. In the end Milkman, already an Isaac figure, born to his father's old age and positioned on the sacrificial rock, becomes the figure of Christ. But by the time he assumes this role, he has come to represent a wholly new idea of a savior. "For now he knew what Shalimar knew: If you surrendered to the air, you could *ride* it." Riding the air substitutes for the idea of flying as escape. Rather, like Pilate, who "without ever leaving the ground . . . could fly," Milkman leaps and wheels, not (as in the words of the song) to go home (meaning either to die or to return to Africa: in African American speech "going home to Africa" means "to die") but to stake the claim in this African American place (rock) *as* home.

By representing Pilate both as black female Christ, displacing the white male Christ of traditional Christianity, and as the mother of a black male Christ, making her more Mary than either Christ or God, Morrison redefines the Christ role away from pure sacrifice (as in the model of the Seven Days or of Christ, who, childless, produced no procreative future) and toward procreativity. She also refurbishes the role of Mary, as mother, for Christianity. Pilate's capacity for nurture is reenforced through the figure of Milkman's literal mother as well. Ruth Foster nurses Milkman far beyond what seems a reasonable or seemly age. She is, as Milkman himself comes to realize, committed to his survival in ways that his father, for example, is not. If there is at the center of the Judeo-Christian Song of Solomon, and therefore of the tradition that the song embodies, a black female beloved, so at the heart of the Christian story of the divine birth is Mary, through whose body the savior is born.

The plotting in *Song of Solomon* of the birth of both the major female and male protagonists recovers the nonbiological line of reproduction that represents Christ's divine parentage. At the same time, it preserves and brings into sharper focus the feature of the immaculate conception/virgin birth that often gets lost within conventional Christology: the birth of the child by the woman without the intervention of any human male. In this line of birth, wholly dependent on the woman, the etymologies of the name Solomon (within either the Judeo-Christian or the African traditions) become meaningless, since the line of descent through the house of David to Joseph is not the line leading to Christ, who is not biologically part of his human genealogy. But then this is to say that in *Song of Solomon*, Morrison recognizes the disjunction between Old Testament and New on which Christianity is based, and reproduces in her own new African American scripture just such a gap. Morrison's song of Solomon is emphatically not the biblical Song of Solomon. But just as in the Christian–Jewish relation, the break, which produces Christianity's ascendancy over its Jewish progenitor, does not simply distinguish earlier from later but, rather, discovers in the earlier text its typological relationship to the later antitype. Morrison's *Song of Solomon*, in staging a new last book of scripture, is necessarily supersessionist. Historical evolution toward the black female Christ becomes antitypological, and the object of its supersession is not simply white Christianity but Judaism as well.

Song of Solomon, then, does not function simply as a work of historical recovery. It does more than discover the culture's origins within its African–white biracialism. It also posits a set of origins (supernatural, African, female) outside white Christian American culture. And it sets up a genealogy of salvation that subverts the terms of cultural dominance. But the novel's move toward the displacement of Judeo-Christian tradition is problematical, for at least two reasons. Insofar as the novel endeavors to expose the dangers of cultural displacement in relation to African and Native American culture, its own strategy of displacement involves it in an act of repetition. The text repeats rather than avoids claims of autonomy and processes of ethnic displacement, which it condemns as features of cultural construction. Even more troubling, however, the object of the novel's displacement is not some general level of white American Christian culture (which, according to the culturally specific terms of this book, constitutes the oppressor culture). Rather, the object is another culture altogether, one that cannot be implicated in the same way in American slavery and racism, and that is itself the victim of just such an act of displacement as the novels both describe and enact. Just as behind *Song of Solomon* there exists a name identical to it yet totally different from it, which it displaces and by which it itself may have been displaced, so there exists behind that biblical Song of Solomon a text identical to it in terms of its words, but not in terms of its language or meaning. *Song of Solomon* displaces this earlier text as well, putting itself in direct conflict with Jewish, as opposed to Christian or Judeo-Christian, culture. And although American Jews, in the twentieth century, certainly do bear responsibility to their fellow African American citizens (and vice versa), they constitute neither the dominant culture in America nor the primary cause of black slavery. Until very recently, Jews (at least in Europe) occupied a position no less oppressed than that of African Americans.

As in Walker's *Meridian*, the history of the Jews does not remain merely the distant foundational text of Christianity. Rather, it enters directly into the text through the voice of the black radical activist Guitar. Needless to say, one must proceed very carefully here because Guitar hardly represents the voice of the text or its author. Nonetheless, throughout the book Guitar speaks important, if hard, truths; and in the case of these particular statements concerning the Nazi extermination of the Jews, there are powerful internal affinities with the structure of the novel itself. "There are no innocent white people," Guitar explains to Milkman, "because every one of them is a potential nigger-killer, if not an actual one. You think Hitler surprised them? You think just because they went to war they thought he was a freak? Hitler's the most natural white man in the world. He killed Jews and Gypsies because he didn't have us. Can you see those Klansmen shocked by him? No, you can't" (p. 156). "What I'm doing ain't about hating white people," Guitar continues, concerning his membership in the radical assassins' organization, the Seven Days. "It's about loving us. About loving you. My whole life is love. ... When those concentration camp Jews hunt down Nazis, are they hating Nazis or loving dead Jews?" (p. 160).

Guitar's enlargement of the field of human suffering to include Jews and Gypsies alongside blacks parallels Morrison's own strategies of expansiveness in the book: her invocation of Native American alongside African American culture as what has been displaced and must now be recovered; and her very inclusion in this book, which has nothing whatsoever to do with the extermination of European Jewry, of a Holocaust reference. Guitar's statement, in other words, seems to carry the force of Morrison's own conviction as she plots the course of racism and human erasure in this novel. But then a fatal swerve in Guitar's argument occurs, and the problem that it poses for reading the novel is whether this part of Guitar's statement also coincides with the deepest strategies and moral convictions of this narrative, and, if so, what we are to do with them.[19]

In response to Milkman's accusation that there is still a difference between the Seven Days and Jewish Nazi-hunters, that whereas Jewish Nazi-hunters arrested and tried guilty people in a court of law, the Seven Days execute innocent people with their bare hands, Guitar responds: "Where's the money, the state, the country to finance our justice? You say Jews try their catches in a court? Do we have a court? Is there one courthouse in one city in the country where a jury would convict them?" (pp. 160–61). The difference between the African American and Jewish experiences, according to Guitar, which legitimates the difference between the post-Holocaust Jewish response to victimization and the contemporary black one, is that while the Jews, in Guitar's view, had power, African Americans do not.

No sooner than the Jewish–African American alliance is formed than it is broken. The Jews are shifted from a position of powerlessness (corresponding to the condition of black Americans) to one of power. They are realigned with the camp of the white enemy, where they become the special antagonists of African Americans, who must now battle not only white racism generally, but the (from Guitar's point of view) inappropriate comparison with the Jews. Quite against what is likely or logical concerning post-Holocaust Jews in Europe, Guitar imagines a recently decimated community rising victorious from the ashes of destruction to wreak vengeance and seek justice. Six million people have been exterminated; hundreds of thousands of refugees – the entire Jewish population of Europe – are rendered homeless; and Guitar can see only Jewish power, Jewish money, and a Jewish "state." Through the words "money" and "state," Guitar repeats a classic anti-Semitic stereotype. He also conflates Jewish survivors immediately after the war with contemporary Jewish Israelis and American Jews (indeed he conflates with each other American Jews and Jewish Israelis). So doing, he fabricates an image of Jewish power that moves the Jews out of the arena of the oppressed into its opposite camp. This move casts its shadow not only on contemporary events (such as the founding of the State of Israel and the Arab–Israeli conflict), but on the whole history of Jewish oppression.[20]

Since it is likely that Morrison intends the reader to reject Guitar's program of blind justice as thoroughly as the Uncle Tomish assimilationism of Dr. Foster and Macon Dead, we can well justify dissociating Morrison's morality from Guitar's. Nonetheless, as already indicated, the book imparts a significant measure of respect for Guitar's position. And just as the moral inclusiveness of the novel as a whole replicates the underlying logic of Guitar's expansion of the Holocaust, so the novel's strategy of displacement, which sets the book in competition first with Christian and then with Jewish history, parallels Guitar's accusations against the Jews. Morrison, in other words, constructs the novel around an act of displacement that is not so different from what Guitar and the Seven Days articulate. And Morrison's displacement displaces the same nation that so preoccupies Guitar.[21]

This displacement is made almost inevitable by the supersessionist play of the text. But Morrison's strategy does not recur simply to general Jewish history or to the Old Testament. Rather, she specifically invokes that particular event within recent Jewish history about which contemporary Jewry, especially in the United States, is most sensitive, the same event that was the basis of painful contention between blacks and Jews in their more direct intellectual exchanges in the 1960s and 1970s and that has emerged in the 1990s as central in the out-and-out warfare between the Nation of Islam and the American Jewish community.

It is with the bitter struggle for the trope of the Holocaust that I will conclude this study, since, in many ways, despite the wounds it has opened, it also leads back again into the possibility of meaningful interethnic exchange between African and Jewish Americans. It also forms the vital nexus between the African and Jewish American identities analyzed in this book, and my own different relationship to Jewish identity and the United States.

5

"The Anguish of the Other": On the Mutual Displacements, Appropriations, and Accommodations of Culture (Toni Morrison, Cynthia Ozick, William Styron, Philip Roth, Grace Paley, and the Jewish–American–Israeli Critic)

The terror beyond evil is the murder that occurred in the Second World War together with the prospect become familiar of entire and utter annihilation. We are all half-dead of it already, and there is to be opposed to it only a more strenuous and more vivid sensing of human community. There is to be opposed to it only the assertion that despite the hatred in everyone, despite violence, despite weakness and sickness, despite the uncertainty of ordinary reality, despite mortality and the seductions of a myth of eternity, despite everything, the human community is possible – and that, so I have wanted to say, is the theme and the occupation of a literature of what I have called "accommodation." . . . "Accommodation" is restoration and love in their ordinary, domestic, painfully contingent instances.

Marcus Klein, *After Alienation*[1]

Even though it is a black critic who first cites the problem of *Beloved*'s relationship to Jewish history, nonetheless my reading of Morrison's novel, through the very slender, perhaps insignificant, opening offered by the dedication and the epigraph, has fundamentally to do with my being a Jewish reader of this text. In a similar way, my uneasiness, in Chapter Three, in relation to the depiction of the Israeli in Bellow's *Mr. Sammler's Planet,* cannot be separated from my being an Israeli, an identity further complicated by the fact that I consider myself an American as well. If blacks and Jews in the United States read each other in order to construct aspects of their own identities, certainly we who are non-American or formerly American, or some other form of self-defining Jews or blacks, cannot but look upon this conversation between them from our own different, and yet related, positions of self-construction.

Bellow and Morrison are both among the most talented writers of our generation. Quite in defiance of general tendencies within the literary world in the 1970s, Bellow discusses, and resists, Zionism; he also takes a reasoned, if harsh, stance against black urban violence. Similarly, at a moment when African Americans are celebrating black cultural strength, Morrison returns to the slave experience to present black people at the moment of their most severe compromise and weakness. Even if most readers defend Sethe's murder of her child, nonetheless the act is, as Paul D and the community interpret it, morally and humanly problematical. As an act of resistance, it follows more the lines of Des Pres's notion of Jewish survival (as represented by Bellow in *Mr. Sammler's Planet*) than it does any fully realized image of heroism. Morrison's novel may, indeed, in more ways than one, owe something to the experience of the Holocaust, in which mothers killed their children to save them and/or their families, and in which surviving became a form of heroism.

Be that as it may, certainly the major point of both Bellow's and Morrison's novels, as of their earlier fiction, is the lesson to be learned from experiences of catastrophe, such as the Holocaust and slavery. My own highlighting of Bellow's condemnation of the Israeli, like my worrying the matter of what amounts to no more than an epigraph and a dedication in Morrison's novel, are certainly legitimate activities within the realm of literary exegesis. The Jewish materials constitute elements of the text, and they demand to be interpreted. Nonetheless, my interpretation of all of these textual features pulls away from what I myself understand to be the major messages of these two texts. Yet, if a major aspect of both of these texts is an effort to defend a certain moral or historical position having to do with questions of power and victimization, then how can a reader, who feels himself or herself to be victimized by this position, not respond to the politics of the text? And how can this response not, in the final analysis, become part of the construction of one's own identity through the (perhaps biased and distorting) rejection of the identity of some other person or group?

Let me recount the following reader-response experience in relation to another of the Jewish American authors I have dealt with, which brings more clearly into view the bias of my relation to American Jewry. When I first read Philip Roth's early writings, in particular the short stories of the 1950s and *Portnoy's Complaint,* and when

I later understood, through reading *The Ghost Writer* and several of
Roth's autobiographical essays, the response of the Jewish American
community to what was perceived of as Roth's indecorous and dangerous assault against them, I could feel only contempt for the folly
of invested readers who refused to see the fun and intelligence of
Roth's fiction. For me, the Jewish community (both in the United
States and abroad) was in no danger of anti-Semitic reprisals. Roth's
unabashed and healthy criticism of newly acquired Jewish materialism and social pretension, not to mention of intransigent and meaningless Jewish neurosis, seemed to me high commendable features
of his art.

And then I read *The Counterlife*. Never had I felt so offended, and
threatened, as by Roth's representation of religious right-wing Israeli
fanaticism. After all, such types certainly existed, but they were not
the majority Israeli population. Furthermore, the threat they opposed was no phantasm. It was real. And it was mine. Even factoring
in the elements of *The Counterlife* that were there to prevent my
taking the text this way, to which I wasn't, even then, completely
blind, what right did Roth have to use the example of embattled,
endangered Israelis to play frivolous postmodernist games concerning *his* uncommitted and rather childish Jewish identity? It took me
a couple of rereadings of *The Counterlife* until I could take it as a
rather brilliant literary representation of just such responses as my
own. This had been the genius of Roth's early stories as well. They
already constituted critiques of the communal criticism that would
reject them.

But there was another turn in this screw of identity politics.

In the winter of 1994, my daughter was assisting in grading papers
for an Arab program. The batch of papers my daughter had been
given to read concerned, of all things, "Defender of the Faith,"
which is the Roth story printed in the *Norton Anthology of American
Literature*, and therefore probably the most widely known Roth text.
The point of the story, which the students were meant to express in
their essays, had to do, it was explained to my daughter, with the
manipulative and aggressive behavior of Jews. Suddenly it occurred
to me that perhaps the Jewish community wasn't wrong to accuse
Roth of writing fiction that, as Judge Wapter puts it in *The Ghost
Writer*, would have warmed the heart of Goebbels and the SS. I
should add to this anecdote that the Roth story taught in the Israeli
high school system for the matriculation exam is "Eli, the Fanatic,"
one of Roth's few stories seriously – to the point of torment – con-

cerned with Jews acknowledging each other and their shared history of catastrophe.

Politics sit on every side of every text. There is no way to prevent a reader's ideological appropriation of a text. The question is how, as an individual reader, to take the measure of a text without either condemning it for pursuing its own, perhaps hostile, agenda, or completely forfeiting one's right to be offended and hurt. Symmetrically, the question for writers is whether there are means by which authors can at least resist (however imperfectly) such appropriations as are likely to encroach on the sensitivities of others. Can the mutual constructions of culture occur without aggression and misunderstanding, or are they necessarily dependent on moments of hostility and displacement?

Take the following knot of mutual constructions, which twist painfully around the Holocaust or, perhaps more accurately, insofar as this knot of mutual constructions is *my* interpretation, reflect one reader's sense of torment and conflict in recognizing the broader implications of a specifically Jewish event.

In a 1991 review of Cynthia Ozick's novella *The Shawl* (1990), critic Bryan Cheyette charged Ozick with seeking to Judaize or re-Judaize the Holocaust. He supported this charge through specific reference to an essay of Ozick's entitled "Primo Levi," in which Ozick had objected to William Styron's use of the Holocaust in his novel *Sophie's Choice*. As Cheyette notes in defense of his argument, Ozick resented Styron's giving us "as the central genocidal emblem of Lager policy . . . a victim who is not a Jew." Ozick is quick to point out in that essay that "the suffering of no one victimized group or individual weighs more in human anguish than that of any other victimized group or individual." Nonetheless, she continues that whereas Catholic Poland still exists today, "European Jewish civilization was wiped out utterly."[2]

Conveniently enough for my purposes in introducing into a discussion of black–Jewish literary relations this controversy between two Jewish critics over the use of the Holocaust in white non-Jewish fiction, Ozick's objections to *Sophie's Choice* mirror analogous charges by African American critics in relation to Styron's incorporation of black history in his earlier novel *The Confessions of Nat Turner* (1966). Although none of the ten writers who respond to *Nat Turner* in a volume published on just this issue, nor Cynthia Ozick in her statement concerning *Sophie*, put the issue of Styron's ethnic identity at the center of their objections, the fact is, of course, that Styron is neither black nor Jewish.[3] He is, however, a southern writer, thus (arguably) representing another minority discourse within American culture. His address, therefore, to slavery and the Holocaust as subjects of his fiction can certainly be understood as acts of identification, whereby a writer from one ethnic group takes on the story of another group in an effort to promote in the reader a more general consciousness of bigotry and to contribute toward the production of a more purely multivocal pluralistic American culture. Styron hints in this direction of the text's all-inclusiveness when he alludes in the *Confessions* to the example of the Jews by depicting a Jewish star (p. 141) and discussing the Jewish exodus from slavery (pp. 308–11). Furthermore, as a member of the dominating class in the South, Styron can also be understood as taking on and confessing collective guilt. The confessions of Nat Turner are not the only confessions in Styron's work. One is certainly entitled to feel in *Sophie's Choice* that the reference to the Holocaust in a book working out a white southerner's relationship to slavery is a similarly motivated gesture.

Read this way, *Sophie* unfolds as follows: recognizing the degree to which his own existence has been enabled through the crimes of slavery perpetrated not only by his community but by his own family, Stingo (like Hawthorne in *The House of the Seven Gables* or Styron himself in the *Confessions*) would seek public expiation. It is for this reason, he reveals to us in the course of the narrative, that he intends one day to tell the story of Nat Turner – which, of course, Stingo's author has already told and has gotten rapped smartly on the knuckles for so doing. Therefore, it is not far-fetched to take *Sophie's Choice* (with a Nathan instead of a Nat) as providing an alternative, less dangerous vehicle for Stingo/Styron's confession. Through exposing the apparatus of fascism and the events of genocide, Styron would reveal as well the systematic oppressions and tortures perpetuated by the institution of slavery.[4] Furthermore, as a white male Christian, he himself would take responsibility in some measure for the sins not only of his immediate southern past, but of even more recent European history.

If these are the novel's intentions, they founder disastrously, as Ozick's indictment of the novel, recalling the responses of black intellectuals to *Nat Turner*, makes clear. Can only Jews write about Jewish history? Only blacks about blacks? The problem is more wide-ranging than this. Philip Roth's *Ghost Writer* landed its author in as much trouble as both Styron's *Nat Turner* and his *Sophie's Choice*.[5] Indeed, it is not beyond the realm of possibility that Roth had Styron's *Sophie* in mind when he wrote *The Ghost Writer*. In haunting ways, *The Ghost Writer* recalls Styron's novel, not only through such details as the name of the major protagonists (Nathan) or such minor details as the description of the accents of both female camp survivors as "fetching," but, more importantly, thematically and structurally. Both represent male author/narrators (Stingo and Nathan) who are doubled through senior, adult mentors (Nathan and Lonoff). All these men are involved in highly sexualized relationships with female Holocaust survivors. In fact, they work through their relationship to the Holocaust through their relationships to these women, and they work through both of these things as part of their bids to become writers. It is even possible to read *The Ghost Writer* as responding to *Sophie's Choice,* perhaps anticipating Ozick (at least in Cheyette's interpretation) in drawing the subject of the Holocaust back out of the hands of the non-Jewish writer and returning it to the terrain of American Jewish fiction.[6]

The issue that Roth's and Styron's novels, both in terms of their subject matter and in the competition between them, puts before us replicates the controversy raised between Styron and the African American community in *The Confessions* and between Roth and American Jewry in *The Ghost Writer* itself: who, if any one, possesses the rights to a particular story of a people's historical suffering? And what constitutes a decorous rendering of such catastrophic events as slavery and the Holocaust? That both *Sophie's Choice* and *The Ghost Writer* are *Bildungsromane* would seem to make them inappropriate vehicles of Holocaust consciousness. For this reason, they raise the question of whether reference to historically fraught and ethnically specific experiences, whether of one's own community or, even more problematically, of another community, may be employed – not to grapple with the sociopolitical or historical implications of these events, but to serve the present needs of a particular group or, for that matter, individual, in the construction of merely personal or ethnic identity.

In a recent essay Walter Benn Michaels has tried to understand the ways in which textual retrievals of slavery and the Holocaust by African American and Jewish American writers respectively have served just such purposes of identity formation. Certainly the possibility exists that specific texts evoke the experiences of slavery and the Holocaust for purposes other than such ideological usage as Michaels claims, whether the texts evoke this event as a memory or produce it as a historical reference; or whether, as I have been claiming, the event alluded to in the text constitutes a part of one's own history or memory or that of some other American ethnic community. Nonetheless, the strong possibility also exists that, as Michaels claims and as Paul Gilroy's analysis also suggests, a fantasy of cultural autonomy informs ethnic fiction, which the fiction supplies both through its recourse to ethnic memory and through its appropriation and displacement of other groups' competing cultural memories.[7]

The question that black–Jewish intertextuality raises, simply but dramatically, is the nature of the relationship of a writer to his or her own specific ethnic past. More complexly, perhaps, for a multiethnic society like the United States, the black–Jewish dyad interrogates the responsibility of any writer to the ethnically specific materials of neighboring communities, which are themselves contributors to, even as they are resisters of, the larger cultural construction in which all of them exist. Is the object of multiethnic culture the synthesis of competing ethnicities? And if so, who determines the synthesis? And what do we do with the ethnically specific elements that are lost in the homogenization of culture, especially if those elements belong to communities whose positions within the cultural whole remain devalued or invisible? The goal of multiethnicity may be the preservation of ethnic discreteness, but if this is so, then we nonetheless need to think about the cost of preserving such ethnic difference. What strategies of ethnic composition are we willing to sanction in the pursuit of ethnic voice, and what are we willing to tolerate, especially if we feel ourselves the particular victims of one or another act of cultural overwriting?

As I have already suggested, the allusions to the Holocaust in both *Song of Solomon* and *Beloved* serve very legitimate literary purposes. To some degree, at least, they evolve from within the textual logic of the fiction. Nonetheless, in both cases the text's supersessionist struggle with white Christian culture necessarily involves it in a similarly hostile relationship to Judaic culture. The text's leap to the Holocaust may, in both cases, reflect a similar inevitability, which is also a confusion of sorts, mistaking Jews for Israelites, modern Jewish history for a much more remote biblical text. Nonetheless, there is within black thinking about Jews an independent position concerning literal Jews and Jewish history. However much the sociological interaction of Jews and blacks incorporates features of their theological relations, it also exists as a feature of contemporary culture and politics.

Therefore, it is impossible to read Morrison's allusions to the Holocaust outside the context of African American relations to the Holocaust. In one early piece on *Beloved,* the reviewer records the contents of a pilgrim's "note" "on a wall of a slave castle off the coast of West Africa," which locates the quite legitimate desire that informs Morrison's novel: "Who will tell of our Holocaust?" The reviewer responds by suggesting that Morrison's novel might just be this telling.[8] But the innocence of this desire cannot be separated from its repetition of earlier longings within black texts that slavery and racism be accorded the same attention bestowed by Americans on Jewish history.

I have cited some of these earlier comments in Chapter Two, in relation to wartime editorials in the *Crisis* and statements by Cruse and Baldwin. These earlier black responses to the Holocaust are not anti-Semitic. Rather, they suggest the degree to which many African Americans, among others, perceived Jewish history as monopolizing certain tropes of enslavement and genocide, and perhaps privileging them.[9] It should not be ignored in this context that as early as 1903 in his *Souls of Black Folk,* W. E. B. Du Bois referred to the post–Civil War black experience (though not slavery itself) as a "holocaust."[10] Nor can we forget the ways in which American authors, including many of the Jewish authors I discuss in this study, have traditionally appropriated the African and Native American experiences for their own fictional purposes, from Cooper's Leatherstocking novels, through Herman Melville's "Benito Cereno" and Mark Twain's *Adventures of Huckleberry Finn,* to more recent works, such as *Mr. Sammler's Planet, The Tenants,* and *The Confessions of Nat Turner.*

Still and all, Morrison's Holocaust references in *Song of Solomon* and *Beloved* also cannot be severed from the sociopolitical context of increasing Holocaust denial worldwide and, in particular, African American challenges to the Jewish community. Obviously, individuals are responsible for their own statements and no one else's. Nonetheless, context cannot be ignored. Therefore it is relevant to thinking about Morrison's references (and Alice Walker's) that in the Nation of Islam's infamous publication *The Secret Relationship Between Blacks and Jews* the chapter concerning the Middle Passage is entitled "Holocaust," while the final chapter listing Jewish slaveowners in the South is called "Jews of the Black Holocaust." In his defense of *The Secret Relationship,* Tony Martin concludes with the observation that "the Jews [who, in his view, controlled the African slave trade] will also derive much moral profit from an emulation of the Germans, who had already paid them 70 billion dollars of reparations as of 1985." Similar statements appeared in the press by figures such as

City College professor Leonard Jeffries and the Reverend Louis Far-
rakhan and Nation of Islam member Khallid Muhammad. Muhammad declares, for example, that the persecution of blacks was "100
times worse than the Jewish holocaust." Therefore, he goes on, we
must "divert attention from the suffering of 'so-called Jews' " to the
"black or African holocaust." Such directly anti-Semitic utterances
also cannot be divorced from the less offensive recent phenomenon
of describing everything from slavery to war as a holocaust, as, for
example, an article on Yugoslavia in the *New York Times* for April 15,
1993, entitled "Does the World Still Recognize a Holocaust?" or
such books as David E. Stannard's *American Holocaust: Columbus and
the Conquest of the New World,* which specifically links the extermina-
tions of both the Jews and the Native Americans, or John Henrik
Clarke, *Christopher Columbus and the African Holocaust.*[11]

These statements may be read as assaults against Jewish history
that inherit, in fairly traditional ways, classical anti-Semitism. They
may also be understood as defensive responses to what is perceived
as an assertion of Jewish power and authority. When a Jewish author
like Malamud has his black character declare to his Jewish character
in *The Tenants* that the Jews are no longer the chosen people, are
we in the realm of a Jew's fantasy of what a black person thinks?
And, by this token, is my own reading of Morrison's fiction the
heightened and irrational sensitivity of someone who cannot get
past racial defensiveness? Yet it is a black intellectual who declares
(as I have already quoted) "that the European experience shows that
when it comes to playing the role of the Chosen People in history,
the danger is that *two* can play this game as well as one."[12] And it is
Morrison herself, in one of her prose statements, who first remarks
(echoing Ellison's similar sentiments on the subject) that "no slave
society in the history of the world wrote more – or more thoughtfully
– about its own enslavement," and then, reading via Martin Bernal's
Black Athena, which is itself a response to classical anti-Semitism that
takes the route of revising black cultural history, goes on to note the
rise of "racial – as opposed to religious – anti-Semitism." Relevant,
too, in this context is Orlando Patterson's *Freedom in the Making of
Western Culture.* Patterson's basic argument is that "freedom was generated from the experience of slavery," where this experience specifically excludes, according to him, Israelite bondage: "Because Israel's bondage was collective, so was its liberation. Its epic history, in
which its Egyptian sojourn was retrospectively reinterpreted as slavery, has no special part in the history of individual freedom. . . .
Freedom . . . was never a central value among the ancient Israelites

and Jews."[13] What does it mean to think of the experience of American blacks as *racial anti-Semitism* or to redefine the Israelite experience (and thus the Jewish experience) as having nothing whatsoever to do with slavery and freedom? Are these unprovoked hostile moves, or do they respond to something in Jewish rhetoric, and, if so, is the response defensible?

In his review of *The Shawl*, Cheyette imagines Ozick as writing her novella in response to what seemed to her another writer's illegitimate recourse to the Holocaust. His critique of Ozick recalls Stanley Crouch's objections to Morrison's *Beloved*, which have to do with what he sees as that book's competitiveness with a Jewish story. In reading *Beloved* as a Holocaust novel, Crouch's criticism of Morrison may be even closer to the mark than one might at first imagine, since there may be a particular Holocaust novel that might have triggered Morrison's response. At the same time, Crouch's comments may also be missing a feature of Morrison's text that Cheyette's criticism of Ozick's novel in relation to Styron helps bring into focus. This is the insistence by Jews on the Jewish character of the Holocaust, and, beyond that, what black intellectuals have long targeted as a Jewish insistence on anti-Semitism as the basic form of racial prejudice in the West, the Jewish story of exodus and liberation *the* motifs of Western cultural thought. Such an insistence on the parts of Jews – like Ozick, and like myself – might not only clash with other, non-Jewish writers' (Morrison's, Styron's) sense of the larger canvas of the Holocaust (Morrison, we recall, notes the extermination of the Gypsies). It might also, especially from the black perspective, seem to repeat the move in American culture whereby the Holocaust, and not slavery, had come to seem the supreme representation of humankind's inhumanity.

While the publication of Ozick's *Shawl* as a novella in 1990 followed the publication of *Beloved* by several years, raising the possibility that the popularity of Morrison's novel might have prompted this particular publishing decision, the publication of the two short stories that make up this novella actually preceded Morrison's novel by several years. In 1980 and 1983 Cynthia Ozick published the two extraordinary short stories, which, whether or not they intended to rival Styron's depiction of the Holocaust (Ozick claims that they do not), nonetheless place the Jewish Holocaust, which has actually received very little direct treatment in American fiction (Jewish and non-Jewish), powerfully center stage of the American cultural scene.[14] These stories, quite eerily, bear striking resemblances to Morrison's *Beloved*.

The similarities between *Beloved* and *The Shawl* go well beyond the contours of their narratives of slavery and Holocaust, which may or may not seem to us comparable experiences. In fact, both books are so historically embedded as to throw into prominence their similarities, since there is no need for recourse by either writer to the experience of the other. The resonances between the two works is therefore nothing less than staggering. In both, the major activity of the text is to conjure up the past through a mother's resurrection of her dead daughter, referred to, in both works, as "beloved" ("Rosa," p. 69). In both, this term "beloved," while also a term of endearment, has specifically scriptural overtones. Despite the Jewish context of Ozick's story, the shawl of the dead daughter Magda is associated with the "True Cross" (p. 32), conveying the connection between shawl and shroud. Even the name of the dead daughter, who is of illegitimate birth, invokes the New Testament context. Magda recalls Mary Magdalene and, through her, features of illegitimacy and sacredness conveyed both in the New Testament and in Morrison's *Beloved*. Beloved herself, in Morrison's novel, is associated with illicit sexuality, both in her conception through the relationship between Sethe and Paul D and in her sexual relationship with her pseudofather.

Furthermore, in both books (although in different ways and to differing degrees) the mother feels responsible for the death of the daughter. For this reason, in both stories the mother experiences a powerful and unremitting sense of not only loss but of guilt as well. The daughter, too, both in *The Shawl* and in *Beloved,* is similarly positioned in competition with a living female relative (a cousin in *The Shawl,* a sister in *Beloved*), to whom the mother also bears some responsibility and who, to some degree, serves to displace the dead daughter. In addition, the mothers in both stories are victims of scientific analysis – in both stories indicated by a reference to a tree. The scientist in *The Shawl* who wants to do a study of camp survivors is named Dr. Tree. Not irrelevantly, in the context of the Morrison relationship, the book he sends Rosa contains a chapter on "Defensive Group Formation: The Way of the Baboons," a title that incorporates along with the slight to the Holocaust survivors a stereotypical racist slur against blacks (p. 60); "A Tree is none of my business?" rages Rosa; "He gets rich on our blood! . . . People respect him! A professor with specimens. He wrote me baboons!" (p. 63). In *Beloved* the slave master who wants to evaluate Sethe's humanness leaves on her back a tree-shaped scar.

In both books, too, the number 3 (an important number for the

Christological affiliations of both texts) figures prominently. In *Beloved* the magical number 3 refers to Sethe, Beloved, and Denver (p. 298). It is the number that is missing at the homestead 124 and that the women try to reinscribe, only to discover themselves locked into a paralyzing and self-destructive relationship as a result of that attempt.[15] In *The Shawl,* the 3 are constituted by Rosa, Stella, and Magda. "I'm left. Stella's left," says Rosa; "out of so many three." "Three?" Persky asks. "How do you count three?" (p. 59).[16] Last but not least, in both books a reconciliation between the mother and a man occasions the final disappearance of the ghost and the affirmation of getting on with the business of living, both for the mother and even more so for the living "daughter" – Stella in *The Shawl* and Denver in *Beloved.* This getting on has fundamentally to do with language and the telling of the story that constitutes both texts. Magda is murdered at the moment of her coming into speech; Beloved is clearly, in the opening scenes of her return, learning how to speak. And in the course of both books, the ascension into language is reached not by the dead infants, but by the people who can go on and tell their stories, whether parents or siblings. In fact, both books end with the ghost's return to silence: in *The Shawl* indicated by Rosa's draping the shawl over the telephone, in *Beloved,* by the child's return into immateriality, to remain present in the world only as weather. One might just imagine Morrison's conjuring act in *Beloved* as conjuring that other beloved who has also so magically disappeared, yet is ever poised for imminent return. Both texts prepare for a second coming.

I do not think it is any more obvious what we are looking at when we cite the traces of Ozick's story in Morrison's text than when we consider the relation of Ozick's work to Styron's or Styron's to Roth's, or of any one of these writers to the events their fictions depict. Nonetheless, we may gain some illumination by looking at one more player in this culture game, who seems in her writing to respond directly to Morrison, but who also exposes what, in the Jewish position, might prove so problematical for the black audience.

In her third and most recent collection of short stories, *Later the Same Day* (1985), Grace Paley produces compelling portraits of ethnic conflict. At the same time, she offers a mode of resolution that, like the culminating image of gender harmony in Morrison's *Beloved,* would preserve stories not in their mutual encroachments but in a relation of what both Morrison's novel and Paley's story present as *nextness to.* In fact, at least one of Paley's stories in *Later the Same*

Day seems to invite our thinking about Morrison's *Song of Solomon* –
the "song of beginnings" of the "Son of Jake," as Paley puts it in the
story entitled "Listening."[17] Nonetheless, it is in "Zagrowsky Tells"
that Paley reveals what it is about the Jewish relation to African
Americans and Jewish history that may have prompted a response to
the Holocaust like the one recorded in *Song of Solomon* and that later
configures aspects of *Beloved* as well.

"Zagrowsky Tells" centers around a confrontation between immigrant Jewish pharmacist Zagrowsky and the heroine of a number of
Paley stories, Faith Darwin. It tells the story not only of Zagrowsky's
rather beautiful and poignant relationship with his illegitimate black
grandson, but also of Zagrowsky's own (earlier?) racism, which had
occasioned Faith's picketing of Zagrowsky's pharmacy. "Zagrowsky
Tells" is a story of race relations in America, a story about how issues
of race do and do not fit into our lives:

> She [Faith] says to me . . . Well, where does Emanuel fit in?
> He fits, he fits. Like a golden present from Nasser.
> Nasser?
> O.K., Egypt, not Nasser – he's from Isaac's other son, get it?
> A close relation. I was sitting one day thinking, Why? why? The
> answer: To remind us. That's the purpose of most things.
>
> It was Abraham, she interrupts me. He had two sons, Isaac,
> and Ishmael. God promised him he would be the father of
> generations; he was. But you know, she says, he wasn't such a
> good father to those two little boys. Not so unusual, she had to
> add on.
>
> You see! That's what they make of the Bible, those women:
> because they got it in for men. Of *course* I meant Abraham.
> Abraham. Did I say Isaac? Once in a while I got to admit it, she
> says something true. You remember one son he sent out of the
> house altogether, the other he was ready to chop up if only
> heard a noise in his head saying, Go! Chop! (pp. 166–67)

There is no mistaking Zagrowsky's cynicism in this passage. He resents having a black grandson (illegitimate, to boot: the problem of
racist stereotyping – the child is produced by the seduction of a
white Jewish girl by a black gardener in a mental institution – cannot
be ignored here). At the same time, however, there is no denying
Zagrowsky's recognition that the originating forefather of his people
was all too willing to send one son into exile and to sacrifice the
other. His black grandchild reminds him of an idea contained
within the scriptures themselves, which (like the racial reference in

Song of Songs) we often forget: that biblical history (within the Old Testament, and, we might add, also in the relationship between Old Testament and New) is the history of doublings and repetitions that (depending on how you view them) either do or do not recognize the relatedness binding brothers and cousins in the community of humankind.

Emanuel, in other words, represents the fact of human related- ness, of our joint origins in a single God and a single ancestry: a single story, which has become painfully divisive and disjointed, one side of the family (male or female, black or white, Jewish, Christian, or Muslim) in opposition to and isolation from the other side. Thus, "in a few days, the rabbi came. He raised up his eyebrows a couple times. Then he did his job, which is to make the bris. In other words, a circumcision. This is done so the child will be a man in Israel. That's the expression they use. He isn't the first colored child. They tell me long ago we were mostly dark. Also, now I think of it, I wouldn't mind going over there to Israel. They say there are plenty black Jews. It's not unusual over there at all" (p. 171). Zagrowsky discovers his relationship to his grandson through the covenant they share and which, he realizes, they have always shared.

Yet Zagrowsky's response to his grandson misses something essen- tial about racism in America, especially vis-à-vis blacks. Let me say first that the other response to racism that the story presents – the response of Faith and her white liberal (and Jewish) friends, which is to picket Zagrowsky's store – is also problematic, as Zagrowsky well realizes. The relation of African American to Jew is as much cause for reflection and concern as that of Jew to African American:

> Let me ask you, if I did you so much good including I saved your baby's life, how come you did *that*? You know what I'm talking about. A perfectly nice day. I look out the window of the pharmacy and I see four customers, that I seen at least two in their bathrobes crying to me in the middle of the night, Help help! They're out there with signs. ZAGROWSKY IS A RACIST. YEARS AFTER ROSA PARKS, ZAGROWSKY RE- FUSES TO SERVE BLACKS. It's like an etching right *here*. I point out to her my heart. I know exactly where it is.
> . . .
> I tried to explain. Faith, Ruthy, Mrs. Kratt – a stranger comes into the store, naturally you have to serve the old customers first. Anyone would do the same. Also, they sent in black peo- ple, brown people, all colors, and to tell the truth I didn't like

the idea my pharmacy should get the reputation of being a cut-
rate place for them. They move into a neighborhood . . . I did
what everyone did. Not to insult people too much, but to dis-
courage them a little, they shouldn't feel so welcome.

. . .

In the subway once she [my wife] couldn't get off at the
right stop. The door opens, she can't get up. . . . She says to a
big guy with a notebook, a big colored fellow, Please help me
get up. He says to her, You kept me down three hundred years,
you can stay down another ten minutes. I asked her, Nettie,
didn't you tell him we're raising a little boy brown like a coffee
bean. But he's right, says Nettie, we done that. We kept them
down.

We? We? My two sisters and my father were being fried up
for Hitler's supper in 1944 and you say we? (p. 159)

I do not cite this rather long passage in order to point out how
classically it represents the phenomenon of racism – the excuses the
racist brings to his defense, the way in which victim becomes victimizer, and so on. Rather, I quote it to show how it figures forth a
complexity of indebtedness and responsibility, which Faith, the liberal Jewish Civil Rights activist, and the African American man in
the subway cannot quite grasp. The fact is that Faith and her friends
do owe Zagrowsky a debt that they cannot simply forget in the process of paying off another debt. As Zagrowsky's comments concerning
his wife remind us, Jewish Americans bear a special burden in relation to other Jews (both American and non-American). Therefore,
not only might the obligation of the Holocaust survivor to African
Americans be different from the obligations of other Americans, but
American Jews have double or triple responsibilities, which mirror
the multiple responsibilities of African Americans. They have responsibilities to African Americans, Jewish Americans, and non-
American Jews.

This, of course, is not to say that one victim (the Jew) has no
responsibility to another victim (the black), or vice versa. It is, however, to suggest why slogans and accusations and indiscriminate political activism (like that of Faith and her friends or of the black man
on the train) are inadequate to the challenge of community. As the
play of words in this passage deftly suggests, debts and responsibilities do not all function within the same sphere of reference. Keeping
people down in history and not helping them up from seats are
simply not the same kinds of things, and just as Zagrowsky is going

to have to get behind the words of the "big colored fellow" with the "notebook" to understand where his words are coming from, so the black man, and Faith, and her friends, are going to have to get behind the events of Jewish history that motivate Zagrowsky's words and deeds.

Paley's story demands of Faith and her readers a consciousness of Jewish history alongside their consciousness of black history. But it is just this consciousness of the untranslatability of one set of historical terms into another, one set of moral responsibilities into another, that makes Zagrowsky's own response to his grandson problematical. Zagrowsky's way of acknowledging his relationship to the child confirms rather than reverses the strategy of cultural appropriation enacted in but also exposed by Morrison's *Song of Solomon*. Zagrowsky, by declaring Emanuel a Jew, renders Emanuel's black origins invisible. He repeats the white Christian and Jewish move that posits Judaism and Christianity as higher evolutions of culture, rendering black culture unnecessary, as once Christian culture had rendered Judaism expendable.

Zagrowsky's response to African Americanism, which is to say, in this instance, to his black grandchild, replicates Guitar's response to the Jews. In the first instance, Zagrowsky, like Guitar, widens the circle of community, incorporating others in the arena once defined by self. But this gesture in no way dissolves the border separating self and other. Rather, it rearranges that border, redesignating positions of anteriority and posteriority, submission and control. Nor does it in any way respect the legitimate anger that the formerly excluded outsider might feel and that might well lead him or her not to want to (re)enter the circle of community. Zagrowsky's response does not grant to African Americans (including his own grandson) what he permits himself: expressions of angry exhaustion and an unwillingness to forgive. It does not grant them cultural specialness and chosenness. "He should eventually know his own people," Faith advises Zagrowsky; "a friend of mine with the same situation moved to a more integrated neighborhood." "Wait a minute," Zagrowsky begins to respond, "we live thirty-five years in this apartment. But I can't talk" (p. 172).

In "Zagrowsky Tells," Paley (possibly in direct response to Morrison's *Song of Solomon*) acknowledges the legitimacy of the problem that prompts Morrison's response (and will account for her dedication to *Beloved*). "At that Time, or The History of a Joke" is a less cautious story than "Zagrowsky Tells," and it delivers us back to the dynamics of cultural conflict and competition that seem to characterize Morrison's two novels. In this little vignette Paley creates a parody of the virgin birth of the "black as night" (p. 94) female savior – exactly the central figure in *Song of Solomon* and *Beloved*. (Paley's story even produces the word "Sing" – p. 94 – which is a crucial key to cultural origins in *Song of Solomon*.) Paley's point is simple and direct. New immaculate conceptions and new saviors (even black female ones) are hardly apt to work out well for the Jews. "Throughout the world, people smiled," we are told. "By that time, sexism and racism had no public life, though they were still sometimes practiced by adults at home. . . . But those particular discontented Jews said again, 'Wonderful! So? Another tendency heard from! So it's a girl! Praised to the most Highest! But the fact is, we need another virgin birth like our blessed dead want cupping by ancient holistic practitioners' " (p. 95).

In point of fact, the Jews do not need another virgin birth. But what if another people does? What if the requirements of cultural cohesion for one people clash with those of another? How do groups within a culture declare the centralities of their positions and narratives? How do we understand, acknowledge, permit, the stories other people tell, even, or especially, when they violate or conflict with our own narratives?

In her 1992 *Playing in the Dark*, Toni Morrison argues against the unwarranted assumption of Americanist critics that "traditional, canonical American literature is free of, uninformed, and unshaped by the four-hundred-year-old presence of, first Africans and then African-Americans in the United States. [The critical tradition] assumes that this presence – which shaped the body politic, the Constitution, and the entire history of the culture – has had no significant place or consequence in the origin and development of that culture's literature." For Morrison, recording the "Africanist" presence in American writing revises our notion of what constitutes the literary tradition, which emerges (as in the arguments of Baldwin and Ellison some decades ago) as always constructed by its African American materials.[18]

But if slavery, segregation, and racism constitute unacknowledged components in the construction of the four-hundred-year-old literature of the United States, how much more potent, and concealed, must be the effects of Jewish culture and its violent rejection on the last two thousand years of Christian, Western culture, including its more recent development in the United States and also including the African American practitioners of that tradition. Just as a repressed relation to black materials may be imagined to vibrate within much American narrative from the seventeenth century on, so within African American fiction, as within white Christian writing generally, an unacknowledged relation (appropriative, displacing, and even hostile) can be understood to structure the text – at least when read by a Jewish reader through the perspective of Jewish history. At the same time, how can Jewish self-conceptions, especially having to do (like Zagrowsky's) with the covenant of chosenness, not force defensive responses on the parts of Christian writers, or, when coupled with the Holocaust, black writers?

The final images of both Paley's *Later the Same Day* and Morrison's *Song of Solomon* (which rewrites the ending of Malamud's *The Tenants*, which rewrites previous passages in Baldwin) to some degree respond to these challenges of cultural accommodation. They are images of irresolution and suspended animation. They pose unanswerable questions and leave them unanswered. "You want my life?" "You need it?" Milkman calls to Guitar, as he leaps toward him, to kill or be killed by him – it isn't clear which (p. 340). Similarly at the end of "Listening," the last story in *Later the Same Day*, Faith and her lesbian friend Cassie do not resolve the differences between them. "Forgive you?" asks Cassie; "She laughed. But she reached across the clutch. With her hand she turned my face to her so my eyes would look into her eyes. You are my friend, I know that, Faith, but I promise you, I won't forgive you, she said. From now on, I'll watch you like a hawk. I do not forgive you" (p. 211).

Perhaps it does not matter, as Morrison puts it in the concluding words of *Song of Solomon*, which brother (or, as in Paley's story, sister) gives up his or her ghost in the killing arms of his/her brother/sister. "If you surrendered to the air, you could *ride* it" (p. 341). Positing as it does a moment of magical or supernatural resolution beyond the everyday world, and beyond the literal end of the story, the climax of Morrison's novel imagines the death struggles of fraternal enemies as, finally, the embrace of lovers. Out of fratricide – perhaps averted, perhaps not (as once out of infanticide – once averted, and once not) – will come salvation. "Here I am," Milkman calls out to Guitar, recalling Abraham's and Isaac's responses to God during the event of the *akedah* – the type of the birth of which Christ, in the Christian tradition, as Pilate/Beloved, in Morrison's retelling of the story, is the antitype. Precisely not forgiving each other, Faith and Cassie will be watchful of each other, mindful of hurts and wrongs, not forgiving, but still friends. This is no ideal solution. But perhaps it is as close to the accommodation of cultures within a national family that individuals can dare to go. And, perhaps, if we are lucky, it is close enough.

Notes

Introduction

1. Werner Sollors, *Beyond Ethnicity: Consent and Descent in American Culture* (New York: Oxford University Press, 1986), and Sacvan Bercovitch, *Rites of Assent: Transformations in the Symbolic Construction of America* (New York: Routledge, 1993).
2. Walter Benn Michaels, *Our America: Nativism, Modernism, and Pluralism* (Baltimore: Johns Hopkins University Press, 1994), p. 13.
3. Paul Gilroy, *The Black Atlantic: Modernity and Double Consciousness* (Cambridge, MA: Harvard University Press, 1993).

Chapter One

1. Cynthia Ozick, "Toward a New Yiddish," *Art and Ardor: Essays* (New York: Alfred Knopf, 1983), p. 177; James Baldwin, "Many Thousands Gone," *Notes of a Native Son* (Boston: Beacon Press, 1955), pp. 24–25.
2. For books concerned with the history of black–Jewish relations, see (among others and in chronological order): *Negro-Jewish Relations in the United States: Papers and Proceedings of a Conference Convened by the Conference on Jewish Social Studies* (New York: Citadel Press, 1966); *Negro and Jew: An Encounter in America: A Symposium Compiled by Midstream Magazine*, ed. Shlomo Katz (New York: Macmillan, 1967); Rabbi Henry Cohen, *Justice, Justice: A Jewish View of the Negro Revolt* (New York: Union of American Hebrew Congregations, 1968); *Black Anti-Semitism and Jewish Racism*, intro. Nat Hentoff (New York: Richard W. Baron, 1969); Max Geltman, *The Confrontation: Black Power, Anti-Semitism, and the Myth of Integration* (Englewood Cliffs, NJ: Prentice-Hall, 1970); Robert G. Weisbord and Arthur Stein, *Bittersweet Encounter: The Afro-American and the American Jew* (Westport, CT: Negro Universities Press, 1970); Lenora

E. Berson, *The Negroes and the Jews* (New York: Random House, 1971);
Ben Halpern, *Jews and Blacks: The Classic American Minorities* (New York:
Herder & Herder, 1971); Hasia R. Diner, *In the Almost Promised Land:
American Jews and Blacks 1915–1935* (Westport, CT: Greenwood Press,
1977); Jonathan Kaufman, *Broken Alliance: Turbulent Times Between Blacks
and Jews in America* (New York: Scribner, 1988); William M. Phillips, Jr.,
*An Unillustrious Alliance: The African American and Jewish American Com-
munities* (New York: Greenwood Press, 1991); Paul Berman, ed., *Blacks
and Jews: Arguments and Alliances* (New York: Delacorte, 1994); Joe
Wood, *Blacks and Jews: Thirty Years of Alliance and Argument* (New York:
Dell, 1994); Murray Friedman, *What Went Wrong? The Creation and Collapse of the Black–Jewish Alliance* (New York: Free Press, 1995), to date,
the most comprehensive history of black–Jewish interrelations; Michael
Lerner and Cornel West, *Jews and Blacks: Let the Healing Begin: A Dialogue
on Race, Religion, and Culture in America* (New York: Penguin Books,
1996); and *Struggles in the Promised Land: Toward a History of Black–Jewish
Relations in the United States,* ed. Jack Salzman and Cornel West (New
York: Oxford University Press, 1997).

3. According to the schematization of one critic, from 1890 to 1914 there
was little interaction between blacks and Jews (which raises the question, why date the alliance from here at all?); between 1915 and 1935
a period of initial bonding occurred, with some philanthropic activity
moving from Jews to blacks; between 1936 and 1946, quiescence set in;
and between 1946 and 1958, rapprochement and close cooperation,
moving into the Civil Rights activism of the mid-1950s to 1960s, after
which occurred schism, division, and (fatal) rupture – William Phillips,
An Unillustrious Alliance, pp. 132–43; see also Hasia Diner, *In the Almost
Promised Land.*

4. Kenneth B. Clark, "Candor About Negro-Jewish Relations: A Social Scientist Charts a Complex Social Problem," *Commentary* 1, no. 4 (1946):
8, 9.

5. I discuss the following texts in this chapter: James Baldwin, *Notes of a
Native Son*; *Nobody Knows My Name: More Notes of a Native Son* (New York:
Dial Press, 1961), and *The Fire Next Time* (New York: Dell, 1963), which
consists of two parts: "My Dungeon Shook: Letter to My Nephew on the
One Hundredth Anniversary of Emancipation" and "Down at the Cross:
Letter from a Region in My Mind," which was originally published in
the *New Yorker,* November 17, 1962: 59–144; Ralph Ellison, "Change
the Joke and Slip the Yoke," in *Shadow and Act* (New York: Vintage
Books, 1972; orig. pub. 1953), pp. 45–59, first appeared in journal as
"The Negro Writer in America: An Exchange," *Partisan Review* 25
(1958): 212–22; "The World and the Jug," *Shadow and Act,* pp. 107–43,
originally published as "The World and the Jug: A Reply to Irving
Howe," *The New Leader,* December 9, 1963: 22–26 and "A Rejoinder,"

The New Leader, February 3, 1964:15–22; Irving Howe, "Black Boys and Native Sons," *A World More Attractive: A View of Modern Literature and Politics* (New York: Horizon Press, 1963), pp. 98–122, originally published in *Dissent* 10 (1963): 535–68; also "A Reply to Ralph Ellison," *The New Leader*, February 3, 1964: 12–14; and "*The New Yorker* and Hannah Arendt," *Commentary* 36, no. 4 (October 1963): 318–19; Stanley Edgar Hyman, "American Negro Literature and the Folk Tradition," in *The Promised End: Essays and Reviews 1942–62* (Cleveland: World Publishing, 1962), pp. 295–318, originally published as "The Folk Tradition" in "The Negro Writer in America: An Exchange," *Partisan Review* 25 (1958): 197–211; Bernard Malamud, *The Tenants* (New York: Farrar, Straus & Giroux, 1971); and Cynthia Ozick, "Literary Blacks and Jews," *Art and Ardor*, pp. 90–112, originally published in *Midstream* (1972); and "Metaphor and Memory," *Metaphor and Memory: Essays* (New York: Alfred Knopf, 1989), pp. 265–83, originally published as "The Moral Life of Metaphor" in *Harper's* (January 1986). All page references are contained within the text.

6. Malamud uses the quotation " 'I got to find the end' – Bessie Smith" as the epigraph to *The Tenants*. *The Promised End* is the title of the novel that the major protagonist is writing; it is also the title of a book of essays by Stanley Edgar Hyman, who was a colleague and friend of Malamud's.

7. See, for example, Edward A. Abramson, *Bernard Malamud Revisited* (New York: Twayne Publishers, 1993), pp. 90–100.

8. See Abramson, *Malamud Revisited*, pp. 1–2.

9. In *Fiedler on the Roof: Essays on Literature and Jewish Identity*, Leslie Fiedler discusses the "Christian-ness of the Jewish-American Writer" (Boston: David R. Godine, 1992), pp. 59–71.

10. Philip Roth, "Writing American Fiction," *Reading Myself and Others* (New York: Farrar, Straus and Giroux, 1975), p. 127. See also Marcus Klein's chapter on Malamud in *After Alienation: American Novels in Mid-Century* (Cleveland: World Publishing, 1962; repr. 1964), pp. 247–93.

11. For example, Abramson, *Malamud Revisited*, does not include "The Jewbird" (p. 90) as one of Malamud's texts about Jews and blacks. In *Defenses of the Imagination: Jewish Writers and Modern Historical Crisis*, Robert Alter suggests that the bird is "what is known in the vernacular as a *shvartser yid*, a Jew who is 'black' not in the racial sense but in the foul oppressiveness of his crude manner and his religious obscurantism" (Philadelphia: Jewish Publication Society, 1977), p. 162. In his recently printed notes and lectures, Malamud repeatedly couples blacks and Jews in his thinking about writing and the American scene: *Talking Horse: Bernard Malamud on Life and Work*, ed. Alan Cheuse and Nicholas Delbanco (New York: Columbia University Press, 1996), pp. 88–89, 111, 115, and 141–42.

12. "Interview," *Jerusalem Post Weekly Overseas Edition* (April 1, 1968), quoted in Abramson, *Malamud Revisited*, p. 2. In "Jewishness in American Fiction," Malamud explains that he meant by this statement that "the Jewish drama is prototypic, 'formed,' and symbolically understandable. If you understand it you realize it is your own, whether you are a Jew or not; and I suppose what I hope by saying that is that recognition of this drama should ally human beings to one another, should ally them, even strangers, to those who have as a people for historical reasons lived through it recurrently" (*Talking Horse*, ed. Cheuse and Delbanco, p. 137).

13. The autobiographical resonances can be detected through comparisons of the text with some of Malamud's own statements concerning himself as author, as reprinted in *Talking Horse*, ed. Cheuse and Delbanco, esp. "Introduction to *The Stories of Bernard Malamud, 1983*," pp. 5–9 and "On Subject Matters": "The ideal is . . . to make art of the message," a statement made directly after praising the art of Ralph Ellison, p. 115.

14. See my *Fiction and Historical Consciousness: The American Romance Tradition* (New Haven: Yale University Press, 1989).

15. Cf. Arthur A. Cohen: "Surely one of the defects of the Jewish personality is that it collects itself (like a derelict rummaging in a junkyard for usable bits and pieces) from its environment, picking and gnawing at the social structures of others for reliable self-images" ("Negro-Jewish Relations in America: A Symposium," *Midstream* 12 [December 1966]: 8). On the self-mirroring, self-conscious quality of the text, see Steven Kellman's "The Tenants in the House of Fiction," *Critical Essays on Bernard Malamud*, ed. Joel Salzberg (Boston: G. K. Hall, 1987), pp. 165–73.

16. James A. McPherson, "To Blacks and Jews: Hab Rachmones," *Tikkun* 4 (1989): 15–18.

17. Quotations in the heading refer to Ellison's "The World and the Jug," *Shadow and Act*. Malamud knew Ellison and Hyman personally: he met Ralph and Fanny Ellison in Europe, and it is pleasant to consider that he named the wife in "Angel Levine" (he was writing the stories of *The Magic Barrel* while in Europe) after Ellison's wife. According to Malamud, Ellison was the best of the contemporary African American authors (*Talking Horse*, ed. Cheuse and Delbanco, p. 141).

18. In her 1993 postscript to the reprinting of "Literary Blacks and Jews" in Paul Berman's *Blacks and Jews* (pp. 42–75), Ozick reiterates her faith in Jewish sincerity vis-à-vis blacks. I myself do not doubt that sincerity. My concern is with what that sincerity doesn't acknowledge.

19. Ellison expresses himself on Jewish–black relations also in "A Very Stern Discipline," *Going to the Territory* (New York: Random House, 1986), pp. 274–83, and in Howard Sage, "An Interview with Ralph Ellison: Visible Man," *Pulp* 2 (1976): 9–11.

20. See, for example, Michael Rogin, "Blackface, White Noise: The Jewish

Jazz Singer Finds His Voice," *Critical Inquiry* 18 (1992): 417–53, and Hasia Diner, *Almost Promised Land.*

21. A similar phenomenon of not saying the word "Jew" even though it is more or less clear from the context that the subject of the debate is Jews occurs in a roundtable discussion on "Liberalism and the Negro", which appears in *Commentary* 37 no. 3 (May 1964): 25–42, among James Baldwin, Nathan Glazer, Sidney Hook, and Gunnar Myrdal. Hook, arguing for limited affirmative action, cites the "influx of refugees from Germany to the United States" (pp. 26–27), to which Baldwin responds by picking up this reference to "German refugees . . . and all the other immigrants . . . who have gotten or not gotten preferential treatment [but] were nevertheless looked upon as white people" (p. 27). Baldwin refers as well to his "playmates" (p. 28) in school, whom he identifies in his other writings, but not here, as Jews. Glazer's contribution then notes that "the appearance of Nazism in Germany" raised similar problems for liberalism (p. 28). The word "Jew" appears only latterly in the discussion. Cf. also the comments of Arthur A. Cohen in the *Midstream* symposium on "Negro–Jewish Relations in America," who understands anti-Semitism in the black community as saying to the Jew that "he's colorless, not white, surely not black, just Jew"; "I'm not a white man, I'm a Jew," the Jew says, and blacks respond (according to Cohen): "White is white and white is Christian and you're *nothing*" (p. 10).

22. *Blacks and Jews,* ed. Berman, p. 74.

23. For good reason, it seems to be everybody's favorite myth in discussing black–Jewish relations. Thus Leslie Fiedler in "Negro and Jew," in *To the Gentiles* (New York: Stein & Day, 1972), p. 166.

24. In this context, see also Harold Rosenberg, "Form and Despair," *Location* 1 (1964): 7–9, who notes that "James Baldwin's *The Fire Next Time* raised the question of the future of Western civilisation, Hannah Arendt's *Eichmann in Jerusalem,* that of the nature of its past."

25. *Commentary* 8, no. 5 (September 1949): 215. Hyman's comments on the subject of the symposium entitled "The Jewish Writer and the English Literary Tradition," which is a response to an essay by Leslie Fiedler, throws light on the problems of Hyman's position, as Malamud adapts it in the novel: "There is this curious parochialism about Fiedler's otherwise useful article and the symposium questions framed, as though only Negro literary men might be assumed to feel hurt and concern over the caricatures of the Negro in our literature (a far more prevalent and violent problem in American writing, incidentally, although one would never guess it from Fiedler's article, than the travesty on the Jew, and one 'men have died of' with equal finality" (p. 214). And he continues: "Let the Jewish writer, then, if he is to censor anything, censor his own covert forms of anti-Semitism, among them self-

pity and parochialism, which is his special occupational disease (and one not unknown to *Commentary*'s pages)" (p. 215). Needless to say, there were few white critics (Jewish or otherwise) so acutely attuned to the question of black rights as Fiedler, but Hyman's desire here – to define himself through black, as opposed to Jewish, culture – is so overpowering as to force an accusation hardly warranted by the facts.

26. Cf. Baldwin, "The Discovery of What It Means to Be an American," *Nobody Knows My Name*, p. 5.

27. Robert G. O'Meally, *The Craft of Ralph Ellison* (Cambridge, MA: Harvard University Press, 1980), p. 166. See also pp. 164–66, where O'Meally notes as well Ellison's argument with Howe.

28. Kerry McSweeney, *Invisible Man: Race and Identity* (Boston: Twayne Publishers, 1988), p. 18. McSweeney lumps Howe's argument together with these ("Howe, a left-wing Jewish literary intellectual") without taking into account that Howe's position originates, much earlier, in a wholly different set of aesthetic assumptions (pp. 19–20).

29. Susan L. Blake, "Ritual and Rationalization: Black Folklore in the Works of Ralph Ellison," reprinted in *Modern Critical Views: Ralph Ellison*, ed. Harold Bloom (New York: Chelsea House, 1986), pp. 77–99.

30. David Bradley made a point similar to Baldwin's in a paper delivered at the 1994 American Literature Association meeting in San Diego, in which he criticized Wright's willingness to be exploited by the white publishing industry. My disagreement with Houston A. Baker Jr.'s extremely fine reading of the Trueblood incident in *Invisible Man*, and, for that matter, with his reading of Ellison's novel as a whole in *Blues, Ideology, and Afro-American Literature: A Vernacular Theory* (Chicago: University of Chicago Press, 1984), pp. 172–99, hinges on the fact that whites did not have trouble with listening to blacks as blacks, just with blacks as Americans. Thus, in my understanding of the book, Ellison does not have to speak two separate languages – one to blacks, the other to whites – even though black people in the real world may have had to dissimulate under such linguistic misrepresentations. White readers were quite prepared to hear the voice of black protest. What they were not prepared to hear was the voice that Ellison was claiming for himself: the voice of mainstream American and Western literature. Cf. Ellison, "A Very Stern Discipline": there were times "when white publishers and the white reading public wished to encounter only certain types of Negroes in poetry and fiction" (p. 281).

31. Paul Gilroy, *The Black Atlantic: Modernity and Double Consciousness* (Cambridge, MA: Harvard University Press, 1993), pp. 146–86.

32. Toni Morrison, "Unspeakable Things Unspoken: The Afro-American Presence in American Literature," *Michigan Quarterly Review* 28 (1989): 1–34, and *Playing in the Dark: Whiteness and the Literary Imagination* (Cambridge, MA: Harvard University Press, 1992); and Ralph Ellison, "What

America Would Be Like Without Blacks," *Going to the Territory,* pp. 104–12.

33. See Shelley Fisher Fishkin's review essay on this flourishing field of scholarship: "Interrogating 'Whiteness,' Complicating 'Blackness': Remapping American Culture," *American Quarterly* 47 (1995): 428–66.

34. Sage, "Interview," p. 9.

35. "What America Would Be Like Without Blacks," *Going to the Territory,* p. 109.

36. *Was Huck Black? Mark Twain and African American Voices* (New York: Oxford University Press, 1993), pp. 129 and 4.

37. Baldwin refers to Christ as a "sun-baked Hebrew" in *The Fire Next Time,* p. 63. He writes at the end of "The Harlem Ghetto," in *Notes of a Native Son:* "The Jew is caught in the American crossfire. . . . Georgia has the Negro and Harlem has the Jew" (p. 72).

38. Cf. "White Americans find it as difficult as white people elsewhere do to divest themselves of the notion that they are in possession of some intrinsic value that black people need, or want. And this assumption – which, for example, makes the solution to the Negro problem depend on the speed with which Negroes accept and adopt white standards – is revealed in all kinds of striking ways, from Bobby Kennedy's assurance that a Negro can become President in forty years to the unfortunate tone of warm congratulation with which so many liberals address their Negro equals. It is the Negro, of course, who is presumed to have become equal" (*Fire,* p. 127).

39. For a consideration of Baldwin's relationship to the theological tradition, with special reference to the image of the father and its autobiographical resonances, see Sondra A. O'Neal, "Fathers, Gods, and Religion: Perceptions of Christianity and Ethnic Faith in James Baldwin," in *Critical Essays on James Baldwin,* ed. Fred L. Standley and Nancy V. Burt (Boston: G. K. Hall, 1988), pp. 125–43.

40. Cf. Baldwin, "The Harlem Ghetto," *Notes of a Native Son,* pp. 66–72.

41. Black anti-Semitism as church-related is the main point of Richard Wright's discussion of the subject in *Black Boy* (New York: Harper & Row, 1966; orig. pub. 1937), pp. 69–71.

42. See David Leeming's *James Baldwin: A Biography* (New York: Alfred Knopf, 1994), which begins: "Illegitimacy and an almost obsessive preoccupation with his stepfather were constant themes in the life and works of James Baldwin. . . . much of Baldwin's early life was concerned with a search for a father . . . for what an ideal father might have been for him. . . . and by extension, his search was a symbolic one for the birthright denied him and all 'colored,' 'negro,' or 'black people' " (p. 3). See again O'Neal, "Fathers, Gods, and Religion."

43. (New York: Viking Penguin, 1989). Penguin reprints the original version of the text.

44. "Du Bois, American Nationalism, and the Jewish Question," *Race and the Invention of Modern American Nationalism,* ed. Reynolds J. Scott-Childress (New York: Garland Press, in press).

45. Cf. W. E. B. Du Bois's images of Jews as black in some of his poetry. Arnold Rampersad writes: "The foundation for this depiction of a black Christ rests on the fact that Jesus Christ was a Jew and that Jews, like blacks, are despised by racists who nevertheless profess Christianity; the Semites are among those 'darker races' for whom Du Bois writes" – *The Art and Imagination of W. E. B. Du Bois* (New York: Schocken Books, 1976, 1990), pp. 180–81. Du Bois's journal, *The Crisis,* was subtitled "A Record of the Darker Races."

46. Alice Walker, *The Temple of My Familiar* (New York: Pocket Books, 1989), p. 365.

47. Cf. "The Discovery of What It Means to Be an American," *Nobody Knows My Name,* p. 5.

48. Nathan Glazer, "Blacks, Jews and the Intellectuals," *Commentary* 47, no. 4 (April 1969): 35.

49. See John Murray Cuddihy, "Jews, Blacks, and the Cold War at the Top," *Worldview* (February 1972), for a reading of the book in these terms, to which Robert Alter, in "Updike, Malamud, and the Fire This Time," *Commentary* 53, no. 4 (October 1972): 68–74, takes exception. See also Steven G. Kellman, "*The Tenants* in the House of Fiction." Relevant in this context is a view of twentieth-century American culture, both at the beginnings of the century and midcentury, as in a state of "dissolution" necessitating on the parts of its writers "accommodation" and the construction of culture. In *Foreigners: The Making of American Literature 1900–1940* (Chicago: University of Chicago Press, 1981), Marcus Klein develops the idea of dissolution from his *After Alienation* and pushes it back to explain the profusion of ethnic literature (in particular Jewish and black) earlier in the century. Writes Klein, it is not surprising that in the initial decades of the century "the business of interpreting American culture should have been conducted so largely by, and under the influence of, marginal Americans. By 1930 an approximate one-half of the population of the United States did in fact consist of marginal Americans, who necessarily were put to the task of discovering a native land from which they might claim rights of nativity. . . . The folk past was . . . created in order to authorize a version of American civilization in the present moment. . . . [A]s a folk-place, the nation also sanctioned and even encouraged assertions of newer typicalities in American life. . . . [The marginal writers] were engaged in making a cultural assertion from utterly dubious cultural materials. . . . On the other hand, their fabrications were not more arbitrary than of those of, for random instances, Sherwood Anderson or James Agee or Ernest Hemingway or T. S. Eliot or William Faulkner. The underlying truth of America it-

self was its cultural dissolution, from which circumstance there followed necessity, in literature, for acts of artifice" (pp.183–226). I would use Klein's observations to support the notion that in this dissolution, everything was up for grabs and that ethnic writers, in producing the terms of their own legitimacy as cultural spokespersons in America, were in active competition with each other for the cultural goods.

50. I have discussed Ellison's revision of the cogito in *Invisible Man* in my *Engendering Romance: Women Writers and the Hawthorne Tradition, 1850–1990* (New Haven: Yale University Press, 1994), pp. 190–92. On the tetragrammaton, see Kimberly W. Benston, "I Yam What I Am: The Topos of Un(naming) in Afro-American Literature," in *Black Literature and Literary Theory,* ed. Henry Louis Gates, Jr. (New York: Methuen, 1984), pp. 151–72.

51. Cf. Baldwin, "The Discovery of What It Means to Be an American," which begins, "It is a complex fate to be an American" (p. 3).

52. Sage, "Interview," p. 10.

Chapter Two

1. Nella Larsen, *Passing,* in *Quicksand and Passing* (New Brunswick, NJ: Rutgers University Press, 1986), p. 169.

2. Stanley M. Elkins, "The Slavery Debate," *Commentary* 60, no. 6 (December 1975): 40–54.

3. *Commentary* 1, no. 1 (November 1945).

4. Although American Jews may take pride in the concern of their community with the issue of Civil Rights, not all blacks have been equally impressed. Writes Harold Cruse: "Throughout this critique we have referred repeatedly to Jews and Negro-Jewish relations. If this shocks or offends certain readers, they might note that the Jewish press deals with these inter-minority imperatives much more often than the diffident Negro press would ever dare to. For example, *Commentary,* the leading organ of Jewish intellectualism, hardly skips an issue in which Negroes and/or Negro-Jewish relations are not analyzed at length. This magazine is a true reflection of what the inner Jewish world really thinks about the Negro problem. Like the pre-Hitler German Jews who were 'more German than the Germans,' some assimilated American Jews become more American than the WASPs in their response to Negro uprisings, and more conservative than the editorial board of *The National Review*" (*The Crisis of the Negro Intellectual* [New York: William Morrow, 1967], p. 476).

   What Cruse does not say is how many articles in *Commentary* are uncompromisingly pro-Civil Rights, integration (both in housing and in schools), and so on.

5. Cruse, *The Crisis of the Negro Intellectual,* pp. 482–83.

6. For a thoroughgoing analysis of the differences between slavery and the Holocaust, see Laurence Thomas, *Vessels of Evil: American Slavery and the Holocaust* (Philadelphia: Temple University Press, 1993). I recur to Thomas's book later in this chapter.

7. See Arnold Rampersad, *The Art and Imagination of W. E. B. Du Bois* (New York: Schocken Books, 1976, 1990), pp. 180–81. The tradition of thinking of Jews as blacks is discussed by Sander L. Gilman in *Difference and Pathology: Stereotypes of Sexuality, Race, and Madness* (Ithaca, NY: Cornell University Press, 1985). See also Bryan Cheyette, "Neither Black nor White: The Figure of 'the Jew' in Imperial British Literature," in *The Jew in the Text: Modernity and the Construction of Identity,* ed. Linda Nochlin and Tamar Garb (London: Thames & Hudson, 1995), pp. 31–41, and Cheyette, *Between "Race" and Culture: Representations of "the Jew" in English and American Literature* (Stanford, CA: Stanford University Press, 1996).

8. Stanley M. Elkins, *Slavery: A Problem in American Institutional and Intellectual Life* (Chicago: University of Chicago Press, 1959). In *The Debate over SLAVERY: Stanley Elkins and His Critics* (Urbana: University of Illinois Press, 1971), Ann J. Lane has collected many of the articles published in response to *Slavery,* plus a response to these responses by Elkins himself, which should be read alongside his later article in *Commentary.*

As Elkins points out, the history of slavery (whether for or against) has always represented a politics of history. Thus writes Jewish Civil Rights activist Herbert Aptheker, in his introduction to the original 1948 publication of *To Be Free: Studies in American Negro History* (New York: International Publishers, 1968): "The Negro's past runs through the warp and woof of the fabric that is America. His history must be understood not only because it is the history of some fifteen million American citizens, but also because American life as a whole cannot be understood without knowing that history.

"This past has been clouded and obscured by distortion, omission, and, at times, by sanctimonious, patronizing sentimentality. This methodology has mirrored and simultaneously bulwarked the super-exploitation of the American Negro people. Denying them a past worthy of serious study and emulation weakens their fight for equality and freedom" (p. 9). Aptheker "reemphasizes" this point in the introduction to the 1968 edition (p. 5). As we shall see later in this chapter, Aptheker anticipates by several decades a later move in African American history away from Elkins's "damage" theory toward a "resistance" theory.

9. Kenneth Stampp, *The Peculiar Institution: Slavery in the Ante-Bellum South* (New York: Vintage Books, 1956). "The peculiar institution" was a designation used already in the nineteenth century to refer to slavery. As Elkins notes in "The Slavery Debate," Stampp's book finally eclipsed any remaining influence of southerner Ulrich Phillips's *American Negro*

Slavery: A Survey of the Supply, Employment and Control of Negro Labor as Determined by the Plantation Regime (Gloucester, MA: P. Smith, 1959; originally published in 1918), which defended plantation slavery.

10. *Slavery,* pp. 81–86.

11. The text of "The Negro Family" can be found in *The Moynihan Report and the Politics of Controversy,* ed. Lee Rainwater and William L. Yancey (Cambridge, MA: MIT Press, 1967), which prints as well many of the essays that appeared in response to the report. Daniel Patrick Moynihan is not, of course, Jewish, but he served as assistant secretary of labor under Arthur J. Goldberg and was co-author of *The Melting Pot* with Nathan Glazer, who wrote prolifically on the issue of black ethnicity and Civil Rights, so, in addition to the mere interest of Moynihan's position, there may be some specifically Jewish elements in it as well, although I wouldn't want to push this too far.

12. *The Moynihan Report,* p. 16.

13. Kenneth B. Clark, "Candor About Negro-Jewish Relations: A Social Scientist Charts a Complex Social Problem," *Commentary* 1, no. 4 (1946): 10.

14. John Higham, *Strangers in the Land: Patterns of American Nativism, 1860–1925* (New Brunswick, NJ: Rutgers University Press, 1955); reprinted with a new preface (New York: Atheneum, 1966). Higham continues: "As a boy in a suburb of New York City, I had known the children of immigrants; I now learned more about their world. I still remained an outsider to it, but this book is a testament to their travail and their endurance."

15. One of the anthropological theories that Elkins is trying in his book to overturn is Herskovits's vis-à-vis African cultures.

16. Franz Boas, *Race and Democratic Society* (New York: J. J. Augustin, 1945). Foreword by Ernst P. Boas.

17. Oscar Handlin, *Race and Nationality in American Life* (Garden City, New York: Doubleday, 1957). Even though the intensity of focus by Jews on the problems of African Americans quickened after the Second World War, the concern clearly predates the Holocaust. As Morris U. Schappes notes, "Outstanding in the fight to prove the absence of scientific basis for white supremacy was the work of such Jewish scholars as Franz Boas, Melville J. Herskovits, Otto Klineberg, Ruth Benedict and their many academic disciples. James S. Allen, Philip S. Foner, and Herbert Aptheker began to make their significant contributions to the study of the history of the Negro People . . . in the forties and fifties" (*The Jews in the United States* [New York: Citadel Press, 1958], p. 233).

Similarly, Ronald Sanders, *Lost Tribes and Promised Lands: The Origins of American Racism* (Boston: Little, Brown, 1978), in the preface in which Sanders accounts for his inclusion of "Jews" along with the "main characters" of his study, "the Black and the Indian," by pointing out that whether or not Jews constitute a race, they have been "victims of a violent and destructive racism" both in "Nazi Germany and in Spain and Portugal" (vii).

18. An editorial reprinted from the *Jewish Frontier* states this same comparison from a Jewish perspective (*Crisis*, January 1939, p. 29); as do a series of letters printed in the same issue, p. 30. The feelings of betrayal and abandonment that the American concern with Jews in Germany produced in blacks can be witnessed as well in the slide away from moral sympathy implicit in the following editorial statement from April 1937: "As frightful as are the tortures and insults heaped upon the Jew by the Hitler government, they are as nothing compared to the damage the governing gang in Germany is doing to the nation itself."

19. Hentoff is quoting Rabbi Alan Miller.

20. Nat Hentoff, "Introduction," *Black Anti-Semitism and Jewish Racism* (New York: Richard W. Baron, 1969), pp. ix–xvii. Cf. the incident reported by Harold Cruse in *The Crisis of the Negro Intellectual:* "At the Village Vanguard when [Leroi] Jones and [Archie] Shepp were reminded of the six million Jews exterminated by Hitler, Jones replies to Larry Rivers, 'You're like the others [whites], except for the cover story.' Shepp added: 'I'm sick of you cats talking about the six million Jews. I'm talking about the five to eight million Africans killed in the Congo' " (p. 486).

21. Ibid., pp. 482–83.

22. In an earlier issue of *Dissent*, Howe writes that "we stand unambiguously with the NAACP in its struggle, with the Montgomery Negroes in their courageous boycott. Nor is it here a question of being a socialist or a liberal or anything but a human being" (Irving Howe, "Reverberations in the North," *Dissent* 3, no. 2 [1956], 121–23; quotation on p. 123).

23. Hannah Arendt, "Reflections on Little Rock," *Dissent* 6, no. 1 (1959): 45.

24. Arendt, "Reflections on Little Rock," pp. 51 and 55.

25. Arendt, "Reflections on Little Rock," p. 49.

26. Arendt, "Reflections on Little Rock," p. 46.

27. Hannah Arendt, "A Reply to Critics," *Dissent* 6, no. 2: 179–81. The two responses printed in the same issue of *Dissent* with Arendt's original essay are: David Spitz, "Politics and the Realms of Being," pp. 56–65, and Melvin Tumin, "Pie in the Sky," pp. 65–71.

28. Arendt, "Reflections on Little Rock," p. 45.

29. Tumin, "Pie in the Sky," p. 67.

30. Charles Chestnutt, *The Marrow of Tradition*, in *Three Classic African-American Novels*, ed. Henry Louis Gates, Jr. (New York: Random House, 1990), p. 538.

31. Irving Howe, " 'The New Yorker' and Hannah Arendt," *Commentary* 36, no. 4 (October 1963): 318–19.

32. Elkins, *Slavery*, p. 89. In "My Jewish Problem and Theirs," Harold Cruse observes just this kind of problem in a *Life Magazine* article in the 1930s, in which a writer condemns Nazi brutalities against the Jews as worse than Japanese violations of the Chinese because "after all, the Germans were *civilized* white people persecuting another civilized white group, the Jews" – in *Black Anti-Semitism and Jewish Racism*, ed. Hentoff, p. 161. Cf. the introduction to "Negro-Jewish Relations in America: A Symposium," *Midstream* 13 (December 1966): "Many Jews . . . react with special resentment to anti-Semitic sentiments among Negroes . . . because [they feel that] Jews have been the victims of the greatest racist crime in human history, perpetrated in our own time by white nations, and they regard it as adding insult to grave injury when they are not only lumped by Negroes together with 'whitey' but are also singled out for special hostility" (p. 3). The symposium was eventually published as *Negro and Jew: An Encounter in America: A Symposium Compiled by Midstream Magazine*, ed. Shlomo Katz (New York: Macmillan, 1967).

33. James Baldwin, "Negroes Are Anti-Semitic Because They Are Anti-White," *The Price of the Ticket* (London: Michael Joseph, 1985), p. 428.

34. James Baldwin, "Open Letter to 'My Sister, Miss Angela Davis,' " *New York Review of Books*, January 7, 1971; Shlomo Katz, "An Open Letter to James Baldwin," *Midstream* 17 (April 1971): 3–5; and James Baldwin and Shlomo Katz, "Of Angela Davis and 'The Jewish Housewife Headed for Dachau': An Exchange," *Midstream* 17 (June/July 1971): 3–7. See also the letters following the exchange, pp. 7–10.

35. Bruno Bettelheim and Morris Janowitz, *Dynamics of Prejudice: A Psychological and Sociological Study of Veterans* (New York: Harper & Brothers, 1950). Bettelheim's "Individual and Mass Behavior in Extreme Situations" was originally published in *Journal of Abnormal and Social Psychology* 38 (1943): 417–52 and was superseded in 1961 by *The Informed Heart* (Glencoe, IL: Free Press, 1961).

36. Richard Pollak, *The Creation of Dr. B: A Biography of Bruno Bettelheim* (New York: Simon and Schuster, 1996).

37. Elkins, "The Slavery Debate," p. 43.

38. The article on Gunnar Myrdal appears as *"An American Dilemma:* A Review," in *Shadow and Act* (New York: Vintage Books, 1972; originally published in 1953), pp. 303–17. The article, as Elkins notes, was written for the *Antioch Review* in 1944 and never published. The interview is reprinted as " 'A Very Stern Discipline,' " in *Going to the Territory* (New York: Random House, 1986), pp. 274–83. Zinn's reference to Elkins's book appears only in a footnote. A fascinating aspect of Zinn's book, which records his several years' experience as a white professor in a black southern university, is that he does not allude to the fact of his Jewishness.

39. " 'A Very Stern Discipline,' " pp. 298 and 287–88.

40. "The Slavery Debate," pp. 53–54. Elkins weights his case, perhaps un-

fairly, by bringing in as the last example of scholarship he examines Robert F. Fogel and Stanley L. Engerman's extremely controversial *Time on the Cross: The Economics of American Negro Slavery* (Chicago: University of Chicago Press, 1974). Fogel and Engerman's claim that plantation slave labor was more efficient than free labor later on, with the potentially offensive implications of that, could be understood, especially in the context of Elkins's defense of his own work, as a version of the "resistance" theory, here reduced to the morally absurd conclusion (which obviously no one intends) that slavery made blacks more productive.

41. Elkins, "The Slavery Debate," p. 49. In *The Seventh Million: The Israelis and the Holocaust,* trans. Haim Watzman (New York: Hill & Wang, 1993; first published 1991), Tom Segev traces the political uses toward which reinterpretation and representation of the Holocaust were directed.

   Despite Herbert Aptheker's long-standing relation with the NAACP and his involvement with Civil Rights, the fact that he wrote his landmark study *American Negro Slave Revolts* in the 1940s may suggest cross-reverberations with the catastrophe ensuing in Europe. Aptheker actually corrected proof on his book as an American GI in Europe (New York: Columbia University Press, 1943; republished New York: International Publishers, 1952 and 1963).

42. Terrence Des Pres, *The Survivor: An Anatomy of Life in the Death Camps* (New York: Oxford University Press, 1976). Des Pres discusses Elkins pp. 151–55.

43. Norman Podhoretz, "Hannah Arendt on Eichmann: A Study in the Perversity of Brilliance," *Commentary* 36, no. 3 (September 1963): 201–8; quotations on pp. 203 and 201.

44. See again Laurence Thomas, *Vessels of Evil.*

45. Hannah Arendt writes very lucidly on this subject in *The Origins of Totalitarianism.*

46. Joe Wood, "The Problem Negro and Other Tales," in *Blacks and Jews: Alliances and Arguments,* ed. Paul Berman (New York: Delacorte, 1994), pp. 102 and 109.

47. Robert G. Weisbord and Arthur Stein, *Bittersweet Encounter: The Afro-American and the American Jew* (Westport, CT: Negro Universities Press, 1970), contains a useful section on Cruse and Podhoretz: "Some Dilemmas for the Intellectuals," pp. 111–32.

48. Anatole Broyard, "Portrait of the Inauthentic Negro: How Prejudice Distorts the Victim's Personality," *Commentary* 10, no. 4 (July 1950): 56–64; quotations on p. 56. Jean-Paul Sartre, *Anti-Semite and Jew,* trans. George J. Becker (New York: Schocken Books, 1965; originally published 1948).

   Drawing these various events closer still is Howe's disagreement with Sartre, which concludes: "Some fifteen years later, engaged in a polemic about black writing with Ralph Ellison, I found myself cast, to my own surprise, in a Sartre-like position. I had written an essay on the fiction of Richard Wright, James Baldwin, and Ellison, stressing the dominance – indeed, the inescapability – of the 'protest' theme in their work. Ellison objected that I had locked the black writers into an airless box – what Sartre would call their 'situation.' Ellison claimed for the blacks, as [Isaac] Rosenberg had for the Jews, an autonomous culture that could not be fully apprehended through the lens of 'protest.' Surely there was some validity to Ellison's argument, yet I could not help thinking that the 'situation' of the blacks had generated more traumas, more scars than he was ready to admit. Perhaps, however, it was easier for me to see this with regard to blacks than Jews. Maybe there can be no clearcut resolution of such differences, first between Sartre and Rosenberg, and then between me and Ellison, since both sides overstress portions of recognizable truth" (*A Margin of Hope: An Intellectual Autobiography* [San Diego: Harcourt Brace Jovanovich, 1982], p. 257).

On the possible anti-Semitic implications of Sartre's book, see Susan Rubin Suleiman, "The Jew in Jean-Paul Sartre's *Réflexions sur la question juive:* An Exercise in Historical Reading," in *The Jew in the Text,* ed. Nochlin and Garb, pp. 201–18.

Also relevant in this context is Franz Fanon's *Black Skin, White Masks,* trans. Charles Lam Markmann (New York: Grove Press, 1967).

49. Broyard, "Portrait of the Inauthentic Negro," p. 64; Sartre, *Anti-Semite and Jew,* p. 143.

50. As Henry Louis Gates, Jr., points out in "White Like Me," Broyard, who was "born black and became white," had severe problems with his own authenticity – *The New Yorker* (June 17, 1996): 66–81; quotation on p. 66. One contributor to *Midstream*'s symposium "Negro-Jewish Relations in America" usefully elides the Jewish question and the Negro problem as the "Negro Question": Jacob Cohen, *Midstream* (December 1966): 11.

51. *Blacks and Jews,* ed. Berman, p. 92.

52. Apparently Baldwin's "Letter from a Region in My Mind" was originally slated to appear in *Commentary,* not the *New Yorker.* According to Alexander Bloom, "in an angry confrontation over selling the piece to another magazine, Baldwin suggested that Podhoretz do an article on his own feelings about race. This appeared as 'My Negro Problem – and Ours,' " in *Prodigal Sons: The New York Intellectuals and Their World* (Oxford: Oxford University Press, 1986), p. 333.

53. Norman Podhoretz, "My Negro Problem – and Ours," *Commentary* 35, no. 2 (February 1963): 93–101; quotations pp. 100–101.

54. Joe Wood, "The Problem Negro and Other Tales," in *Blacks and Jews,* ed. Berman, pp. 97–130.

55. "My Jewish Problem," p. 188.

56. *The Crisis of the Negro Intellectual,* p. 480. Cruse's singling out of Hansberry's response expresses the other object of his anger: not the Jews but Jew-loving blacks like Hansberry, who "had not simply married a man who 'just happened to be of Jewish antecedents' as the liberal-humanist-moralists would have it; she 'assimilated' into white Jewish cultural life" (p. 484).

57. "Postscript (1993)" to "My Negro Problem – and Ours," reprinted in *Blacks and Jews,* ed. Berman, p. 92.

58. "My Negro Problem – and Ours," p. 99. The responses to the essay appeared in *Commentary* in April through August 1963; the final installment of "Responses and Reactions," by Norman Mailer, was in the October issue. Critics who applaud Podhoretz's bravery include such famous figures as Kenneth Clark, Paul Goodman, Hilton Kramer, and John Fischer (editor in chief of *Harper's*) – all in the April issue.

59. "Letters from Readers," *Commentary* 35, no. 4 (April 1963): 341.

60. *Commentary* 35, p. 347.

61. *Commentary* 35, pp. 342–43.

62. *Commentary* 35, no. 3 (June 1963): 529.

63. *Commentary* 36, no. 3 (May 1963): 430.

64. In *On Modern Jewish Politics* (New York: Oxford University Press, 1993), Ezra Mendelsohn provides the useful set of terms: acculturationist or integrationist and assimilationist. According to Mendelsohn, what the integrationists "wanted the Jews to do was to integrate into the majority society without being entirely swallowed up by it" (p. 16), whereas the assimilationists proposed the absolute absorption of and by Jews into the majority culture. When Podhoretz uses the terms "assimilation" and "integration," however, I think he is closer to meaning more what Mendelsohn is calling acculturation/integration: as Mendelsohn points out, there is a lot of slipping and sliding among these terms. Miscegenation is for Podhoretz what assimilation is for Mendelsohn, and therefore, in my understanding, is closer to conversion than integration.

65. "*Jewishness and the Younger Intellectuals:* A Symposium," *Commentary* 31, no. 4 (April 1961): 306–59; reprinted as *Jewishness and the Younger Intellectuals* (New York: *Commentary,* 1961), pp. 45–46.

66. Compare Franz Fanon's statement in *Black Skin, White Masks* concerning the need to "prove the existence of black civilization to the white world" (p. 34).

67. Nella Larsen, *Passing,* in *Quicksand and Passing,* p. 169 (originally published 1929).

68. Harold Cruse, *The Crisis of the Negro Intellectual,* p. 490.

69. Ibid., p. 497.

70. Ibid., pp. 147, 148, 149, 158, and 168.

71. Ibid., pp. 480–81.

72. Ibid., p. 482.

73. Although David Levering Lewis is concerned with an earlier period in black–Jewish relations in "Parallels and Divergences: Assimilationist Strategies of Afro-American and Jewish Elites from 1910 to the Early 1930s," *Journal of American History* 71 (1984): 543–64, nonetheless his thesis concerning the ways in which black and Jewish elites conspired with each other to facilitate the total assimilation of their peoples is exactly relevant to what I am observing in Cruse and Podhoretz. His "argument, simply stated, is that there was a time when a small number of socially powerful and politically privileged Jews and Afro-Americans embraced an ideology of extreme cultural assimilationism; that, although this ideology was emphatically not without paradox or illogic, its ultimate consequence entailed the abandonment of identity; and that these two elites – one, wealthy and of primarily German-Jewish descent; the other, largely northern, college-trained Afro-Americans – reacting to threats to their hegemony both from within and from outside their ethnic universes, decided to concert many of their undertakings in the belief that group assimilation could be accelerated through strategies of overt and covert mutual assistance" (pp. 543–44). Thus Franz Boas, who did such thorough research into race and race prejudice and wrote so effectively against it, is quoted by Lewis as saying that "it would seem that man being what he is, the negro problem will not disappear in America until the negro blood has been so much diluted that it will no longer be recognized just as anti-Semitism will not disappear until the last vestige of the Jew as a Jew has disappeared." In a similar vein, James Weldon Johnson in 1928 saw the preference of African American men for marrying "light-skinned women as a positive example of racial natural selection" (p. 544).

74. Irving Howe, *A Margin of Hope*, pp. 11–14 and 47. Writes Grace Paley, "I . . . really felt that to be Jewish was to be a socialist." Quoted by Ezra Mendelsohn, *On Modern Jewish Politics*, p. 94, who also discusses the similar attitudes of Alfred Kazin, Lionel Trilling, and Sidney Hook (pp. 93–103). In the same vein, see Alexander Bloom's discussion of the New York intellectuals generally in *Prodigal Sons*. In *Writers on the Left: Episodes in American Literary Communism* (New York: Octagon Books, 1979), Daniel Aaron quotes an editorial from a 1927 issue of the *New Masses* (Mike Gold's publication), which depicts the artist in just the kind of Jewishly resonant terms that suggest the transfer from religious to secular identity that I am suggesting: "Are artists people? If you prick an artist does he bleed? If you starve him does he faint?" – quoted on p. 165. Aaron also cites Arthur Koestler's comment that Marxism is the extension of the Judeo-Christian tradition. See also Aaron's 1965 essay in *Salmagundi* 1:23–36: "Some Reflections on Communism and the Jewish Writer."

75. Irving Howe and Stanley Plastrik, "Comments and Opinions: After the Mideast War," *Dissent* (July/August, 1967): 387–94, quotation on p. 387. See also Howe's *Margin of Hope*, pp. 276–77; and, for a discussion of the war and American Jewry, see Nathan Glazer, *American Judaism*, rev. ed. (Chicago: University of Chicago Press, 1972), pp. 171–72 and 198.

76. David Levering Lewis, "Parallels and Divergences," p. 554. See also Ezra Mendelsohn, *On Modern Jewish Politics*, pp. 132–39. Mendelsohn essentially agrees with Cruse that for American Jews, Zionism was a way of strengthening *American* Jewish identity. Thus, Mendelsohn quotes Louis Brandeis that "to be good Americans, we must be better Jews, and to be better Jews, we must become Zionists," and Horace Kallen, "the reestablishment of the Jewish homeland [is] an essential element in the 'harmonious adjustment of the Jew to American life' " (pp. 133–34). Mendelsohn discusses Cruse on pp. 134–35.

77. *Crisis of the Negro Intellectual*, p. 484. Note as well the following statement: "In the April 30, 1954, issue of the *Jewish Press*, an article on the Black Muslims compares them with American Nazis like Lincoln Rockwell. For Jews of this newspaper's persuasion, Muslims are racists and extremists. They conveniently forget, of course, that the Irgun Zvai Leumi and the Stern Gang (the Lehi) in pre-1948 Israel were called the same things – 'Jewish racists and extremists,' yet it was these very people who truly forged Israel" (p. 495).

   Cruse may not have been the first African American to yield uncritically to the example of Jewish Zionism. As Paul Gilroy notes, "it is often forgotten that the term 'diaspora' comes into the vocabulary of black studies and the practice of pan-Africanist politics from Jewish thought." *The Black Atlantic: Modernity and Double Consciousness* (Cambridge, MA: Harvard University Press, 1993), p. 22. Afrocentric black nationalism finds its original articulation in the first half of the nineteenth century in the writings of Martin Robison Delany, whose 1852 *The Condition, Elevation, Emigration and Destiny of the Colored People of the United States Politically Considered* makes explicit reference to the Jewish example: "Such also are the Jews scattered throughout not only the length and breadth of Europe but almost the habitable globe, maintaining their national characteristics, and looking forward in high hopes of seeing the day when they may return to their former national position of self-government and independence let that be in whatever part of the habitable world it may." In inheriting the mantle of black nationalism, Marcus Garvey, who had many accusations to level against the Jews, and some considerable sympathy for Hitler, took on as well its affinities with Jewish Zionism. As Murray Friedman – *What Went Wrong? The Creation and Collapse of the Black–Jewish Alliance* (New York: Free Press, 1995) – has pointed out, "his call for an African exodus bore a striking similarity to the ideas of Jewish thinkers like Pinsker and Herzl," while some of his statements directly invoke the Jewish example (p. 78). His biographer entitled his book *Black Moses.*

78. See Joel Carmichael's contribution to "Negro-Jewish Relations in America: A Symposium," *Midstream,* pp. 6–7.

79. Murray Friedman, *What Went Wrong?* notes Vernon J. Williams's statements to this effect, p. 9.

80. *Crisis of the Negro Intellectual,* pp. 484 and 481.

81. Ibid., pp. 482, 489, 494.

82. See, for example, Daniel Boyarin and Jonathan Boyarin, "Diaspora: Generation and the Ground of Jewish Identity," *Critical Inquiry* 19 (1993): 693–725, and Jonathan Boyarin, *Storm from Paradise: The Politics of Jewish Memory* (Minneapolis: University of Minnesota Press, 1992).

83. See, again, Ozick's postscript to the republication of "Literary Blacks and Jews," where she cites Howe's reluctance to having his comments to Ellison read as Jewish (*Blacks and Jews,* ed. Berman, p. 74), and Podhoretz's postscript to "My Negro Problem – and Ours" in the same volume, where he also denies that he is speaking as a Jew (p. 92).

84. Pp. 481–82 and 496; cf. Cruse's comment concerning "Nathan Glazer's article 'Negroes and Jews: The New Challenge to Pluralism' ": "What is behind Nathan Glazer's insistence that Negroes be integrated as fast as possible, and by any means?" "Whether or not Nathan Glazer is Zionist, pro-Zionist or anti-Zionist, the fact remains that pro-Zionist policies in Civil Rights organizations are pro-integrationist for Negroes and anti-assimilationist for Jews. Frankly, Jews can take integration, or leave it" (pp. 496–97). Glazer's article appears in *Commentary* 38, no. 6 (December 1964): 29–34. The roundtable "Liberalism and the Negro: A Round-Table Discussion" appears in *Commentary* 37, no. 3 (May 1964): 25–42.

85. "Negro-Jewish Relations," pp. 26–27. Another, related, statement is Earl Raab's "The Black Revolution and the Jewish Question," *Commentary* 47, no. 1 (January 1969): 23–33, which is reprinted in Hentoff, *Black Anti-Semitism and Jewish Racism,* pp. 15–41. Raab provides the following useful history of American Jewish assimilation into liberalism and the problems this produced for black–Jewish relations: "America seemed to emerge from the war as a nation in which the Jewish Question was miraculously dead. American Jews, of course, felt that the war had been fought – and won – around the Jewish Question. . . . American Jews settled down to a new security.

"At the same time . . . the Jewish Question was apparently being supplanted by the Negro Question. And the defensive energies and apparatus of the Jewish community moved from one to the other. At least, that is the way it turned out. A surface theory relating to Jewish security rationalized the move: Equal opportunity for one means equal opportunity for all. But no one examined this dubious axiom very closely. . . .

"[The] preeminent concern with Civil Rights swiftly and inevitably became a predominant concern with the needs and aspirations of the Negro community. . . . The second stage reflected the shift from the goal of equal opportunity to the goal of equal achievement . . . from the Civil Rights Revolution to the Negro Revolution [and then, stage three] the Black Revolution" (p. 24).

86. "Liberalism and the Negro," p. 25. Podhoretz is quoting from David Danzig, "The Meaning of Negro Strategy," *Commentary* (February 1964). In this context, see also Glazer's "Negroes and Jews: The New Challenge to Pluralism," pp. 29–34.

87. "Liberalism and the Negro," pp. 27–32.

88. Ibid., p. 41.

89. Ibid., pp. 27–28 and 34.

90. Ibid.

91. Ibid., pp. 35–36. Hook points out that Podhoretz's proposal is a "variation of an old one. Bruno Bauer in the 19th century said that the best way for Jews to get their Civil Rights was to stop being Jews" (p. 36). Hook objects to Sartre's *Anti-Semite and Jew* in similar terms in "Reflections on the Jewish Question," *Partisan Review* (May 1949): 463–82.

92. In "Ralph Waldo Ellison: Anthropology, Modernism, and Jazz," Berndt Ostendor cites Leslie Fiedler as having called Ellison a "black Jew" – *New Essays on Invisible Man,* ed. Robert O'Meally (Cambridge: Cambridge University Press, 1988), p. 119. "White Negro" is Norman Mailer's phrase, picked up by Ellison.

93. Ben Halpern, in "Negro-Jewish Relations," pp. 44–46; and *Jews and Blacks: The Classic American Minorities* (New York: Herder & Herder, 1971).

94. Myron Fenster, in "Negro-Jewish Relations," p. 22.

95. Leslie A. Fiedler in "Negro-Jewish Relations," p. 23; reprinted as "Negro and Jew" in *To the Gentiles* (New York: Stein & Day, 1972), pp. 164–74.

96. Norman Mailer, "The White Negro: Superficial Reflections on the Hipster," *Dissent* 4, no. 3 (1957): 276–93; pp. 277, 290, and 291.

97. Ibid., p. 277.

98. Stanley Cavell, "Emerson's Constitutional Amending: Reading 'Fate,' " *The Translatability of Cultures: Figurations of the Space Between,* ed. Sanford Budick and Wolfgang Iser (Stanford, CA: Stanford University Press, 1995), pp. 101–26.

99. Stanley Cavell, "Hope Against Hope," *Conditions Handsome and Unhandsome* (Albuquerque: Living Batch Press, 1989), p. 138. See also "Aversive Thinking" in the same volume.

100. A similar moment occurs in *Walden,* when Thoreau seems, rather tastelessly, to use southern slavery as a figure for conformity: "I some-

times wonder that we can be so frivolous, I may almost say, as to attend to the gross but somewhat foreign form of servitude called Negro slavery, there are so many keen and subtle masters that enslave both North and South. It is hard to have a Southern overseer; it is worse to have a Northern one; but worst of all when you are the slave-driver of yourself. Talk of a divinity in man! Look at the teamster on the highway, wending to market by day or night; does any divinity stir within him? His highest duty to fodder and water his horses! What is his destiny to him compared with the shipping interests?" As I have argued elsewhere, this passage does not dissolve suffering into metaphor. Rather, it locates the genuine offense of slavery: that it functioned in America despite the realization of Americans that it was wrong; and that it was permitted to exist for purely financial, monetary reasons. See my *Engendering Romance: Women Writers and the Hawthorne Tradition, 1850–1990* (New Haven: Yale University Press, 1994).

101. Norman Mailer, "The White Negro," p. 278.
102. Ibid., pp. 288–89.
103. Ibid., pp. 280–81.
104. Ibid., pp. 279 and 291–92.
105. Reprinted in *To the Gentiles,* pp. 124–28. In this article, Fiedler calls "The White Negro" "inchoate and sentimental." Nonetheless, Fiedler would, if he had to make a choice, "stand with Mailer, whose enemies," he goes on, "at least seem more like my own" (p. 125).
106. Leslie A. Fiedler, "Race – The Dream and the Nightmare," *Commentary* 36, no. 4 (October 1963): 297–304; quotation on pp. 302–3.
107. Ibid., pp. 28–29. This image of illegitimate birth may be in Grace Paley's mind when she writes the story entitled "Zagrowsky Tells," a story I discuss later.
108. "Liberalism and the Negro," p. 41.
109. "Race," p. 297.
110. "Race," pp. 303 and 300.
111. Norman Mailer, "Responses and Reactions VI," *Commentary* 36, no. 4 (October 1963): 320–21; quotation on p. 321.

Chapter Three

1. Philip Roth, *Operation Shylock: A Confession* (London: Jonathan Cape, 1993), pp. 170–71.
2. Philip Roth, *Goodbye, Columbus* in *Goodbye, Columbus and Five Short Stories* (London: Penguin Books, 1986), pp. 14–17. All future citations in text.
3. For a discussion of three modern American novels that stresses the mutual identification of whites with black characters, see William T. Stafford, *Books Speaking to Books: A Contextual Approach to American Fiction*

(Chapel Hill: University of North Carolina Press, 1981): "The Black/ White Continuum: Some Recent Examples in Bellow, Malamud, and Updike," pp. 73–102. See also Barry Gross, "American Fiction, Jewish Writers, and Black Characters: The Return of 'The Human Negro' in Philip Roth," *Melus* 11 (1984): 5–22.

4. Leslie A. Fiedler, "Negro and Jew," *To the Gentiles* (New York: Stein & Day, 1972), p. 164; originally published in "Negro-Jewish Relations in America: A Symposium," *Midstream* 13 (December 1966): 22–28.

5. Fiedler, "Negro and Jew," p. 164.

6. H. J. Kaplan, "The Mohammedans," *Partisan Review,* 10 (1943): 210–92; and Lionel Trilling, "The Other Margaret," *Partisan Review* 12 (1945): 481–501; citations in text. Leslie Fiedler cites these stories, along with Isaac Rosenfeld's "The Pyramids" and Delmore Schwartz's "In Dreams Begin Responsibilities," in his essay on "Saul Bellow" in *Collected Essays of Leslie Fiedler,* vol. 2 (New York: Stein & Day, 1971), p. 57.

7. Quoted by Alexander Bloom in *Prodigal Sons: The New York Intellectuals and Their World* (New York: Oxford University Press, 1986), p. 159; see also Bloom's discussion of the relationship between *Commentary* and *Partisan Review,* pp. 158–59. Richard H. Pells notes in *The Liberal Mind in a Conservative Age: American Intellectuals in the 1940s and 1950s* (Middletown, CT: Wesleyan University Press, 1989) that already by the 1940s the *New Republic* was also printing numerous articles on the massacre of European Jewry (pp. 40–44).

8. Trilling's story vividly recalls Gerard Manley Hopkins's "Spring and Fall," in which the child's mourning for the death of summer is her grieving for her own mortality.

9. See my essays "Lionel Trilling and the 'Being' of Culture," *The Massachusetts Review,* 35 (1994): 63–82, and "The Holocaust and the Construction of Modern American Literary Criticism: The Case of Lionel Trilling," in *The Translatability of Cultures: Figurations of the Space Between,* ed. Sanford Budick and Wolfgang Iser (Stanford, CA: Stanford University Press, 1995), pp. 127–46.

10. H. J. Kaplan, "A Minor Scandal in the Middle East," *Partisan Review* 16 (1949): 604–20.

11. Saul Bellow similarly concludes his *To Jerusalem and Back: A Personal Account* (Harmondsworth: Penguin Books, 1985), which I have argued inherits an anti-Zionist tradition: "*To Jerusalem and Back:* Reflections on the Place of Israel in American Writing from Melville and Mark Twain to Saul Bellow," *South Central Review* 8 (1991): 59–70.

12. For a discussion of Rosenfeld and the novel, see Alexander Bloom, *Prodigal Sons,* esp. pp. 172–73.

13. *Jews Without Money* (New York: Carroll & Graf, 1984), p. 14.

14. "The Situation of the Jewish Writer," in *An Age of Enormity: Life and Writing in the Forties and Fifties,* ed. Theodore Solotaroff (Cleveland:

World Publishing, 1962), pp. 67–69. Rosenfeld records similar thoughts in his review of Jo Sinclair's *Wasteland* ("From Marx to Freud: Adjust to Belonging") and in his essay entitled "The Young Richard Wright" – all reprinted in *An Age of Enormity*.

15. "The Situation of the Jewish Writer," in *An Age of Enormity*, ed. Solotaroff, pp. 67–69. On modernist alienation and the figure of the writer, see Marcus Klein, *After Alienation: American Novels in Mid-Century* (Chicago: University of Chicago Press, 1964).

16. *Passage from Home* (Cleveland: World Publishing, 1961), p. 117; originally published 1946. Hereafter cited in text.

17. *Writin' Is Fightin': Thirty-Seven Years of Boxing on Paper* (New York: Atheneum, 1988), p. 7.

18. Grace Paley, *Enormous Changes at the Last Minute* (New York: Farrar, Straus, & Giroux, 1974), p. 198.

19. "Adam and Eve on Delancy Street," in *Age of Enormity*, pp. 186–87. This essay, which appeared in *Commentary*, produced a storm of protest by Jewish leaders. See Alexander Bloom's discussion of this in *Prodigal Sons*, pp. 163–64.

20. Saul Bellow, *Mr. Sammler's Planet* (Harmondsworth: Penguin Books, 1977), p. 42; all citations hereafter in text.

21. For readings along this line, see Max F. Schulz, "Mr. Bellow's Perigee, Or, The Lowered Horizon of *Mr. Sammler's Planet*," in *Contemporary American-Jewish Literature: Critical Essays*, ed. Irving Malin (Bloomington: Indiana University Press, 1973), pp. 117–33; Sol Gittleman, "*Mr. Sammler's Planet* Ten Years Later: Looking Back on the Crisis of 'Mispocha,' " *Judaism* 30 (1981): 480–83; S. Lillian Kremer, "The Holocaust in *Mr. Sammler's Planet*," *Saul Bellow Journal* 4 (1985): 19–32, and *Witness Through the Imagination: Jewish American Holocaust Literature* (Detroit: Wayne State University Press, 1989), pp. 44–62; Gloria L. Cronin, "Holy War Against the Moderns: Saul Bellow's Antimodernist Critique of Contemporary American Society," *Studies in American Jewish Literature* 8 1 (1989): 77–94; and Kurt Dittmar, "The End of Enlightenment: Bellow's Universal View of the Holocaust in *Mr. Sammler's Planet*," in *Saul Bellow at Seventy-Five: A Collection of Critical Essays*, ed. Gerhard Bach (Tübingen: Gunter, Narr, 1991), pp. 63–80.

22. On the internal affinities between Sammler and the pickpocket, see Jonathan Wilson, *On Bellow's Planet: Readings from the Dark Side* (Rutherford, NJ: Fairleigh Dickinson University Press, 1985), pp. 148–49; Hana Wirth-Nesher and Andrea Cohen Malamut, "Jewish and Human Survival on Bellow's Planet," *Modern Fiction Studies* 25 (1979): 65; and Regine Rosenthal, "Memory and the Holocaust: *Mr. Sammler's Planet* and *The Bellarosa Connection*," in *Saul Bellow at Seventy-Five*, p. 86.

23. Even where critics have noted the possibility of racism, they have understated its potential implications. For example, Max Schulz lets his

criticism remain with the suggestion that Bellow's choice of a black
pickpocket is "an expression of Bellow's conservative Jewish outrage at
the state of the nation" ("Mr. Bellow's Perigee," p. 122); while Hana
Wirth-Nesher and Andrea Cohen Malamut caution that "we should be
careful not to assume that the use of a black man as physical force and
'other' to Sammler's cerebral nature constitutes a blatant straightforward reaffirmation of an ugly racist stereotype. It would violate the
novel's verisimilitude to give us access to personal information about a
character our perceiving consciousness, Mr. Sammler, could never
know" ("Jewish and Human Survival," p. 66). Like Wirth-Nesher and
Malamut, Kurt Dittmar suggests that the pickpocket must be understood as fitting the book's "body-mind antithesis. The black man represents the human as purely physical existence" ("End of Enlightenment," p. 76).

   Two critics who do note Sammler's racism, although they do not
dwell on it, are Susan Glickman, "The World as Will and Idea: A Comparative Study of *An American Dream* and *Mr. Sammler's Planet*," *Modern
Fiction Studies* 28 (1982–83): 577, and Jonathan Wilson, *On Bellow's
Planet*, p. 146, who notes as well that Sammler is also a misogynist. Both
these readings of the book depend on separating Bellow from Sammler
and assigning the racist position to Sammler, which will be my own
strategy as well.

24. See, again, Max Schulz, "Mr. Bellow's Perigee," and Gloria Cronin's
    "Holy War Against Modernism."
25. Susan Glickman, "The World as Will and Idea," p. 569.
26. Earl Rovit, "Saul Bellow and the Concept of the Survivor," in *Saul Bellow
    and His Work,* ed. Edmund Schraepen (Brussels: Centrum Voor Taal–
    Literatuurwetenschap, 1978), pp. 115–27, bases many of his ideas on
    Terrence Des Pres, *The Survivor: An Anatomy of Life in the Death Camps*
    (New York: Oxford University Press, 1976). Des Pres is specifically ar-
    guing against people like Stanley Elkins and their assumptions that
    heroism is defined by acts of resistance.
27. Judie Newman, *Saul Bellow and History* (New York: St. Martin's Press,
    1984), pp. 133–56. Also see my *Fiction and Historical Consciousness: The
    American Romance Tradition* (New Haven: Yale University Press, 1989).
28. See, again, Rovit, "Saul Bellow and the Concept of the Survivor." On
    Sammler as the voice of morality in the book, especially in relation to
    making moral distinctions, see M. A. Quayum, "Finding the Middle
    Ground: Bellow's Philosophical Affinity with Emerson in *Mr. Sammler's
    Planet*," *Saul Bellow Journal* 8 (1989): 24–38, who sees Sammler as the
    exponent of Emersonian "mediation, moderation, and middle ground"
    (p. 24), and Dittmar, "The End of Enlightenment." Wirth-Nesher and
    Malamut, "Jewish and Human Survival," read the book as "Bellow's
    most forceful defense of humanism" (p. 59).

29. Dittmar, "End of Enlightenment," p. 72.
30. Saul Bellow, *To Jerusalem and Back*, p. 160. See, again, my essay "*To Jerusalem and Back:* Reflections on the Place of Israel."
31. Andrew Furman, *Israel Through the Jewish-American Imagination: A Survey of Jewish-American Literature on Israel 1928–1995* (Albany: State University of New York Press, 1997), pp. 59–82.

Chapter Four

1. James Baldwin, *The Fire Next Time* (New York: Dell, 1963), p. 54.
2. *Beloved* (New York: Signet, 1987). Hereafter cited in text.
3. Quoted in Walter Clemons, "A Gravestone of Memories," *Newsweek,* September 28, 1987, p. 75. According to recent figures compiled by Herbert A. Klein (*The Middle Passage: Comparative Studies in the Atlantic Slave Trade* [Princeton: Princeton University Press, 1978]), based upon other work in the field by Philip Curtin, Morrison's number seems exaggerated. Of course, what do numbers matter where human suffering is involved? And how can they not matter?
4. Mae G. Henderson, "Toni Morrison's *Beloved:* Re-membering the Body as Historical Text," in *Comparative American Identities: Race, Sex, and Nationality in the Modern Text,* ed. Hortense J. Spillers (New York: Routledge, 1991), p. 64.
5. Paul Gilroy, *The Black Atlantic: Modernity and Double Consciousness* (Cambridge, MA: Harvard University Press, 1993), pp. 222–23. Further references appear in text.
6. Stanley Crouch, "Aunt Medea," *Notes of a Hanging Judge: Essays and Reviews 1979–89* (Oxford: Oxford University Press, 1990), p. 205; first published in the *Village Voice* on October 19, 1987.
7. Silko, *Almanac of the Dead* (New York: Simon and Schuster, 1991); see inside cover and p. 26. Walker, *Temple of My Familiar* (New York: Simon & Schuster Pocket Books, 1989), pp. 334, 308, 310. Let me also take note of, without venturing to explicate it, Gloria Naylor's decision in *Bailey's Cafe* to represent female circumcision (a subject that concerns Alice Walker as well in *The Secret of Joy*) not simply, as Walker does, through the example of black African tribes, but through the example of black African Ethiopian Jews.
8. Chester Himes, *Lonely Crusade* (New York: Thunder's Mouth Press, 1986), p. 394; hereafter citations in the text.
9. Alice Walker, *Meridian* (New York: Simon & Schuster, Pocket Books, 1976), p. 78; all further citations in the text.
10. Chester Himes, *If He Hollers Let Him Go* (New York: Thunder's Mouth Press, 1986), pp. 39, 56, 113, 112–15, 155, 160, and 198.
11. Caroline Walker Bynum, *Holy Feast and Holy Fast: The Religious Significance of Food to Medieval Women* (Berkeley: University of California Press,

1987). See also Rudolph M. Bell, *Holy Anorexia* (Chicago: University of Chicago Press, 1987).

12. Walker represents a much harsher version of this statement in *The Temple of My Familiar,* which was written during the height of the Palestinian uprising in Israel: "The child will always, as an adult, do to someone else whatever was done to him when he was a child. . . . I shudder to think what Hitler's childhood was like. . . . But anyone can see that the Palestinians and their children are reliving it under the Israelis today" (p. 310).

13. Much of the criticism of *Song of Solomon* has focused on the novel's recovery of a black past that empowers contemporary African Americans to perpetuate their own cultural heritage. See, for example, Kimberly W. Benston, "I Yam What I Am: The Topos of Un(naming) in Afro-American Literature," in *Black Literature and Literary Theory,* ed. Henry Louis Gates, Jr. (New York: Methuen, 1984), pp. 151–72 and "Re-Weaving the 'Ulysses Scene': Enchantment, Post-Oedipal Identity, and the Buried Text of Blackness in Toni Morrison's *Song of Solomon,*" in *Comparative American Identities,* ed. Spillers, pp. 87–109; Jane Campbell, *Mythic Black Fiction: The Transformation of History* (Knoxville: University of Tennessee Press, 1986); Cynthia A. Davis, "Self, Society, and Myth in Toni Morrison's Fiction," *Contemporary Literature* 23 (1982): 323–42; Dorothy H. Lee, "The Quest for Self: Triumph and Failure in the Works of Toni Morrison," in *Black Women Writers 1950–80: A Critical Evaluation,* ed. Mari Evans (Garden City, NY: Doubleday, Anchor Books, 1984), pp. 346–60; Genevieve Fabre, "Genealogical Archaeology of the Quest for Legacy in Toni Morrison's *Song of Solomon,*" in *Critical Essays on Toni Morrison,* ed. Nellie Y. McKay (Boston: G. K. Hall, 1988), pp. 105–14; Joseph T. Skerrett, Jr., "Recitation to the *Griot:* Storytelling and Learning in Toni Morrison's *Song of Solomon,*" in *Conjuring: Black Women, Fiction, and Literary Tradition,* ed. Marjorie Pryse and Hortense J. Spillers (Bloomington: Indiana University Press, 1985), pp. 192–202; Valerie Smith, *Self-Discovery and Authority in Afro-American Narrative* (Cambridge, MA: Harvard University Press, 1987); Jan Stryz, "Inscribing an Origin in *Song of Solomon,*" *Studies in American Fiction* 19 (1991): 31–40; and Susan Willis, *Specifying: Black Women Writing the American Experience* (London: Routledge, 1990), pp. 83–109.

14. *Song of Solomon* (New York: Signet, 1977), pp. 333–34; hereafter cited in text. Compare Benston, "Re-Weaving the 'Ulysses Scene.' "

15. A similar insight into biblical culture is contained in Walker's *Temple of My Familiar,* when Lissie, revealing one more of many previous incarnations, admits her desire to have initiated a "tribe" of her own. "That, anyway, is *my* fantasy," she goes on. "It is also the fantasy upon which the Old Testament rests . . . but without any mention of our intimacy

with the other animals or of the brown and black colors of the rest of my folks" (p. 365).

16. References to the biblical text are to the standard King James version. Morrison is quite correct to object to the slighting of the implications of "black" in this passage. According to the Anchor Bible, commentators have consistently attempted to "mitigate the blackness" by retranslating the text – *Song of Songs: A New Translation with Introduction and Commentary*, ed. Marvin H. Pope (Garden City, NY: Doubleday, 1977), p. 307. Pope's commentary on the connotations here of blackness go on for some time, covering, among others, Rashi and his problems with the passage, and discussing black Madonnas and black goddesses, among other things. While he discusses "The Song of Songs and Women's Liberation," he does not discuss the "Song" and African Americanism (pp. 308–9).

17. *Ruth: A New Translation with Introduction, Notes, and Commentary,* ed. Edward F. Campbell, Jr. (Garden City, NY: Doubleday, 1975).

18. I have discussed this dimension of *Beloved* at length in *Engendering Romance: Women Writers and the Hawthorne Tradition, 1850–1990* (New Haven: Yale University Press, 1994), pp. 204–6.

19. What is fascinating about Guitar's account of Jewish Nazi-hunters is that the dissimilarity it claims between the African American and Jewish situations is hardly what Guitar imagines it to be. Not only did the courts in Europe *not* try the majority of Nazi war criminals (and when they did try them, the sentences were almost never commensurate with the crimes), but Jewish Nazi-hunters, realizing this, set upon a course of action not so very different from that of the Seven Days. Not that the Jewish Nazi-hunters set out to kill innocent people, but they did on more than one occasion take justice into their own hands; and they did conceive a plot (ultimately foiled by other Jews) to poison the drinking water in a major German city (Michael Elkins, *Forged in Fury* [London: Corgi, 1971], pp. 252–55).

20. See, again, Walker's reference to the Palestinian–Israeli conflict in *Temple of My Familiar,* p. 310.

21. Samuel Allen notes that "the Weimaraner dogs, Horst and Helmut, in the decaying house of the grandfather's murderers, suggest but fall short of the name of the Munich beer-drinking song" (untitled review, in *Critical Essays,* ed. McKay, p. 31). This might constitute another quasi allusion to the Holocaust, reappropriated to the story of African American history. In this context the name of the book's major protagonist and Christ-figure, recalling the betrayal of Christ, may also be relevant. Although, as in *Beloved,* the novel intends a subversion of Christian culture, nonetheless the name does recall the story of the Jewish role in the crucifixion of Christ.

Chapter Five

1. Marcus Klein, *After Alienation: American Novels in Mid-Century* (Chicago: University of Chicago Press, 1964), pp. 295–96.
2. Bryan Cheyette, "Life after the Holocaust," *TLS,* June 14, 1991, p. 26; Cynthia Ozick, "The Shawl" (letter), *TLS,* July 5, 1991, p. 13. Cynthia Ozick, "Primo Levi's Suicide Note," *Metaphor and Memory: Essays* (New York: Alfred Knopf, 1989), p. 43. Cf. Alvin H. Rosenfeld, "The Holocaust According to William Styron," *Midstream* (December 1979): 43–49, and Irving S. Saposnik, "Bellow, Malamud, Roth . . . and Styron? or One Jewish Writer's Response," *Judaism* 31 (1982): 322–32.
3. *William Styron's Nat Turner: Ten Black Writers Respond,* ed. John Henrik Clarke (Boston: Beacon Press, 1968). Cf. Harvard Sitkoff and Michael Wreszin, "Whose Nat Turner? William Styron vs. the Black Intellectuals," *Midstream* (November 1968): 10–20, and Styron's response, printed in *The Confessions of Nat Turner* (New York: Random House, 1992), pp. 433–55.
4. For a set of compelling reasons for not comparing slavery and the Holocaust, see Laurence Thomas, *Vessels of Evil: American Slavery and the Holocaust* (Philadelphia: Temple University Press, 1993).
5. I have discussed the relationship of both of Styron's novels and Roth's *Ghost Writer* in my essay "Silent Inscriptions of the Holocaust in American Literary Culture," in *Living with America, 1946–1996,* ed. Cristina Giorcelli and Rob Kroes (Amsterdam: VU University Press, 1997), pp. 191–210.
6. *Ghost Writer* (New York: Random House, 1995; originally published 1979), pp. 28 and 125; William Styron, *Sophie's Choice* (New York: Random House, 1976), p. 122; all future references in the text. Other affinities between Roth and Styron include the interest in ghosts and a general literary allusiveness, especially to the writings of James Joyce; also, in the later Zuckerman novel *The Counterlife,* the fact that Nathan Landau's brother is, like Nathan Zuckerman's, a dentist.
7. " 'You who never was there': Slavery and the New Historicism, Deconstruction and the Holocaust," *Narrative* 4 (1996): 1–16.
8. Marcia Anne Gillespie, "Out of Slavery's Inferno," *Ms* 16 (1987): 68.
9. On Nation of Islam and recent black–Jewish tensions, see Murray Friedman, *What Went Wrong? The Creation and Collapse of the Black-Jewish Alliance* (New York: Free Press, 1995), pp. 1–16. Toni Morrison, "Site of Memory," in *Inventing the Truth: The Art and Craft of Memoir,* ed. William Zinsser (Boston: Houghton Mifflin, 1987), p. 109, and "Unspeakable Things Unspoken: The Afro-American Presence in American Literature," *Michigan Quarterly Review* 28 (1989): 7. Morrison is referring to Martin Bernal, *Black Athena: The Afroasiatic Roots of Classical Civilization,* vol. 1: *The Fabrication of Ancient Greece 1785–1985* (New Brunswick, NJ:

Rutgers University Press, 1987). In *The Holocaust in Historical Context: The Holocaust and Mass Death before the Modern Age* (New York: Oxford University Press, 1994), Steven T. Katz discriminates the differences between the Holocaust and other large-scale human catastrophes (such as slavery, witch-hunts, the extermination of the Indians, and so on), not to claim for the Holocaust superiority on the scale of human atrocities but to clarify its uniqueness.

10. W. E. B. Du Bois, *The Souls of Black Folk* (New York: Penguin, 1989), p. 8.

11. *The Secret Relationship Between Blacks and Jews,* prepared by The Historical Research Department, The Nation of Islam (Chicago: Latimer Associates, 1991); Tony Martin, *The Jewish Onslaught: Despatches from the Wellesley Battlefront* (Dover, MA: The Majority Press, 1993), p. 78; Khallid Muhammad, quoted in "Howard puts off Jewish scholar," *Boston Globe,* April 19, 1994. Cf. "Divided by a Diatribe," *New York Times,* December 29, 1993. See Harold Brackman's response: *Jew on the Brain: A Public Refutation of The Nation of Islam's The Secret Relationship Between Blacks and Jews* (n.p., 1992). David E. Stannard, *American Holocaust: Columbus and the Conquest of the New World* (Oxford: Oxford University Press, 1992); John Henrik Clarke, *Christopher Columbus and the African Holocaust* – cited in Haki R. Madhubuti, "Blacks, Jews and Henry Louis Gates, Jr.," *Black Books Bulletin: WordsWork* 16 (1993/94): 6. See also Walter F. Pitts, *Old Ship of Zion: The Afro-Baptist Ritual in the African Diaspora* (Oxford: Oxford University Press, 1993), which represents another recent phenomenon: the application to other diaspora communities of traditional Jewish discourse concerning the diaspora. Alan M. Dershowitz discusses recent developments in black–Jewish relations in *The Vanishing American Jew: In Search of Jewish Identity for the Next Century* (Boston: Little, Brown, 1997), pp. 118–35. Cf. for uncanny anticipations of the present moment, "Negro-Jewish Relations in America: A Symposium," *Midstream* (December 1966): 3–91.

12. Harold Cruse, *The Crisis of the Negro Intellectual* (New York: William Morrow, 1967), pp. 482–83.

13. Orlando Patterson, *Freedom,* vol. 1: *Freedom in the Making of Western Culture* (New York: Basic Books, 1991), pp. xiii and 33–34. I note in passing that in presenting the impetus for his desire to explain "how freedom became such a powerful value," Patterson cites the fact that "during the long nightmare of the Cold War [we] were prepared to risk nuclear holocaust in order to defend [the] sacred ideal we call freedom" (p. ix).

14. "The Shawl," *The New Yorker* 56 (May 26, 1980): 33–34; "Rosa," *The New Yorker* 59 (March 21, 1983): 38–71; and *The Shawl* (New York: Vintage Books, 1990). Quotations hereafter cited in text – unless otherwise specified – are from the 1990 edition. I have discussed the absence of

the Holocaust as a major subject of American writing in two essays: "Acknowledging the Holocaust in Contemporary American Fiction and Criticism," in *Breaking Crystal: Writing and Memory after Auschwitz*, ed. Edraim Sicher (Urbana: University of Illinois Press, 1998), pp. 329–44; and "Silent Inscriptions of the Holocaust in American Literary Culture," *Living with America*, ed. Giorcelli and Kroes.

15. I discuss this at length in *Engendering Romance: Women Writers and the Hawthorne Tradition, 1850–1990* (New Haven: Yale University Press, 1994), pp. 202–18.

16. On the book's philosophical concern with counting, see, again, my essay on *Beloved* in *Engendering Romance*.

17. *Later the Same Day* (Harmondsworth: Penguin Books, 1985), p. 203; cf. p. 185; hereafter, cited in text.

18. Toni Morrison, *Playing in the Dark: Whiteness and the Literary Imagination* (Cambridge: Harvard University Press, 1992), pp. 4–5.

Index